# THE THOMAS CODE

# THE THOMAS CODE

## S. P. LAURIE

HYPOSTASIS

*London · 2018*

Published by Hypostasis Ltd.
71-75 Shelton Street, Covent Garden
London WC2H 9JQ

www.hypostasis.co
Email: info@hypostasis.co

Book cover design by BespokeBookCovers.com

ISBN: 978-1-912029-71-6

$3 \cdot 2 \cdot 3 \cdot 2 \cdot 3$

*"When I broke the five loaves for the five thousand, how many baskets full of broken pieces did you take up?"*

*They said to him, "Twelve."*

*"And the seven for the four thousand, how many baskets full of broken pieces did you take up?"*

*And they said to him, "Seven."*

*And he said to them, "Do you not yet understand?"*

— (The Gospel of Mark, 8:19-21 ESV)

# CONTENTS

**1** The enigma gospel                                    1

### PART ONE

**2** One hundred and eight sayings                         15
**3** Five trees in paradise                                33
**4** Five in a house                                       49
**5** Three threes, two twos, and a single one              67
**6** Dividing by two                                       79
**7** Powers of ten                                         87

### INTERLUDE

**8** Five and seven loaves                                 95

### PART TWO

**9** The structure of Thomas                              113
**10** The first eighteen                                  125
**11** The second eighteen                                 135
**12** The third eighteen                                  163
**13** The fourth eighteen                                 177
**14** The fifth eighteen                                  191
**15** The sixth eighteen                                  207
**16** Postscript                                          231

Note from the author                                      237

THE GOSPEL OF THOMAS                                      239

Acknowledgements                                              271

### APPENDICES

I  The "five in a house" saying in Luke and Matthew          275
II  Reconstruction of the "three gods" saying               281
III  Links between the beginning and the end of the Gospel  287
IV  Reconstructing the last eighteen                        291

Notes                                                        299
Bibliography                                                 307
About the author                                             311

# 1

# The enigma gospel

*"It is not just the sayings themselves that shock and surprise, but also the bizarre juxtaposition of apparently contrasting ideas, side by side. This is the key point: if the author of Thomas is aiming at coherence he has failed. It is unlikely, however, that he is attempting to be coherent. Rather, his Gospel is aiming at enigma, and this is why it announces itself as an enigma from the beginning (Incipit, 1), and why it orders sayings in this apparently incomprehensible way." (Mark Goodacre, Thomas and the Gospels, p16).*

The Gospel of Thomas is the world's most enigmatic manuscript. To qualify as truly enigmatic, a manuscript should be old, having been secreted in some hidden place where it has lain for centuries; it should be puzzling to the point of indecipherability; and when finally deciphered, it must contain a secret with profound significance. Such enigmas are common in fiction and all but impossibly rare in reality. Yet all of these are true of the Gospel of Thomas.

Most scholars doubt that the enigma that is Thomas has a solution. The Gospel has occupied the time of numerous researchers over the years, and although progress has been made, the central mystery is unresolved. This breeds a certain skepticism or even cynicism. Many think that the Gospel is essentially a random collection of sayings, some of which may be early, but others much later. Others would agree with Mark Goodacre in his book *Thomas and the Gospels* that the Gospel has no meaning, but is mysterious for the sake of being mysterious. In this view, Thomas is an ancient con trick to lure in the foolish with fake promises of secret knowledge. It is unsurprising that such a view is attractive to conventional Christians and scholars who fervently wish that the Gospel of Thomas could be buried in the sands again.

This book proposes that the doubters are wrong. The Gospel of Thomas is not random. It is not enigmatic for the sake of enigma, but rather it uses enigma to hide and protect its secrets from those considered unworthy. It offers us a series of riddles that we must solve to progress to a deeper understanding. Thomas is clever, very clever. And the biggest surprise of all is that the organizing principle is mathematical.

The mathematical secrets of Thomas do not require a computer to analyze them. The authors of Thomas were inspired by the Greek mathematics of prime numbers, and their mathematics is simple. Their interest in mathematics was not abstract, but mystical. The numbers represented sacred truths. The authors saw relationships between the primes as more fundamental than the physical world, as expressing a revelation that the ultimate God had hidden for men and women to find. Mostly this mathematical symbolism has been lost, but fragments still survive. The concept of the Holy Trinity is a remnant of this mystical-mathematics.

## The discovery of a lost gospel

The first modern glimpse of Thomas came at the end of the Victorian era. Two Oxford archaeologists, Bernard Grenfell and Arthur Hunt, were excavating the remains of the Egyptian provincial town of Oxyrhynchus when they discovered an ancient rubbish heap containing a huge number of fragmentary papyrus manuscripts.[1] The dry climate in Oxyrhynchus had excluded water and enabled the preservation of the manuscripts for almost two thousand years. The condition of the manuscripts was poor. They had, after all, been thrown away at the end of their useful life and had then spent two millennia in a rubbish heap. What was recovered was an enormous number of fragments, so many that most have still not been studied in detail. This rich haul gave a unique window into the ancient Roman world. Much of what was found was utilitarian; business records and the like. Yet there were also a large number of classical and pagan texts. The great hope of the time was to find evidence for early Christianity. The dating of the rubbish heap was just right, the early centuries AD when Christianity was expanding rapidly throughout the Roman Empire and might have even reached an outpost like Oxyrhynchus. Could the heap contain fragments of the Gospels that were earlier than anything then known? Grenfell and Hunt did find fragments of the New Testament Gospels, but they found something else, something completely unexpected. They found a damaged papyrus leaf containing several sayings introduced by the words "Jesus said."[2] Some of these sayings were well known from the Gospels, but others were very strange. Were these lost sayings originally spoken by Jesus?

After Grenfell and Hunt's initial excavation in 1897, they returned again in 1903 and found two more fragments with "Jesus said" sayings.[3] One of these fragments contained the beginning of the Gospel, which recorded that the sayings were spoken by the living Jesus and written down by Thomas. It seemed that the mysterious sayings came from the long-lost Gospel of Thomas, a work mentioned several times in the writings of the church fathers, but which had disappeared without a trace. The fragments were among the earliest surviving physical evidence for Christianity, with the oldest dated to c200 AD and other two before 250 AD. But no more were found, and with only a handful of sayings, the papyrus fragments were little more than an intriguing curiosity. All that was to change in 1945. Just as the most destructive war in the history of the world was coming to an end, another remarkable find was made from the dry Egyptian sands.

The discoveries this time were not made by Oxford archaeologists, but rather by an Arab peasant farmer named Muhammed 'Ali al-Samman and his brothers.[4] When asked years later about his discovery, Muhammed 'Ali told a dramatic tale of a blood feud. Their father had recently been murdered, and they were sworn to revenge his death. It was at around this time that the brothers went to Jabal al-Tarif, a mountain with a large number of caves, to dig for fertilizer for their crops. Digging in the soft soil, they found a buried earthen jar about a meter high. At first, they were fearful that it might contain a Jinni, yet plucking up their courage, they broke it open. Inside were twelve ancient codices, books bound in leather and written in an old, unreadable language. They took the books home and left them in a pile on the floor. As well as the bound books, there were some loose leaves from a thirteenth codex, some of which their mother used as kindling for the fire.

About a month after the discovery they came across their father's assassin who was sleeping by the roadside. They took a brutal revenge, hacking off his limbs before killing him and eating his heart. Fearing that they would be interrogated by the police for the murder they had committed, they sent some of the books to a local Christian priest for safe keeping. There they were seen by a local history teacher, who recognized the volumes as being potentially valuable. A book was sent to a dealer in Cairo for his opinion, and they all eventually found their way onto the black market. The books were so sensational that they attracted the attention of the Egyptian authorities who managed to buy or seize most of them for the Coptic Museum in Cairo.

Recently, this account has been questioned.[5] The dramatic nature of the story suggests that it has been considerably embellished. A cynic would say that the brothers knew exactly what they were doing – searching illegally for buried antiquities to sell to wealthy Western collectors.[6] There is a long history of looting treasures from the Egyptian sands, and the idea that the brothers would have been unaware of the value of a number of books contained in an ancient jar is questionable to say the least. Some of the more incredible features of the story, such as eating the heart of the murdered man, are indicative of macho fiction rather than remembered fact. It has, in fact, all the signs of a tall story made up to impress questioning Westerners.[7]

What is not in doubt is the importance of the Nag Hammadi discovery. The thirteen codices have been securely dated to the late fourth century from documents found in the bindings. They are written in Coptic, a version of ancient Egyptian which used the

Greek alphabet rather than hieroglyphics. Egypt, before the Islamic conquest, was a hotbed of Christianity and the center of the monastic movement. Coptic was the language of these Egyptian Christians (the surviving Christian community in Egypt are called Copts to this day). The codices were found just a few miles from the monastery of St. Pachomius, and the scholar Frederik Wisse has suggested that the codices originated from the library at this monastery. The date of the codices is consistent with an order made in 367 AD by Athanasius, Archbishop of Alexandria, to purge monastic libraries of heretical works. When the monks were ordered to remove the forbidden books from their library, perhaps they chose to hide them rather than destroy them. Presumably, they hoped to retrieve the books when the political winds changed, but this never happened.[8]

The Nag Hammadi codices contained fifty-two separate works, almost all of which could be characterized as "Gnostic."[9] The Gnostics were well known from the writings of the church fathers. In particular, Irenaeus, bishop of Lyons, wrote extensively against the Gnostics in his book *Against Heresies*, which was produced around 180 AD. The word Gnosis meant "knowledge." It was not physical, factual, or philosophical knowledge that the Gnostic sought, but spiritual knowledge of hidden things. The Gnostic view contrasted with that of the proto-orthodox church which emphasized belief. The proto-orthodox Christian was expected to trust in the authority of their minister and bishop, to believe in Jesus as revealed in the New Testament Gospels, and in God as revealed by the Jewish scriptures. This was not enough for the Gnostic who desired direct experience of a spiritual reality.

Before Nag Hammadi, scholars had not been able to read the Gnostics in their own words but only through the writings of those who opposed them. The fact that the young church had been infected with a large number of "heretical" sects was one of the secrets that the clergy liked to keep from their flock. Many a young man studying for the priesthood must have been shocked and titillated by the stories in Irenaeus and other early sources, hinting as they did at bizarre sexual practices. So extreme were the stories told about the beliefs of the Gnostics, that the more sober considered them to be exaggerations, made up to blacken the Gnostics by their opponents. In terms of behavior, the Nag Hammadi gospels revealed the Gnostics as typically being strongly ascetic—as rejecting the things of this world, including sexuality. However, Irenaeus had not exaggerated their beliefs at all. Reading their own words made these beliefs seem even more extreme and "weird."

A great deal has been written about the Gnostics, but it has to be said that the general reader today will find the majority of the fifty-two works found at Nag Hammadi disappointing. The literary quality is mostly poor. They are obsessed with hierarchies of angels and involve explanations on how the universe came to be, arising as it did from the fall of Wisdom from the Pleroma, the totality of the Godhead. Most of this is, quite frankly, absurd. But there are exceptions, such as the beautiful work "Thunder: Perfect Mind" with its female narrator expressing a series of paradoxical "I am" statements. Then there is the fascinating Gospel of Philip, which is best known for its hints of a relationship between Mary Magdalene and Jesus. But the most interesting work of all was found in Codex II immediately before the Gospel of Philip. This was a complete copy of the Gospel of Thomas.

## *Academic views*

Thomas has been the subject of considerable academic controversy. From the start, a debate has raged about the dating of the gospel. There are those (perhaps the majority) who would place it firmly in the second century, after the four New Testament Gospels. But among the specialists in the study of the so-called Apocrypha (works excluded from the Bible) there has always been a strong strand of belief that elements of Thomas are earlier than, and independent of, the four Gospels.

The fact that Thomas was found in a collection of Gnostic texts originally led scholars to believe that it also was Gnostic and relatively late. The first scholar to study the gospel, Gilles Quispel, dated it to around 140 AD, a dating which would still appeal to many conventional scholars today. It was Grenfell and Hunt who first argued that the Gospel could not be later than c140 AD to allow time for it to be copied in sufficient volume to reach a backwater like Oxyrhynchus. So it is perhaps no coincidence that many scholars date the Gospel to around 140 AD as the latest date consistent with the papyrus fragments.[10]

The comforting idea that Thomas was dependent upon the four Gospels was challenged by Professor Helmut Koester of Harvard. Although he agreed with a date of 140 AD for the final compilation of Thomas, he argued that many of the individual sayings were much earlier, going back to 50–100 AD, with some preserving versions of parables earlier than those in the New Testament gospels.[11] Koester was very influential, and many scholars from the more liberal wing of Gnostic studies have worked for him or with him. His students include Elaine Pagels, who went on to write the best-selling book *The Gnostic Gospels* which brought the whole subject to wider attention.

A few scholars went further than Koester in suggesting a very early Thomas. Stevan Davies did not teach at an elite institution, such as the Harvard school of Divinity or Princeton, but at the relatively obscure College Misericordia. But he made two significant contributions to the study of Thomas. The first was the discovery of links between the Gospel of Mark and Thomas.[12] Most spectacularly, he showed how a section of the Gospel of Mark must be dependent upon a Thomas saying, and this the very saying Thomas 22 (quoted above) that appears to be so weird to conventional Christians. This was the first hard evidence that a saying in Thomas was not just earlier than Mark, the first of the New Testament Gospels to be written, but was used by the author of Mark as a source. His second contribution was an influential book, *The Gospel of Thomas and Christian Wisdom*. This book disputed the conventional belief that Thomas was Gnostic, suggesting that it was closer to the Jewish Wisdom tradition. Davies assigned a date of 50–70 AD for Thomas.[13]

Another former student of Koester who argued for an early date for Thomas was Stephen Patterson. His book, *The Gospel of Thomas and Jesus*, which was published in 1993, defended Thomas against the established view that it was dependent upon the other Gospels.

He showed that where there was an overlap, the version of a saying in Thomas preserved an independent, or even earlier version of the saying, compared to the Gospels. The few cases in which Thomas did appear to copy the New Testament Gospels, could be explained by copyists harmonizing texts by reverting to the familiar gospel version. He suggested that the Gospel was compiled at the same time as the New Testament Gospels were being written at around 70–80 AD.[14]

At the other end of the dating spectrum was Nicholas Perrin who believed that Thomas was written in Syriac and was dependent upon Tatian's harmony of the four Gospels, the Diatessaron, which would date the Gospel to no earlier than the 170s AD.[15] Such a late dating has not commanded much support, not the least because it conflicts with the physical evidence of the papyrus fragments.[16]

More influential was another scholar, April DeConick, who wrote two back-to-back books about Thomas.[17] She offered the theory of a Gospel that had arisen through waves of accretions. Under this theory, parts of Thomas (the so-called kernel sayings) are very early and may go back to original apocalyptic sayings from Jesus. However, this original Gospel was substantially added to over a period of about a century. These accretions reflected the gnostic worldview of those making the additions.

Scholars had long noticed a special relationship between the Gospel of John and the Gospel of Thomas. Conventional scholars explained this by Thomas copying John. However, in her best-selling book *Beyond belief*, Elaine Pagels, following the theories of Gregory Riley, challenged this view. She proposed that not only was the author of the Gospel of John aware of Thomas, but also that the Gospel of John was in fact written against the Christians who used the Gospel of Thomas.

More recently there has been push-back for the idea that Thomas is independent of the four Gospels. Leading the attack are two heavyweight British scholars, Simon Gathercole from Cambridge University and Mark Goodacre from Duke University. They independently wrote two books, working along similar lines and coming to similar conclusions.[18] They argue that many sayings in Thomas are too close to the synoptic versions for this to be chance and that Thomas was compiled as a Gnostic Gospel which borrowed from the New Testament Gospels. Goodacre takes us full circle in dating Thomas to c140 AD.[19]

Beyond the dating of the Gospel is another central question: What does it all mean? It has been over seventy years since a full copy of the Gospel was discovered, and in that time it has been subject to intense academic research. And yet it has remained an enigma. The academic study has deepened rather than resolved the mystery. There are some things that everyone agrees on. It is clearly a spiritual gospel that shows gnostic tendencies, although not the developed form of Gnosticism found in the other Nag Hammadi texts. The Gospel promises hidden knowledge and delights in paradox and contradiction. The sayings are mostly short and often resemble riddles. All of which point to the idea that Thomas is clever, and that there is something mysterious about the Gospel, some hidden key that we must find and turn to unlock its secrets.

And yet, in the accepted view, Thomas is little more than a random accumulation of sayings. It is true that scholars have searched for a structure, but because no one has found anything that is completely convincing, many have concluded that there is nothing to be found. Yet there are hints that something is going on beneath the surface. It is well known that successive sayings are often (but by no means always) linked by one or more keywords. And there are themes that seem to run through some sections of the Gospel. Steven Davies proposed some ideas on structure, including four keystone sayings on searching and finding that he believes may play a special role. And in her own work, April DeConick suggested that the original kernel Gospel consisted of five separate speech gospels which she believes were verbally transmitted before being written down.[20] Yet in a 2009 interview, Stevan Davies gives a gloomy conclusion. After discussing a few links between sayings at the beginning and end of the Gospel, which he believes are genuine, he adds: *"Since nobody has ever liked my attempt to find organization in the other sayings, and I don't like anybody else's attempt or even my own, I think the other sayings are just a list, not mathematically random but conceptually so."*[21] The idea that Thomas is not "mathematically random" is fascinating, but he does not elaborate on what he means by this. Perhaps it goes back to a theory he posited in a 1994 paper, later added as an appendix to the second edition of *The Gospel of Thomas and Christian Wisdom*, that the Gospel was used for divination. It was this paper that gave me the initial idea that sparked the current book.

## *The Thomas Code*

This book will show that the organization of the Gospel is far from random. It is, in fact, exquisitely structured around a mathematical formula that I have called the Thomas Code. This key was lost at a very early stage. Without knowledge of the organizing principle, people found the Gospel unordered and strange. In fact, the secret to understanding Thomas was hiding in plain sight. Typically, the Gospel itself tells us just this: *"Know what is in front of you and that which is hidden from you will be revealed to you."* The truth is staring us in the face. The Gospel tells us about its own structure, and that structure is mathematical. Several sayings allude to and specify this structure. In retrospect, the clues are obvious. The simple fact that Thomas is a carefully demarcated collection of sayings, with all those "Jesus said" statements, rather than a narrative gospel, lends itself to a mathematical organizing principle. And there are a lot of numbers in Thomas, ranging from the "five trees in paradise" to the strange expression "single one" for someone in the kingdom of heaven. Then there is the way in which the numbers tend to be found in the most mystifying of sayings. And the very name the Gospel of Thomas, meaning the Gospel of the Twin, will turn out to be a clue to the formula.

This book offers an abundance of evidence for the Thomas Code. It has been arranged into two main parts, separated by an interlude:

- Part 1 goes through the sayings which specify and allude to the structure.
- The interlude covers the miracles of the loaves and fishes.
- Part 2 shows how the structure is reflected in the Gospel.

At the end of the book is a complete version of the original Gospel ordered according to the principle of the Thomas Code.

The key test of any theory is what insights it brings beyond the things it sets out to explain. The two miracles of the loaves and fishes, in which Jesus feeds five thousand and four thousand, have long been suspected of hiding some mathematical secret. In these miracles, numbers are very prominent and specific. The Thomas Code was developed to explain Thomas, so it was a complete surprise to find that it also explained the miracles of the loaves and fishes. The inventor of the Thomas Code must also have written the source that lay behind the account of the miracles in the first gospel, that of Mark. The feeding of the multitudes by loaves and fishes was a mathematical conundrum which has been misunderstood and turned into a literal miracle.

The link with the miracle of the loaves and fishes is a key piece of evidence for Thomas being earlier than even the earliest of the New Testament Gospels. This is supported by one of the most important sayings specifying the Thomas Code, which was used as a source by both Matthew and Luke. This means that Thomas must be older than either of these Gospels. Moreover, because the Thomas Code is used to structure the Gospel, this conclusion applies not just to individual sayings, but to the Gospel as a whole. This has profound implications for our view of early Christianity. The Gospel of Thomas reveals a Jesus movement that will seem very strange to anyone brought up on the four Gospels, yet the evidence shows that it is the original.

One of the delights of writing this book has been finding the many clues and features that have been hidden in the Gospel of Thomas. The Gospel wants to be read. At the same time, those who assembled the Gospel did not want to make things easy for us. The meaning has been deliberately obscured. They wanted us to work hard, to be worthy of the revelations that the Gospel would provide. Yet they were also kind, for they did not set us an impossible task. They placed numerous clues within the Gospel. After almost two thousand years, we can discover these clues and begin the task of decoding the Gospel's meaning. I invite the reader to accompany me on this task.

# PART ONE

# 2

# One hundred and eight sayings

*"The Gospel of Thomas uses the phrase "Jesus said" over ninety times, but the phrase does not primarily function to communicate the simple fact that the sayings are to be considered those of Jesus. That fact is established in the first sentence of the text and surely one cannot presume the text's audience was staggeringly stupid as to require such constant reinforcement." (Stevan Davies, Does the Gospel of Thomas have a meaning?).*[22]

I stumbled across the Thomas Code quite by chance. It all started in a coffee shop with the number one hundred and eight. I was sitting reading Stevan Davies' classic book *The Gospel of Thomas and Christian Wisdom*. At the end of the book was a paper called "Does the Gospel of Thomas have a meaning?" which Davies had originally presented to an SBL conference in 1994. The paper set out his theory that the Gospel of Thomas was used for divination. I had read the book before but did not recall this paper. (It was actually only attached to the second edition.) I had, however, heard about the divination theory and did not like it. Thomas was a repository for mysteries, not a tool for fortune telling. Does not the very introduction of the Gospel tell us that it contains the secret words of Jesus, which must be understood to obtain eternal life? Yet I was intrigued by the paper because it asked a question that was tantalizingly simple: "How many sayings were in the Gospel?" This prompted the corollary: "Could it be that the number of sayings was important?" I had thought of Thomas as a fairly random collection without any real structure. But under the divination theory, the number of sayings had to be precise.

Davies drew attention to the fact that most sayings included the words "Jesus said." What other purpose could this serve than to demarcate the sayings? But why should the sayings be separated one from another and not just merged together as we find in other sayings collections from the time? The implication was that there was some structure to Thomas that required individual sayings to be distinguished.

Davies analyzed the number of sayings and came to the conclusion that the traditional count was wrong and there were actually 108.[23] This was the number which, under his divination hypothesis, could be selected by a roll of dice. His attempt at determining the number was intriguing, but some of his decisions were contrived. My count gave 112. But then what mattered was not how many sayings were in our surviving fourth-century copy of the Gospel but how many were in the original. Almost certainly some sayings had been added to the collection over the centuries; there was a suspicious clustering of duplicates near the end of the Gospel. So it was quite possible that the original had 108 sayings.

Sitting in the coffee shop, I began to play with the number 108. The number seemed to have a lot of divisors; you could divide it by 2, 3, 4, 6, 9, 12, 18 and 36. This meant that you could group a collection of 108 sayings in many different ways. The number intrigued me. There was something special about it, but it took me a while to figure out what it was. Every number has what is called a prime factorization, a unique way in which it can be expressed as a group of prime numbers multiplied together. (This will be explained further below. Please do not panic if you do not like mathematics! The mathematics here are very simple and will be set out in a way that I hope is easy to follow.) When I reduced 108 to its prime factorization, I saw it was the first two primes raised to their own powers:

$$108 = 2^2 \cdot 3^3$$

The number was actually unique. If you wanted to generate numbers from successive primes raised to their own powers, then only 108 could be used practically for a collection of sayings. It was a pleasant intellectual game to work out how the formula could be used to organize the Gospel. It would have to be structured as a multi-level hierarchy. This required the factors to be put in order, and I immediately saw there was one very attractive way of organizing two twos and three threes. It is this order of the factorization that I call the Thomas Code. Of course, this was nothing more than a game. It could not really be like this. There was no other early Christian text—indeed, no other ancient text as far as I knew—that was organized in such a complex mathematical way.

As I left the coffee shop and strolled around the town, certain sayings in Thomas went through my mind. These were sayings that had puzzled me for years, sayings which I had attempted to explain, some of which I thought I had explained. These sayings involved numbers. Now, I suddenly saw that all my previous attempts and explanations were wrong. The sayings were talking about the very sequence I had just come across in the coffee shop! Moreover, the placing of one of these sayings (the five trees in paradise) was very significant. It came precisely at the end of the first important section as predicted by the Thomas Code. Commentators had noticed that the Gospel appeared to be signaling an end at this point even though it had scarcely got going. But no one had known why.

I went hurriedly home and sat down with a copy of the Gospel and a pencil and marked out the pattern. There were some decisions to be made but surprisingly few until the end section. Even from the start, there were some intriguing clues that I was on the right lines. Over the next few days, I puzzled out the main outlines of the structure set out in the second section of the book. Within a few weeks, I began to write this book and fill in the details. The link with the miracle of the loaves and fishes came much later and was a marvelous confirmation of the theory. But before we explain all this, we must go back to the beginning. The reader may be wondering why there should be any doubt about the number of sayings in Thomas, so we will start with Stevan Davies' theories.

## How many sayings?

If you pick up any modern edition of the Gospel of Thomas, you will find a collection of sayings numbered from 1 to 114. Before the first saying there are a few lines of text, which scholars call "the Incipit," and at the end is the title, *"The Gospel Of Thomas."* The neat numbering of sayings, however, is a modern invention and not in the original. Ancient documents did not use numbering systems. Indeed, they did not even use any punctuation marks, nor did they have any blank spaces between words, but instead they ran all the letters together. In the Roman world, documents were produced by professional scribes and mostly read aloud by other scribes. The professional does not want to make things easy for the amateur. Before you could read a text, you would have to parse it, to decide where one word ended and the next began. Today even the experts find it impossible to read an ancient work straight off like a modern text.

In the original Thomas manuscripts, the sayings are all merged together in a continuous stream. So how can we tell one saying from another? In other early Christian texts, such as the Gospels, we must take our clues from the narrative. In Thomas, we do not have a narrative, but we do have a unique feature found in no other text; most sayings include the words "Jesus said." Normally this is the start of the saying, although sometimes a disciple or some other person makes a statement or asks a question, followed by a "Jesus said" reply. It would be nice and neat if every saying included a "Jesus said," but nothing is ever that easy in Thomas! Instead of "Jesus said" some sayings have "he said" although it is clear that it is Jesus who is speaking. Things get harder when the subject matter changes completely without a "Jesus said" or "He said" to indicate a new saying. In these cases, do we have two sayings or one?

The first editors of the Coptic Thomas made decisions to divide the Gospel up into the individual sayings which they then numbered 1 to 114. Later scholars disputed some of these decisions (no two scholars ever agree on anything!). Some scholars go further and divide up the individual sayings into component parts. So, for example, you will come across sayings referred to as 33a, 33b, and so on.

However, to split sayings up in this way goes against the grain of those "Jesus said" statements.

The "Jesus said" statements stop us from reading the Gospel of Thomas as one continuous whole as we would the letters of Paul or the four Gospels. They bring us up short and force us to think more about each saying before going on to the next. The second-century Gospel of Philip, which was bound immediately after Thomas in Nag Hammadi Codex II, is also a sayings gospel but has no such individual saying marker. So we tend to read it differently from Thomas, as more of a continuous document. Other Jewish sayings sources, such as Proverbs or the Wisdom of Solomon are similar to Philip in this respect. The "Jesus said" statements impose a structure on Thomas which is not found in these other texts, and this structure must have had some significance to the early users of the Gospel.

In *Does the Gospel of Thomas have a meaning*, Stevan Davies asks why the "Jesus said" statements should be so monotonously repeated (see the quotation at the head of this chapter). Davies suggested that the reason it was necessary to distinguish one saying from another was that the Gospel was used for divination.

Although Davies has made major contributions to the study of Thomas, he has always modestly admitted that he does not understand the Gospel. However, there were other ancient documents equally enigmatic. The Chinese I Ching is also divided into a large number of mystifying sayings. The seeker would approach the I Ching, as an oracle, to ask a question. They would throw sticks into the air and from the pattern the sticks made on the ground, a saying would be selected. The seeker would then have to ponder the meaning of the saying to understand the answer that the universe had revealed. The I Ching came from a different culture, but a similar example from the Roman world was the Oracle of Homer. This consisted of 216 sayings selected from the writings of Homer. These sayings, stripped as they were of their original context, were equally mystifying. To consult the oracle, you would throw three dice. There are 216 combinations from such a throw, so the result would point to a single saying from the collection that gave the seeker a suitably ambiguous answer to their question.[24]

What Davies noticed was the number of sayings in Thomas was very close to 108, which is half of 216. If the Gospel originally contained 108 sayings, three throws of the dice could easily have been used to select a unique saying from Thomas. All that would be required was one small change; if one of the dice read 4,5,6, then this throw could be repeated (or perhaps replaced by 1,2,3). There would then be 108 different combinations, enabling one saying from Thomas to be selected. So did Thomas function as a type of Christian I Ching?

It was necessary to determine the exact number of sayings to support this hypothesis. Davies was proposing that the Gospel had been used continuously for divination up to and including the complete Coptic version that has come down to us. This meant that the number of sayings had to remain constant as the Gospel was transmitted and translated. The "Jesus said" and "he said" dividers would play a vital role in enabling the selection of the correct individual saying. But were there 108 sayings? By keeping more rigorously to the "Jesus said" and "he said" statements, Davies concluded that some sayings had been incorrectly split by the first editors. By counting these as one saying, he was able to get to exactly 108 sayings. However, he had to make some subjective judgment calls and admitted that other scholars would probably come to a different answer.[25]

Davies did not really offer any evidence for his divination theory other than the number of sayings. And because of the doubt as to how many sayings the Gospel originally contained, the case he made was quite weak. There were some obvious objections. If the copy of the Gospel that had come down to us had been used actively for divination with dice, would there not be some marks on the manuscript to make this easier? It would have been a cumbersome process to count through all the sayings to find the correct one. And why would Thomas have been bound as part of a book containing many other texts that were certainly not used for divination? This would be awkward because a divination tool would need to be regularly consulted. In any case, unlike 216 the number 108 is not that special for a method of selecting from dice throws. Any multiple of 36 would do as well. For example, if there were 72 sayings then on the third dice odd numbers could be interpreted as 1, with even numbers being 2. Or if there were 144 sayings, then one dice could be thrown again if it read 5 or 6.

The divination theory did not command much support. Personally, I subscribed to the standard theory that the sayings would originally have been transmitted orally. At some point, they were written down, but the order of the sayings was probably unimportant. Indeed, the lack of order was one reason why some scholars considered Thomas to be early. They regarded it as a haphazard collection of sayings, some potentially going back to Jesus with others added later. Its scholarly value was as a collection of sayings that were potentially independent of the other Gospels.

My view of an oral Thomas began to crumble as I worked on my book, *The Rock and the Tower*. In the final stages of editing that book, I realized that the Gospel of John's account of the last supper was based on the Gospel of Thomas.[26] Eventually, I detected no less than 20 sayings in Thomas that had been used by the author of John in this one section of his Gospel. Sometimes the use of a saying was quite loose, other times it was very specific. But it was significant that the 20 sayings were not randomly scattered over Thomas. Most came from a small section of Thomas, and the sayings in this section were used in almost the same order in John as they appear in our Coptic Thomas. This meant that a written Gospel of Thomas that looked very similar to our Coptic copy (except that it would have been in Greek!) must have been in existence and well accepted by the time the Gospel of John was written at around 100 AD. My work on John also gave me a new respect for the Coptic version of Thomas, which seemed to be closer to the copy that the author of John possessed than the Greek fragments.

While writing *The Rock and the Tower*, I had stopped reading what others had written on Thomas. I wanted to spend my time on the original sources and not be swayed by other interpreters. But this changed as I was finishing the book. I began to catch up on my reading, and I turned again to Davies' book. And so started my fascination with 108.

# *Prime factors*

Most people are aware of prime numbers. These are defined as numbers that cannot be divided by any number other than itself and 1. For example, the number 11 is prime because there is no number other than 11 or 1 that can divide it without leaving a remainder. However, the number 10 is not prime because it is equal to 2 times 5 (which I will write as $2 \cdot 5$ using a $\cdot$ for multiplication). Prime numbers form the foundation of number theory. In the first century, the importance of prime numbers was already well established. The most famous work of ancient mathematicians was Euclid's Elements, which dates from c300 BC. It contains two important proofs concerning prime numbers. One is that there are an infinite number of primes. The other, now called the Fundamental Theory of Arithmetic or the Unique Prime Factorization Theorem, states that every integer (whole number) greater than 1 is either a prime or can be written as a unique product of primes. So, for example, the number 120 has the prime factorization of $2 \cdot 2 \cdot 2 \cdot 3 \cdot 5$. The order of the factors is not important, but if you try and reduce 120 to prime numbers, you will always end up with the same five factors.

To date, an enormous number of prime numbers has been discovered, mostly by computer. But the sequence of prime numbers starts simply enough:

$$2, 3, 5, 7, 11, 13, 17, 19, 23 \ldots$$

The number 108 has a very special prime factorization involving the first two primes, 2 and 3. The prime factorization has two twos and three threes.

$$108 = 2 \cdot 2 \cdot 3 \cdot 3 \cdot 3$$

Or using modern notation:

$$108 = 2^2 \cdot 3^3$$

So, it is equal to the first two primes raised to their own powers. How special is this? Well, it is one of a sequence of numbers that starts with these four:

$$2^2 = 4$$

$$2^2 \cdot 3^3 = 108$$

$$2^2 \cdot 3^3 \cdot 5^5 = 337{,}500$$

$$2^2 \cdot 3^3 \cdot 5^5 \cdot 7^7 = 277{,}945{,}762{,}500$$

After this, the numbers get huge! No one would get very far with just four sayings, so the only practical number in this sequence for a collection of sayings is 108. In this sense, we can say that 108 is unique. But why should the compilers of Thomas select the number of sayings based on mathematics? People would not normally associate any connection between mathematics and Christianity, but we will see that the connections are there! The reason is that to the ancients, these mathematical discoveries had religious significance.

Unlike modern mathematicians, the ancients attached mystical meanings to numbers and mathematical properties. This goes right back to the first Greek mathematician, Pythagoras. He kept his mathematical discoveries secret as mysteries to be taught only to those who joined his religious cult, the Pythagoreans. At its origins, mathematics was indistinguishable from mysticism. The Greeks had a myriad of gods led by Zeus, but as their pantheon arose by a process of accretion of many local deities, it lacked logical cohesion. Indeed, the Greek origin myths for the universe are quite vague. In the most prominent version, the first of the gods was Gaia, the earth, who emerged from primordial Chaos. But what is certain is that Zeus was seen as a relative latecomer, the supposed child of the Titan Cronus, son of Gaia. Zeus might rule the world, but he had not created it. Now imagine what would happen when a culture holding to these beliefs began to uncover mathematical truths that seemed more fundamental than anything in the visible world. Surely it was not Zeus who created the idea of a right-angled triangle, or the precise mathematical relationship between the lengths of its sides? Such mathematical properties must have come before anything visible, before even Gaia. But if mathematical truth was not created by Zeus or the other gods, then humans were beginning to penetrate to a level of knowledge beyond the gods themselves.

There is a vital difference between the Jewish God and Zeus, in that YHWH, unlike Zeus, was believed to have created the universe. The early Jesus movement did not share the Jewish mainstream's view of the YHWH as revealed in the Jewish Scriptures, but they did believe in an ultimate God, YHWH, the Father. The world, however, was not under the direct control of this ultimate God because his divine nature meant that he was too remote to communicate directly with humans. Instead, the world was ruled by lesser divine beings, angels who had rebelled against YHWH. These angels had introduced evil into the creation. The Jesus movement believed that Jesus was the Son of God the Father, a part of the ultimate God who had been sent to assume human nature and redeem humanity from the evil rule of these angels.

The importance of mathematics was that it must have been created before the creation of the visible world. Mathematics could not be created after physical things since such objects can only exist in a physical space which is ruled by the laws of mathematics. But if mathematics came before physical things, then it must have been created by the ultimate God, the Father, before he created the physical universe, and even before he created the angels, the sons of God. So mathematics was uncorrupted by these lesser entities, a rare glimpse into the mind of the ultimate God himself. From this came the belief that God the Father would have somehow encoded some of the secrets of his plan for mankind and the universe in mathematical form.

This, I think, is why the early Jesus movement searched for religious meaning in mathematics, a meaning which they found and expressed in the Thomas Code. If so, it comes from a collision of Jewish and Greek culture, and so probably does not go back to the very first stage of the Jesus movement in Judea in the 20s and 30s AD. Instead, we can see the mathematical ideas as being formed in the 40s and 50s, when the expanding Jesus movement was coming into contact with Greek ways of thinking.

The prime numbers then were all part of God's secret plan. So we should not be surprised to find out that 108 was special because the Jesus movement attached a special religious meaning to the first primes.

## *The Thomas Code*

The order of the prime factorization is not important in modern mathematics. But if the numbers had some special significance then the order would have been very important. How can we express "two twos and three threes" in an order that would have intuitive appeal to the ancient mind? There is one pattern that immediately stood out to me, and it is this I have called the Thomas Code:

$$3 \cdot 2 \cdot 3 \cdot 2 \cdot 3$$

The reason for choosing this order was simple; aesthetics. It seemed more special than other orderings. But we can analyze the features of the aesthetic attraction below.

Symmetry: The most important property is that the ordering is symmetrical around the central 3. The sequence is the same whether read in reverse or forward. Symmetry was of vital importance to the ancients, and they loved symmetrical patterns. They even composed whole passages of text in a symmetrical structure, called a chiastic composition. It is well known that the early Christians were fascinated by chiastic structures. They are particularly important in the first narrative gospel to be written, that of Mark, where scholars have discovered a number of chiastic passages. The requirement for symmetry eliminates all but one other ordering of the five factors. The sequence $2 \cdot 3 \cdot 3 \cdot 3 \cdot 2$ is also symmetrical, but the sequence above seems to me to be far preferable.

Twin twos:

$$3 \cdot 2 \cdot 3 \cdot 2 \cdot 3$$

The pattern has the two twos encased by threes. The twos are placed as twins on either side of the central three. Two is, of course, the number of twinship, and "Thomas" is not a real name but means "twin." We will explore this further once we have seen the significance of the twos.

Three threes:

$$3 \cdot 2 \cdot 3 \cdot 2 \cdot 3$$

The threes form a triad pattern. They are the most important element, occupying both the center and the two ends, being the first and the last. The placing of the threes means that the pattern has both two-fold symmetry with the twos and a three-fold symmetry with the threes. I think it is this combination of both a two-fold and three-fold nature, which makes the pattern so attractive. We will see later what the twos and threes represent.

## The first three primes

We have seen how the number 108 is generated by the first two primes raised to their own powers. The numbers two and three are also special because they are the only two consecutive numbers that are both prime. And there is another feature that would have appealed to the mystical-mathematicians who created Thomas. The Thomas Code is not just created from the first two primes but is intimately related to the third prime, the number 5. There is, in fact, a unique relationship between the first three primes because the third is the sum of the first two:

$$5 = 2 + 3$$

This also means that:

$$3 = 5 - 2$$

These two relations occupy a key role in the mathematical symbolism of the early Jesus movement. In a mathematical sense both properties are unique:

- If we add any two successive primes, there is only one case in which we get another prime, and that is 2 and 3, which sum to the next prime 5.[27]

- There are an infinite number of prime pairs where the difference between the two primes is 2; for example, 5 and 7; 11 and 13; 17 and 19. But there is only one pair of primes where the difference is 3, and that pair is 2 and 5.[28]

A modern mathematician would see these unique properties as deriving from the fact that 2 is the only even prime. However, to the religious mathematicians of the early Jesus movement, the ultimate father created these relationships to express a spiritual truth. So the three prime numbers, 2, 3, and 5 were intimately linked together to signify a secret not known to the angelic powers who ruled the world. The Thomas Code was an expression of this relationship because although it was made up from 2 and 3, it gave the total 5 in three different ways:

- There are 5 factors in the Thomas Code.
- If we add the two prime numbers that feature in the factorization, we get 5.
- If we add any two consecutive factors, we also get five.

The first two are consequences of the prime factorization of 108. The last point, though, is only true for our particular sequence. In fact, this is the only way in which the factors can be organized so that if we add up any consecutive pair of numbers, we get the same answer.[29] For example, if we were to take the other symmetrical sequence $2 \cdot 3 \cdot 3 \cdot 2$ then the first pair adds to 5 but the second pair adds to 6.

## *The Thomas hierarchy*

If the Thomas Code was used to structure the 108 sayings, then the Gospel must be structured as a hierarchy. This would be unique among Christian texts or indeed among any other text from the ancient world. It is much more familiar in our modern information age because it is the natural way in which computers organize collections. Electronic computers work in binary structure, which is equivalent to a prime factorization involving twos, such as $2 \cdot 2 \cdot 2 \cdot$

$2 \cdot 2 \cdot 2 \cdot 2 \cdot 2 = 256$. If Thomas is organized using a similar structure, albeit involving 2s and 3s, then it has anticipated the development of computers by almost two thousand years!

Hierarchies may not have been used for texts, but they were very familiar in the ancient world as the way to organize people, and in particular, armies of soldiers.

Suppose we had an army of 108 men and wanted to organize it using the Thomas Code. We would do it in this way:

The first factor is 3. So we would start by grouping our soldiers into threes. Let us call each of these groups a "squad."

The next factor is 2. So we would take each pair of squads and combine them to make a "platoon." Each of these platoons would have 6 soldiers.

The following factor is 3 again, and we would then group our platoons into threes. Let us call such a group a "regiment." Each of our regiments would have 18 soldiers.

The next to last factor is 2. So we must double our regiments up to make "divisions" consisting of 2 regiments, or 36 soldiers.

The last factor is 3. Our three divisions would make up our army, giving a total of 108 soldiers.

So each soldier belongs to a squad, a platoon, a regiment, and a division. Instead of 108 soldiers, we have 108 sayings, but the principle of the ordering is the same. There are two consequences of applying the Thomas Code to the sayings in this way.

## The ordering is multi-level

Each saying belongs to a group of 3, 6, 18 and 36 sayings as well as the whole Gospel of 108 and being an individual. Moreover, the smaller groups relate to the larger groups. So, for example, we can analyze an eighteen into six threes. This gives a much more complex structure than simply dividing the Gospel into sections. It explains

# The Thomas Code structure and renumbering

| | 1st thirty-six | | 2nd thirty-six | | 3rd thirty-six | |
|---|---|---|---|---|---|---|
| *Divisions within the eighteen:* | 1st eighteen | 2nd eighteen | 3rd eighteen | 4th eighteen | 5th eighteen | 6th eighteen |
| **1st six** — *1st three* | 1.1 | 2.1 | 3.1 | 4.1 | 5.1 | 6.1 |
| | 1.2 | 2.2 | 3.2 | 4.2 | 5.2 | 6.2 |
| | 1.3 | 2.3 | 3.3 | 4.3 | 5.3 | 6.3 |
| *2nd three* | 1.4 | 2.4 | 3.4 | 4.4 | 5.4 | 6.4 |
| | 1.5 | 2.5 | 3.5 | 4.5 | 5.5 | 6.5 |
| | 1.6 | 2.6 | 3.6 | 4.6 | 5.6 | 6.6 |
| **2nd six** — *3rd three* | 1.7 | 2.7 | 3.7 | 4.7 | 5.7 | 6.7 |
| | 1.8 | 2.8 | 3.8 | 4.8 | 5.8 | 6.8 |
| | 1.9 | 2.9 | 3.9 | 4.9 | 5.9 | 6.9 |
| *4th three* | 1.10 | 2.10 | 3.10 | 4.10 | 5.10 | 6.10 |
| | 1.11 | 2.11 | 3.11 | 4.11 | 5.11 | 6.11 |
| | 1.12 | 2.12 | 3.12 | 4.12 | 5.12 | 6.12 |
| **3rd six** — *5th three* | 1.13 | 2.13 | 3.13 | 4.13 | 5.13 | 6.13 |
| | 1.14 | 2.14 | 3.14 | 4.14 | 5.14 | 6.14 |
| | 1.15 | 2.15 | 3.15 | 4.15 | 5.15 | 6.15 |
| *6th three* | 1.16 | 2.16 | 3.16 | 4.16 | 5.16 | 6.16 |
| | 1.17 | 2.17 | 3.17 | 4.17 | 5.17 | 6.17 |
| | 1.18 | 2.18 | 3.18 | 4.18 | 5.18 | 6.18 |

why previous attempts to find a structure have not been successful, although there have been many hints that such a structure exists.

## The ordering is symmetrical

We can either start with the individual sayings and amalgamate them into groups. Or we can start with the whole and divide it up. Either way, we apply the same factors in the same order of 3, 2, 3, 2, 3. This is a consequence of the symmetrical nature of the Thomas sequence. Perhaps the best way to show the symmetrical nature of the hierarchy is to set out the different levels:

> 108 groups of 1 saying
> 36 groups of 3 sayings
> 18 groups of 6 sayings
> 6 groups of 18 sayings
> 3 groups of 36 sayings
> 1 group of 108 sayings

At the end of this book, I have included a copy of the full Gospel renumbered and organized using this structure. In theory, no level of the hierarchy is any more important than any other. To reflect this, we could number each saying by its position in each level the hierarchy. This would give us numbers such as 1.1.3.2.3. In this example, the saying would be in the first thirty-six, the first eighteen of that thirty-six, the third six of the eighteen, the second three of the six, and the third saying of the three. Such a numbering system would be correct but almost incomprehensible. However, in practice, it is difficult to develop a multi-level hierarchy without anchoring it at one level. So we will find that the creators of Thomas attached particular importance to the six groups of eighteen. To reflect this, I have adopted a numbering system based upon the eighteens. The first number is the eighteen (1 to 6) and the second the position of the saying within the eighteen. So instead of numbering the example as 1.1.3.2.3 it now becomes 1.18, meaning that it is the last saying of the first eighteen. The use of the eighteens is convenient, but the reader should remember that the hierarchy is more complex than just eighteens. The full structure in the different levels but organized primarily by eighteens is illustrated by the diagram.

So far, we have not offered any proof that the Thomas Code is the structure behind the Gospel. It is not even certain that the Gospel had 108 sayings. All we can say is that 108 is in a credible range for the original number of sayings. So it is now time to look at how the Gospel itself tells us it is encoded using the Thomas Code. And we will start with that saying 1.18.

# 3

# Five trees in paradise

*1.18 Jesus said: "Blessed is he who was before he came into being. If you should be my disciples and listen to my words, these stones will minister to you. For you have five trees in Paradise which do not move summer and winter, and their leaves do not fall. He who knows them will not taste of death." (Th. 19)*

It was in the above saying that I first found a trace of the Thomas Code. It had always been one of the most mysterious sayings in the whole Gospel. The meaning of the five trees has confounded all commentators. There were two trees in the Garden of Eden, but five? Even those who are most confident in giving their own interpretation of each saying have pulled up at the five trees. For a while, I favored the possibility that the five trees meant the five senses but eventually rejected this idea because there was nothing in the saying to support it.

There was, however, one clue to the meaning of the five trees. Many years ago, I had come across a posting to a Gospel of Thomas group that suggested that the five trees must mean the Gospel of Thomas. The reason for thinking this was that the language of Thomas 19 matched the Incipit in which it is promised that one who knew the meaning of the words (the Gospel) would not taste death. In Thomas 19, one who knows the trees will not taste death. So logically both the "words" and the "trees" should mean the same thing. If this were the case, then the leaves that do not fall would be a reference to the individual sayings. But there was much that did not fit this explanation. Why should the trees not "move" during both summer and winter? Would there even be summer or winter in paradise? And then there was the odd image of the stones that minister. What did this mean?

There was something else though that supported the idea that the five trees were the Gospel. There were clear clues that the Gospel was coming to an ending at this exact point. This was puzzling because the Gospel would then have just eighteen sayings (this assumes that we regard Thomas 1 as being part of the Incipit as most scholars do). But it did, of course, continue for another 95 sayings! Some people thought that perhaps this first part of Thomas was originally a separate work, a mini-gospel that was then expanded by the addition of many more sayings. If so then the five trees would have been the very last thing in this original Gospel, so it was fitting that they applied to the whole.

Nor was it unreasonable that the Gospel should be compared to trees in paradise. There were clues linking the saying to the story of the creation in Genesis. It is well known that in Eden there were two trees; the tree of life and the tree of the knowledge of good and evil. Adam and Eve were permitted to eat of any tree except the tree of the knowledge of good and evil. But Eve was seduced by the promise of the serpent that if she ate she would not die but would have knowledge like God. She goes ahead and eats of the tree and persuades Adam to also eat. But when YHWH finds out, he exiles them from paradise:

> Then the Lord God said, "Behold, the man has become like one of us in knowing good and evil. Now, lest he reach out his hand and take also of the tree of life and eat, and live forever—" (Genesis 3:22 ESV)

It is fascinating that YHWH seems to agree with what the serpent has told Eve. By tasting of the fruit of good and evil, they have become as "one of us," that is like the Elohim, the gods. But they have yet to eat from a second tree, the tree of life. If they ate from this tree, they would live forever. This ties into Thomas 19 where one who "knows" the trees will not taste death.

The Gnostics attached huge importance to this story in Genesis, and some of them equated the apple to Gnosis. In this view, YHWH was the lower god, the demiurge, who was deliberately keeping knowledge from mankind. So we might see the five trees as a Gnostic element that has crept into Thomas. Except for the frustrating detail that we have five trees and not one or two. After grappling with the saying over the years, I concluded that it was essentially unsolvable because we were missing a vital piece of the puzzle. I thought there must be a work featuring the five trees but that it had been lost.

Now, however, the five trees were staring me in the face:

$$3 \cdot 2 \cdot 3 \cdot 2 \cdot 3$$

They were the five factors of the Thomas Code! And I saw something else. That odd phrase that the five trees "do not move summer and winter" suddenly made sense. Suppose we go through the sequence a pair at a time. We start with 3 and 2, then we have 2 and 3 and so on. This gives a series of pairs that we can think of as two seasons:

[3, 2]  (summer)

[2, 3]  (winter)

[3, 2]  (summer)

[2, 3]  (winter)

Yet regardless of whether it is summer or winter we still get the same total:

$$3 + 2 = 2 + 3 = 5$$

Which equals the number of factors. The five trees do not move summer or winter because each pair sums to five. Of all the ways in which we could order the five factors, this is only true for the Thomas Code ordering. So, if we started with the concept of the prime factorization of 108 and combined this with the information in Thomas 19 that the trees do not move summer or winter, then the

Thomas Code would be determined uniquely. There is no other way we can structure the factors.

It was the five trees saying that first led me to the importance of 5 in the Thomas Code and the fact that if we sum any successive factors, we get the total number of factors. Whoever composed Thomas 19 understood this property and wanted to draw our attention to it.

This was not the only thing that the Thomas Code explained. The very positioning of the saying was a powerful confirmation. The Gospel was not coming to an end, nor were the first eighteen sayings originally a separate gospel. The Thomas Code predicted that the Gospel should be organized by eighteens. As the Jesus movement attached particular importance to the principle of "first and last," the first and the last eighteens were particularly important. The Gospel was marking the end of this first eighteen by linking back symmetrically to the beginning. The five trees saying was positioned as the very last of the eighteen and was symmetrical to the first saying about seeking and finding. If the five trees meant the Thomas Code and hence the Gospel, then this was exactly where it should be. It was the culmination of the theme of seeking and finding that ruled the first group of eighteen.

It was clear that "their leaves do not fall" must represent the sayings, which are eternal. But what did the stones that minister mean? We will come to this shortly and show how it is explained by the Thomas Code. But first, we will take a more detailed look at the placing of the saying in the first eighteen.

## *The first eighteen*

The diagram shows the structure of the first eighteen. The Gospel starts with a brief introduction, which scholars call "the Incipit":

> *These are the hidden words that the living Jesus spoke, and Didymus Judas Thomas wrote down. And he said this: "Whoever finds the meaning of these words will not taste death." (Th. Incipit and Th. 1 — Coptic)*

# The First Eighteen - symmetries and links between beginning and end

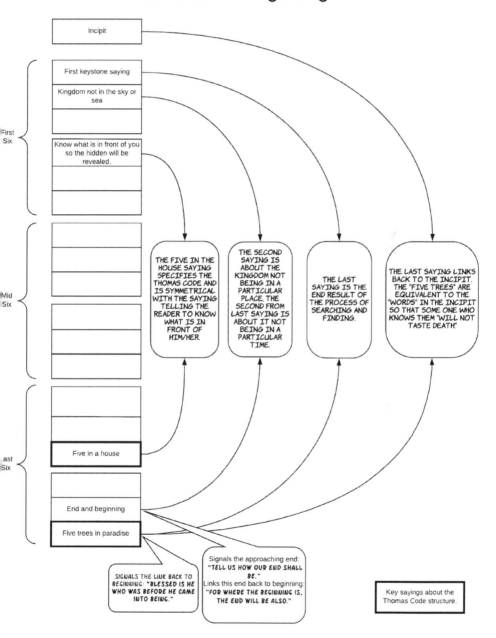

Incipit

First keystone saying

Kingdom not in the sky or sea

Know what is in front of you so the hidden will be revealed.

**First Six**

**Mid Six**

**Last Six**

Five in a house

End and beginning

Five trees in paradise

THE FIVE IN THE HOUSE SAYING SPECIFIES THE THOMAS CODE AND IS SYMMETRICAL WITH THE SAYING TELLING THE READER TO KNOW WHAT IS IN FRONT OF HIM/HER.

THE SECOND SAYING IS ABOUT THE KINGDOM NOT BEING IN A PARTICULAR PLACE. THE SECOND FROM LAST SAYING IS ABOUT IT NOT BEING IN A PARTICULAR TIME.

THE LAST SAYING IS THE END RESULT OF THE PROCESS OF SEARCHING AND FINDING.

THE LAST SAYING LINKS BACK TO THE INCIPIT. THE "FIVE TREES" ARE EQUIVALENT TO THE "WORDS" IN THE INCIPIT SO THAT SOME ONE WHO KNOWS THEM "WILL NOT TASTE DEATH".

SIGNALS THE LINK BACK TO BEGINNING: "BLESSED IS HE WHO WAS BEFORE HE CAME INTO BEING."

Signals the approaching end: "TELL US HOW OUR END SHALL BE." Links this end back to beginning: "FOR WHERE THE BEGINNING IS, THE END WILL BE ALSO."

Key sayings about the Thomas Code structure.

The second half ("*And he said this ...*") is conventionally numbered as the first saying, Thomas 1. However, I follow Stevan Davies and others in taking Thomas 1 and the Incipit as one whole.[30] Finding the meaning of the words and not tasting death links back to the "hidden words that the living Jesus spoke" in the first part of the Incipit.

The first proper saying then, is conventionally numbered as Thomas 2:

> *1.1 Jesus said: "Let him who seeks not stop seeking until he finds, and when he finds he will be troubled, and if he is troubled he will become amazed, and he will become king over the all of it." (Th. 2—Coptic)*

This is one of the most significant sayings in the Gospel. It is one of three "keystone" sayings, each relating to searching and finding and each located in one of the three thirty-sixes where it occupies a specific position. As the first saying of the whole Gospel, this keystone saying does double-duty; it rules both the first thirty-six and also the Gospel as a whole.

Saying 1.18 is symmetrical to 1.1 within the eighteen; one is last and the other first. We will see that 1.18 is also closely linked to the Incipit. There is also a link between the second saying 1.2 and the second from last 1.17. Not only does this indicate the symmetrical nature of the eighteen, but 1.17 also gives us a clear clue that the eighteen is coming to an end.

## The end and the beginning

> *1.17 The disciples said to Jesus: "Tell us how our end shall be." Jesus said: "Have you discovered then the beginning, that you seek after the end? For where the beginning is, the end will be also. Blessed is he who will stand in the beginning, and he will know the end and not taste of death." (Th. 18)*

In this saying, the very idea of linear time is challenged. The disciples expect the apocalypse and kingdom of heaven to come at the end of time, but Jesus points them back to the beginning, the first spiritual creation in Genesis. To those in the kingdom of heaven all time is one; if they exist at the beginning, they will exist also at the end. Although this is the first and most substantive level of meaning, it is normal for Thomas sayings to do double or triple duty. The deeper spiritual meaning exists simultaneously with a lighter "riddle" meaning. So we will see how this saying cleverly alludes to the structure of Thomas as well as expressing the philosophy of the Jesus movement towards time.

**Links between 1.17 and 1.2**

Sayings 1.2 and 1.17 are symmetrical within the eighteen:

> *1.2 Jesus said: "If those who lead you say to you: 'Behold, the kingdom is in the sky' then the birds of the sky will become first before you. If they say to you: 'It is in the sea' then the fish will become first before you. Rather the kingdom is inside you and outside you. When you should know yourselves, then you shall be known, and you shall realize that you are the sons of the living Father. But if, however, you do not know yourselves, then you are in poverty, and you are poverty." (Th. 3)*

The two sayings are linked, with one concerned with the location of the kingdom in physical space and the other with its location in time:

- In 1.2, "those who lead you" say that the kingdom of heaven is in the sky or under the sea. However, the idea that the kingdom is located in a particular place is rejected; it is "inside you and outside you."

- In 1.17, the disciples think that the kingdom is at the end. But Jesus tells them that the kingdom is not at a particular time; "where the beginning is, the end will be also."

In both sayings, the end result of "knowing" is the kingdom of heaven; in 1.2 those who know themselves will be *"sons of the living father"* whereas in 1.17 one who knows the end *"will not taste death."*

The symmetry between 1.17 and 1.2 is important because it shows that the next saying must be the end of the section, the eighteen. But this is also indicated by other clues.

## The end is nigh

Most obviously 1.17 contains a strong clue to the approaching end:

> *"Tell us how our end shall be?"*

This is very typical of the riddling nature of Thomas. The question is telling us that the end is imminent and will come with the next saying.

## Symmetry

Jesus' reply expresses the symmetry and chiastic structure of the eighteen, and indeed of the Gospel as a whole, by linking the end to the beginning:

> *Have you discovered then the beginning, that you seek after the end? For where the beginning is, the end will be also.*

The link of beginning and end applies at different levels:
1. To the eighteen.
2. To the Gospel as a whole.
3. The structure of time itself.

Some of the symmetries of the eighteen are illustrated by the diagram, and we will see additional expressions of this symmetry when we analyze the first eighteen in more detail. But there is also symmetry within the whole Gospel, between the first and last eighteens. Most obviously the second saying 1.2 is closely linked with our second to last saying 6.17 as two "bookends." We will see that 1.17 comes into this structure and is also linked with 6.17 as well as 1.2.

The symmetry of the Gospel is a reflection of the symmetry of time itself. And the same symmetry is found in the Thomas Code:

$$3 \cdot 2 \cdot 3 \cdot 2 \cdot 3$$

This also can be read either backward or forward with the same result, so that "where the beginning is, the end is also."

## Will not taste death

Let us walk through 1.18 in its entirety. It starts with a blessing:

> *Blessed is he who was before he came into being*

This is connected with the last line of 1.17:

> *Blessed is he who will stand in the beginning, and he will know the end and not taste of death.*

In 1.17, one who stands at the beginning is blessed, whereas in 1.18, it is the one who existed before he came into existence who is blessed. What does this strange idea of existing before you came into being mean? In fact, both blessings relate to the creation story in Genesis. A person can exist "before he came into being" because in Genesis there are two accounts of the creation of man, Adam. In the first creation, Adam was made hermaphrodite, male and female.[31] In the second creation, he was made again out of dust and the female, Eve, separated from his rib.[32] The Jesus movement believed that the first creation was a spiritual creation which took place before the second physical creation. This first creation resulted in a spiritual reality that was more fundamental than the degraded physical reality around us. By entering the kingdom of heaven, a Christian would return to this first spiritual reality. They could only do this if they had an existence which transcended physical reality, by existing in the first creation, before their physical birth. Time was an aspect of the physical universe and did not exist in the spiritual creation. So one who entered into the kingdom of heaven and the first spiritual reality transcended time. The saying continues:

> *If you should be my disciples and listen to my words, these stones will minister to you.*

This links back to the Incipit:

> *These are the hidden words that the living Jesus spoke, and Didymus Judas Thomas wrote down. And he said this: "Whoever finds the meaning of these words will not taste death."*

The Incipit says that Jesus spoke the hidden words and that one who finds the meaning of the words "will not taste death." Now in the last saying of the eighteen, it is promised that if you should be a disciple and listen to Jesus' words "these stones will minister to you." We will see what this odd expression of the stones means in the next section, but we will first look at the remainder of the saying:

> *For you have five trees in Paradise which do not move summer and winter, and their leaves do not fall. He who knows them will not taste of death.*

So one who listens to the words and knows the trees will not "*taste of death,*" the same expression we find in the Incipit. We have seen how the five trees stand for the Thomas Code and hence the Gospel of Thomas. So the words and the trees are the same thing, the Gospel of Thomas which brings life.

We can now see how the last line of the previous saying (1.17), cleverly alludes to 1.18. It starts with

> *Blessed is he who will stand in the beginning…*

Which, as we have seen, links to the beginning of 1.18. It continues:

> *…and he will know the end…*

Linking to the end, the last saying of the eighteen 1.18, and specifically the five trees.

> *...and not taste of death.*

The identical expression that ends 1.18 and links back to the Incipit.

## *The stones that minister*

There is one element of 1.18 left to explain:

> *If you should be my disciples and listen to my words, these stones will minister to you.*

To minister is to supply with food and drink. So what can be meant by saying that stones will minister? And how can this tie in with the idea that the five trees are an allusion to the Thomas Code?

There is one story in Matthew and Luke that does talk about stones becoming bread, and that is when Jesus goes into the wilderness and is tempted by the devil:

> *And the tempter came and said to him, "If you are the Son of God, speak that these stones might become loaves of bread." But answering he said, "It is written, 'Man shall not live by bread alone, but by every word that comes from the mouth of God.'" (Matthew 4:3-4)*

This is expressing a close parallel to the Thomas saying. Not only do we have the stones turning into bread but also the concept of the "word" from the mouth of God. In 1.18 and the Incipit, the words that bring life come from the mouth of Jesus. So, has Thomas taken the idea of stones that minister from Matthew or Luke? No, because the Matthew story is literal and the Thomas saying is metaphorical. Whatever the saying means in Thomas, it is certainly not that stones will magically begin dispensing food or turn into tasty loaves of bread. The metaphor comes first and it is then misunderstood and literalized as a miracle story. Matthew/Luke have taken the metaphor from Thomas and not the other way around.

To understand the real origins of "the stones that minister" we must look at the two elements separately. First, who is it that ministers? And second, what was the meaning of the stones to the Jesus movement? We will see that the two questions point to the same answer.

### Those who minister

The word to "minister" is the Greek, *diakonei*. Although the general meaning was to supply the wants of someone, such as to give them food and drink, to the Jesus movement it meant something very specific. It applied to the role of ministering in the spiritual sense to those in the movement. It has given us the word "deacon" as well as the English "minister" for those who look after a flock.

To the Jesus movement, it was spiritual food and drink that was ministered, the bread and wine of the Eucharist, the substance of Jesus. It is the food that can be infinitely divided and shared. Although given by all "ministers," the power and authority derived from the original disciples/apostles whom Paul calls simply "the Twelve." In Acts, we find the Twelve in a story about ministering:

> *Now in these days when the disciples were increasing in number, a complaint by the Hellenists arose against the Hebrews because their widows were being neglected in the daily ministration (diakonia). And the twelve summoned the full number of the disciples and said, "It is not right that we should give up preaching the word of God to minister (diakonein) at tables. Therefore, brothers, pick out from among you seven men of good repute, full of the Spirit and of wisdom, whom we will appoint to this duty. But we will devote ourselves to prayer and to the ministry (diakonia) of the word." (Acts 6:1-4)*

We have here a tradition that both the Twelve and the Seven were involved in ministering to the movement. We should not get too distracted by the literal elements of this story. The person who wrote both Luke and Acts is a very able novelist who invents shamelessly. But behind the literal elements we can see the original source:

- The Twelve were first involved in ministering to the disciples.
- The Twelve were supplanted in this task by a new group called the Seven.

In Acts, the Seven are ministering to the Hellenists, that is the Gentiles. This suggests that the appointment of the Seven was connected with the expansion of the movement away from Judea and across the Roman Empire. In the Acts story, the food and drink become literal. But this was not the real meaning of "ministering" to the movement. It was spiritual food and drink that was the true sustenance. Neither should we give any credibility to the names of the Seven in Acts, which are a complete invention by the author of Acts. Most likely the real Seven were the same group that Paul calls "the brethren of the Lord" with James as their leader. The evidence of Paul's letters shows that the brethren were in charge of the movement when Paul was writing his epistles in the AD 50s and that they were not the same group as the Twelve.

We have answered the question of who ministers to the disciples; it was the Twelve followed by the Seven. But what is the connection to the stones?

## The twelve stones

The reason why the Twelve should be called stones is found in the Torah in the stories about Moses and his successor Joshua. Moses led the Israelites out of the land of Egypt, parting the waters of the Red Sea so that they could pass over safety and escape the pursuit of Pharaohs' army, who were drowned when the waters closed again. Although Moses was to lead the Israelites to within sight of the Promised Land, he was forbidden to cross over by YHWH and died at Moab. It was Joshua who crossed the Jordan, in a miracle that is very similar to, but less spectacular than, the crossing of the Red Sea. Joshua commanded the priests to carry the Arc of the Covenant to the edge of the waters, which then parted in front of them. They were then able to walk on the dry riverbed to the center of the river, even though the waters were swollen by the rains. As the priests hold the Arc, the people walk across the river. Joshua then orders twelve men, one for each of the twelve tribes, to take a stone from the river bed where the priests stand and erect it on the bank. The twelve stones are a memorial to the twelve sons of Israel (Joshua 3:1-4:9).

We find a similar story about twelve stones applying to Moses. Before ascending Mount Sinai and receiving the Law from YHWH, he erects twelve stones to represent the twelve tribes:

> And Moses wrote down all the words of the Lord. He rose early in the morning and built an altar at the foot of the mountain, and twelve pillars, according to the twelve tribes of Israel. And he sent young men of the people of Israel, who offered burnt offerings and sacrificed peace offerings of oxen to the Lord. (Exodus 24:4-5 ESV)

The "young men" are a group of twelve young men that follow Moses around to represent the twelve tribes. The link to Jesus and the Twelve has been noted by scholars, who believe that Moses' twelve are the prototype for the Christian Twelve.

So we find stories about both Moses and Joshua in which twelve stones represent the twelve sons of Israel, and that the same stories are behind the appointment of Twelve special disciples in the Jesus movement. It is clear that the "stones that minister" must represent the Twelve. But how is this connected to the Thomas Code?

### The stones that minister in the Thomas Code

We can, in fact, find both the Twelve and the Seven from the Thomas code. Let us look at the sequence again, this time emphasizing the central three:

$$3 \cdot 2 \cdot 3 \cdot 2 \cdot 3$$

Like the whole sequence, this three is also symmetrical. It is positioned at the heart of the Thomas code so we should not be surprised if it is significant. Suppose we multiply it out, what do we get?

$$2 \cdot 3 \cdot 2 = 12$$

It gets us to the Twelve! The stones that minister, meaning the Twelve, are encoded at the very center of the Thomas Code! We have seen that adding factors was also important—this was how we got 5 from two successive factors. So suppose we add the three central factors instead of multiplying them:

$$2 + 3 + 2 = 7$$

This gives us the other group who minister, the Seven.

The original "stones that minister" must be the Twelve as only the twelve are related to the stones in scripture. There are two possibilities. Either the person who put the Thomas Code together has noted the coincidence that the central triplet multiplies to twelve, and put an allusion to this in 1.18. Or the whole idea of the Twelve has come in the first place from the Thomas Code. If so, then this central twelve has been connected to the stories about Moses and Joshua, from which the idea of the twelve disciples and apostles has come. As the Twelve are a very early feature, this second possibility would require the Thomas Code to have been in existence from the very beginning of the movement, which seems unlikely.

We can be more confident that the concept of the Seven has been generated from the Thomas Code. The Seven come on the scene much later than the Twelve. They are only connected to the stones indirectly, through the Thomas Code. So it seems that when a replacement to the Twelve was desired, the central three factors were added to justify Seven. As the original Twelve were intimately connected to the twelve tribes of Israel, it makes sense for the Seven to be associated with the new mission to the Gentiles.

# The importance of eighteen

The significance of the central triplet in the Thomas Code leads to another insight. There are actually three such triplets in the sequence. The other two are positioned at the beginning and end:

$$\mathbf{3 \cdot 2 \cdot 3} \cdot 2 \cdot 3$$

and:

$$3 \cdot 2 \cdot \mathbf{3 \cdot 2 \cdot 3}$$

These both give the triplet:

$$3 \cdot 2 \cdot 3$$

This is also symmetrical and multiplies out to eighteen:

$$3 \cdot 2 \cdot 3 = 18$$

We will see how vital the eighteens are in the organization of the Gospel. The fact that the triplet at the beginning and end of the sequence gives 18 provides a reason why the compilers of Thomas should attach particular importance to the eighteens.

# 4

# Five in a house

*1.15 Jesus said: "Perhaps men think that I am come to cast peace upon the world, and know not that I am come to cast divisions upon the earth; fire, sword, war. For five will be in a house, three will be against two, and two against three, the father against the son and the son against the father; and they shall stand as single ones." (Th. 16)*

This is perhaps the most important of the structural sayings in the Gospel. It is positioned fourth from the end of the first eighteen. It is the last saying of the fifth three whereas the five trees saying 1.18 is the last saying of the sixth three. The symmetrical saying within the eighteen is 1.4:

*1.4 Jesus said: "Know what is in front of you and that which is hidden from you will be revealed to you. For there is nothing hidden that will not appear." (Th. 5)*

The Incipit tells us that what is hidden is the meaning of the words. So if we can *"know what is in front of you,"* we can understand the Gospel. So what is *"in front of you"*? If you were reading saying 1.4 in its original setting, then the Gospel of Thomas would be in front of you! You must see what is staring you in the face in the Gospel to understand the hidden things, the meaning of the words. The purpose of the saying is to challenge us. The clue to the Gospel is somewhere right in front of us. And the riddle is solvable—*"there is nothing hidden that will not appear."* If we solve it, we will have the clue that will help us understand the hidden meanings. We just need to use our eyes. It is 1.15 that is *"in front of you,"* as the symmetrical saying ahead of us in the eighteen.

Versions of 1.15 are also found in Luke and Matthew.[33] This is one of few times when Jesus seems to be promoting violence. In fact, the other times Jesus seems to suggest violence can all be traced back to this one saying. But what is most important for now are the numbers. Five, three, two, and one are all present. We show how the Thomas Code can explain the whole of this saying before looking at the revolutionary implications for the origins of all the Gospels.

## Casting fire upon the Earth

Let us start with the first line:

> *Perhaps men think that I am come to cast peace upon the world, and know not that I am come to cast divisions upon the earth; fire, sword, war.*

At face value, Jesus here is saying that he comes to bring war rather than peace. This conflicts with the Christian emphasis on non-violence and pacifism. Unlike other Jewish groups, the Jesus movement did not believe in fighting the Romans. The contradiction is a sign that we are not supposed to read this at face value. It is a riddle. Jesus' paradoxical words are challenging us to find the solution.

### What is cast upon the earth?

The word for "cast" is repeated twice in the line. Jesus has not come to *"cast peace upon the world"* but to *"cast divisions upon the earth."* There are two other sayings in Thomas where something is cast onto the earth or the world, and both are found together in the first eighteen. They are in the third three of the eighteen, starting with the parable of the sower:

> *1.8 Jesus said: "Behold, the sower came out, he filled his hand, he cast. Some indeed fell upon the road; the birds*

*came and gathered them. Others fell onto the rock, and sent*
*no root down to the earth nor did they sprout any sheaths*
*up to the sky. And others fell onto the thorns; they choked*
*the seed, and the worm ate them. And others fell onto the*
*good earth, and gave good fruit up to the sky, sixty per*
*measure and a hundred and twenty per measure." (Th. 9)*

The meaning of the parable is not explained in Thomas, and in Mark, Jesus also first gives the parable to the multitude without explanation. But later, in private, he tells his inner circle that the seed represents the "word."[34] This explanation in Mark is surely on the right lines. The seed represents the gospel, which when it falls upon good soil has a superabundant yield (sixtyfold and a hundred and twenty fold). Those who hear the gospel and yield the fruit will then go out and sow the gospel seed to others. So the saying is describing the start of the process of exponential increase. Whoever composed the parable of the sower had faith that the Jesus movement would greatly expand as indeed it did.

So the thing that is cast upon the earth is the word or gospel and the person who does the first sowing is Jesus. In Thomas, the word means the Gospel of Thomas; it is the Gospel itself that is cast upon the earth.

**Casting fire**

The other example of something cast upon the world is in the very next saying:

*1.9 Jesus said: "I have cast fire upon the world, and behold*
*I watch over it until it burns." (Th. 10)*

The fire is not the apocalypse as some think.[35] If this were about the apocalypse, then Jesus would be a sadist. Not only does he set the world alight, but he guards the fire until it blazes. If this were a literal fire, then he would watch while men, women, and children catch fire and die, all the time fanning and spreading the flames. Instead, we must understand this saying in relation to the parable of the sower, which occurs immediately before. Just as the sower spreads the seed so starting an exponential increase of the gospel, so Jesus casts the fire and guards it, until it also spreads across the world. Those who are the fruits of the initial sowing will become sowers in their own right; those who are ablaze with the spiritual fire will set others alight. The two sayings are parallel ways of describing the same thing, the exponential increase of the Jesus movement. This interpretation of "fire" is supported by another Thomas saying:

> Jesus said: "He who is close to me is close to the fire, and
> he who is far from me is far from the kingdom." (Th. 82)

To be close to Jesus is to be close to the fire and also close to the kingdom. This is not consistent with the fire being something destructive. The fire is spiritual, not literal. We find the idea of the "Holy Spirit" as a fire that descends upon the apostles at Pentecost in Acts:

> They saw what seemed to be tongues of fire that separated
> and came to rest on each of them. (Acts 2:3 ESV)

The spirit was called both a wind or breath, *pneuma*, and fire, so the author of Acts makes up a story where the spirit is literal wind and literal fire. We find the original "fire" in Thomas, where it is not tongues of flame from heaven, but the spiritual fire spread by the word, the Gospel.

## It is the Gospel of Thomas that is cast upon the world

The evidence all points in the same direction; the thing that is cast upon the world/earth is the Gospel of Thomas, and it is the Gospel that is the subject of 1.15. Jesus in this saying is not advocating violence; he is not a sadist, and he is not talking about the apocalypse. The saying is a riddle about Thomas.

## A gospel not of peace

*Perhaps men think that I am come to cast peace upon the world...*

The riddle meaning of this line is about people's false expectations of the Gospel. Most of those who read or listen to the Gospel expect "peace," meaning that they expect it to be harmonious and consistent, at peace with itself. They are looking for something that tells them what to believe and how to behave. Something that sets out clear moral principles that they can agree with and follow. But that is not the gospel that Jesus gives them:

*...and know not that I am come to cast divisions upon the earth;*

Instead of a "peace," Jesus brings a gospel of "divisions." This word refers to two things. First, it is alluding to the structure of the Gospel. We can apply the Thomas Code either by accumulating sayings in groups of three, two, three, etc., or by dividing up the 108 sayings into three, and then two, and then three, etc. So one meaning of "divisions" is this way of dividing up the Gospel.

The second meaning of "divisions" is that the Gospel appears, to those who seek "peace," to be divided against itself. At face value, the sayings are opposed to each other. The Gospel expresses its truths through paradox and contradiction. It loves to confound our expectations, even to the extent of expressing the exact opposite of what we are expecting. So we find sayings telling the believer not to pray, fast or give alms, even though we know perfectly well that early Christians did pray, fast and give alms. Those with tidy, rational minds will explode trying to cope with these contradictions. Which is why many Christians, in both the ancient and modern worlds, have rejected the Gospel of Thomas at first acquaintance.

*fire, sword, war.*

This phrase expands upon "divisions." At face value, it is talking about armed conflict, but again we are being presented with a riddle! These three words cover both meanings of "divisions."

## Fire, sword

We start with two words that point us to the way the Gospel is organized into divisions and the main structure of eighteens. Each suggests a saying in the first and last eighteens respectively.

Fire in the first eighteen: We have seen Jesus casting fire onto the world in saying 1.9 above.

Sword in the last eighteen:

> 6.6 [Jesus said: The kingdom of the Father is like a man who wanted to kill a great man. He drew the sword in his house and drove it into the wall, that he might know that his hand would be strong. Then he slew the great man.] (Th. 98)

So, both "fire" and "sword" are linked to sayings, one in the first eighteen and one in the sixth. They summarize the main divisions of the Gospel by reference to the first and last eighteens.

## War

We might be tempted then to think that war also means one of the divisions of the Gospel. The sayings in the first and last eighteens are also in the first and last thirty-sixes. So are the three words intended to point to the three thirty-sixes? There is no saying in the whole Gospel that explicitly mentions war, but the closest we come is the parable of the tenants, 4.10, which is indeed in the middle thirty-six. In this parable, a good man rents out his vineyard to tenants who refuse to give him the fruits. He first sends two servants who are beaten and then his son who is killed. There are two problems though with identifying this saying with "war." First, the sequence would be out of order; it should be "fire, war, sword." Second, to call the dispute in this parable "war" is stretching things!

Instead, we should see "war" as contrasting with the "peace" that men expect. If so then "war" refers to the second meaning of "divisions"; the civil war that the Gospel is raging against itself and which defies the reader's expectations for harmony. The contrary nature of the Gospel of Thomas has been well remarked by modern readers and conventional commentators. For example, in his recent book on the Gospel, Mark Goodacre offers the view that Thomas is deliberately enigmatic and unclear (see the quotation at the start of the first Chapter).

It would seem that the first readers shared the same unease. In places, the Gospel is downright contradictory. For example, Thomas 95 says that you should not lend money at interest but give it away without asking anything back in return. However, Thomas 109 approves of lending at interest; when a man finds a treasure in a field, he can lend money at interest to whom he wishes. It is no coincidence that both these sayings are in the last eighteen, and we will see that these two sayings are placed symmetrically within the eighteen; one is third from the beginning, the other third from the end. The opposition between the two is quite intentional.

The use of paradox and contradiction is woven through the Gospel, and we find it within the individual sayings. As an example, look at a group of sayings that constitute a "three" within the fifth eighteen:

> *5.7 Jesus said: "Whoever has known the world has found the body, and whoever has found the body, the world is not worthy of him." (Th. 80)*

> *5.8 Jesus said: "Whoever has become rich, let him become king, and he who has power let him renounce it." (Th. 81)*

> *5.9 Jesus said: "He who is close to me is close to the fire, and he who is far from me is far from the kingdom." (Th. 82)*

The three are linked by the same paradoxical form. The Gospel is continually playing with its readers, challenging them to resolve the paradoxes. Every saying is its own riddle, which we must solve. A favorite technique of the Gospel is to assign to a word a spiritual meaning that draws upon, and yet contrasts with, the physical meaning. So in 5.8, riches are the spiritual riches of the kingdom of God, as well as the mundane riches of physical gold. And the apparent paradox of 5.8 is resolved once we realize that the "fire" is the spiritual fire with which we burn if we are close to Jesus.

## Five in a house

After threatening war, the saying comes down to squabbles in a household. Under conventional explanations this makes no sense. But with the realization that the saying is specifying the Thomas Code, it all becomes clear. So the saying starts with an allusion to the divisions of the Gospel. It then specifies the mathematical structure of these divisions:

> *For five will be in a house, three will be against two, and two against three, the father against the son and the son against the father; and they shall stand as single ones.*

We will go through it part by part.

> *For five will be in a house,*

This is parallel to the five trees in Thomas 19. It refers, of course, to the five factors in the Thomas Code. The line continues:

> *three will be against two, and two against three,*

Combined with the information that there is "five in a house" this completely specifies the factorization. It tells us that we start with 3 and this is followed by 2. The 2 is then followed by 3. To extend to the five in a house, we must have:

$$[3,2]$$
$$[2,3]$$
$$[3,2]$$
$$[2,3]$$

Which is the Thomas Code order:

$$3, 2, 3, 2, 3$$

To get the whole sequence, we have to extend it beyond the first two pairs. However, we can do better than that! Consider the next line:

*the father against the son and the son against the father;*

This line disrupts the flow between the "three" and "two" in the previous line and the "single one" in the line following. Does it go against our mathematical interpretation? No, it confirms that interpretation beautifully! It was a common convention in Semitic literature to repeat something twice using two expressions which appear to be different but which mean the same thing. This gives us the clue to understanding the line. We need to take it together with the first part:

*three will be against two, and two against three*

*the father against the son, and the son against the father;*

See how these are exact parallels! All we have to do is replace the parallel terms:

father = three

son = two

Now if we expand this is what we get:

| | |
|---|---|
| three will be against two | [3,2] |
| two against three | [2,3] |
| the father against the son | [3,2] |
| the son against the father | [2,3] |

Which specifies the Thomas Code:

$$3 \cdot 2 \cdot 3 \cdot 2 \cdot 3$$

The son, of course, is Jesus and the Father is God. So under this interpretation, Jesus, the Son, is represented by "2" and God, the

Father, by "3." This will have profound significance and is the first clue to the mystical meaning of the Thomas Code.

The last line continues the numerical symbolism:

*and they shall stand as single ones.*

The Coptic word translated here as "single ones" is *monachos,* which came to mean those who lived in monasteries. However, the first evidence for this monastic meaning dates from the fourth-century, long after Thomas was written.[36] The same word *monachos* is also found in Thomas 49 and 75. The word literally meant "singles" and is very similar to the Greek loan word expression "single one," which is also used in Coptic Thomas. It was Klijn who proposed that the original expression was indeed "single one" and that in these few places it has been translated into Coptic as *monachos.*[37] I think this is the most likely explanation and have followed Grondin[38] in using "single ones" for *monachos* in the English translation. We should remember that those who produced the Coptic translation of Thomas would have been *monachos* (monks) themselves and would have had a strong incentive to use this word.

The "single ones" in Thomas generally means the chosen, those who are in the kingdom of heaven. Here it has two meanings. The first is an extension of the numerical mysticism of the previous line. This meaning relates the "single ones," the chosen, to the two (Jesus) and the three (God the Father). We shall explore this meaning later.

The second meaning relates to the individual sayings. The Gospel is at war with itself, and the last line literally means "they shall stand alone." The previous lines referred to the structure of the Gospel, and this is now telling us that each saying must be understood on a "stand-alone" basis. Each and every saying has an individual meaning apart from any meaning connected with the Gospel as a whole. The riddle that is the Gospel of Thomas has 108 sub-riddles!

# The structure of 1.15

We can now look at the structure of the saying as a whole. One aspect of this structure is that it is carefully constructed around numbers:

> We start with 2 contrasting things (peace and divisions).
> We then have 3 things (fire, sword, war).
> We then have 5 in a house (5=2+3)
> This 5 is then split into 3 and 2 which are opposed
> We then have 2 opposed things (the father and son)
> We end with 1, a "single one."

It is a play on the three prime numbers, 2, 3, and 5. It first ascends to 5, which is resolved into 3 and 2, and then descends, ending with 1.

There is also a close similarity with the other structural saying, 1.18, about the five trees in paradise. They both approach the Thomas Code in the same way, as a sequence of pairs. This can be seen in the comparison below:

| **1.18 (Th. 19)** | **1.15 (Th. 16)** |
|---|---|
| *For you have five trees in Paradise* | *For five will be in a house,* |
| This specifies the five factors. | This specifies the five factors. |
| *which do not move summer and winter,* | *three will be against two, and two against three* |
| This is a reference to the pairs [3,2}, [2,3], [3,2], [2,3]. | *the father against the son, and the son against the father;* |
| These give two seasons "summer" meaning [3,2] and "winter" meaning [2,3]. The trees do not move because the pairs all sum to 5. | This specifies the pairs [3,2], [2,3], [3,2], [2,3]. |
| *and their leaves do not fall.* | *and they shall stand as singles ones.* |
| The leaves are the individual sayings that will not fall (fail). | The individual sayings stand alone—they all have their own meaning. |

The two have been crafted by a single person and reflect that individual's way of thinking about the Thomas Code. It is only the Thomas Code that can explain 1.15 as a whole. Conventional commentators have been confused by the apparently disparate elements of this saying. So they have seen it as an accumulation of separate parts. Yet the structure shows that it is a beautifully crafted whole. But the saying is not just found in Thomas, it is also found in the Gospels of Matthew and Luke. And all three are clearly related to a passage in Micah. If 1.15 has been specifically designed around the Thomas Code, then how does it relate to these other versions?

## *Which came first?*

The Luke version of the saying is very close to Thomas. The Matthew version is less similar but is close to the passage in Micah. However, Matthew also has features which are not found in Luke but which it shares with Thomas. The conventional explanation for this is that we start with Micah, then get the Matthew version, then Luke, and then Thomas, which must have been influenced by both Luke and Matthew. This is illustrated by the diagram below:

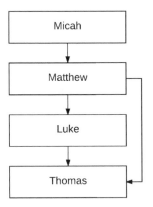

There are two problems with this. The first is that, as we shall see, there are features in Luke which are impossible to explain if it is only based on Matthew/Micah. In fact, Luke must be copying a source that looks very like the version of the saying in Thomas! This means that Thomas cannot be dependent upon Luke. Instead, either the Thomas version must come before both the Matthew and Luke versions, or it must come after Matthew but before Luke.

The explanation that the purpose of 1.15 is to give the Thomas Code has explosive consequences. The features that Thomas shares with Matthew are actually integral to this explanation. It is impossible to see how we could start with Matthew and construct the inter-related structure of 1.15 as an expression of the Thomas Code. So there are only two possibilities:

- Our explanation of 1.15 is wrong.

Or

- Thomas has come first, and Matthew has used Thomas as a source.

If the Thomas Code is the organizing principle for Thomas, and this whole book gives the evidence that it is, then 1.15 must be about the Thomas Code, for it matches it too perfectly for this to be chance. Also, if our explanation of 1.15 were wrong, then we could not explain how the Thomas version came into existence from Matthew, or how the Luke version came to reflect Thomas. So we must reject the first option. The only explanation that makes sense is that the author of Matthew, like the author of Luke, was aware of 1.15.

The reason that this is so significant is that 1.15 encodes the structure of Thomas. It makes no sense unless the whole of the Gospel, the full 108 sayings, were in existence at the same time. So Thomas in its entirety must be earlier than both the Gospels of Matthew and Luke.

So we are proposing that the real order was as follows:

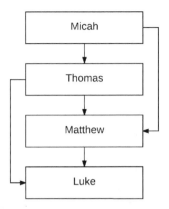

It is disturbing that 1.15, which was intended as a playful riddling reference to the structure of the Gospel, may ultimately have been used to justify violence by Christians. The Christians who wrote the New Testament Gospels were literal-minded, and the knowledge of the real meaning of 1.15 was not available to either the authors of Luke or Matthew. Neither of those authors liked the idea that Jesus was suggesting violence, yet the suggestion remained in their Gospels where it would be interpreted literally by some later Christians.

Appendix I shows why Luke and Matthew must have used the Thomas version. The evidence is particularly strong for Luke. It is impossible to explain how the Luke version could have been generated from Matthew unless the author of Luke was also aware of the Thomas version. If the author of Luke uses Thomas, then they keep "fire" but remove "war" and the "sword." However, if we look closely, we can see where these other two elements have been repositioned.

## *Why two swords?*

Christianity is a religion of peace, love, and nonviolence. This has disgusted many fighting men over the ages who have wanted to justify their wars by their Christian faith. Islamic warriors have labored under no such disadvantage. There are several passages in the Qur'an that are clear calls to Jihad. So it is a tribute to the intellectual ingenuity of Christians that many have found it possible to justify a level of violence often in excess of their Islamic equivalents.

It is true that those wanting to justify a "just war" can find plenty of material in the Old Testament scriptures. In the book of Joshua, YHWH is not even above genocide (although ironically the conquest of Canaan is probably fantasy; the Jews were a Canaanite people and had been there all along). Still, the fighting Christian could never be entirely content if their only justification was in the Old Testament that Jesus had come to supersede. There are, however, a few passages in the Gospel where Jesus does seem to be advocating violence. One of these is the Matthew version of 1.15. Another is an episode in Luke:

> He said to them, "But now let the one who has a moneybag take it, and likewise a knapsack. And let the one who has no sword sell his cloak and buy one. For I tell you that this Scripture must be fulfilled in me: 'And he was numbered with the transgressors.' For what is written about me has its fulfillment." And they said, "Look, Lord, here are two swords." And he said to them, "It is enough." (Luke 22:36-38 ESV)

One of these two swords will be used later to strike off the ear of the high priest's servant. Jesus attempts to stop this violence and cures the ear immediately. The episode of the ear is also in the other gospels, but the two swords appear only in Luke. The author of Luke obviously wants to show Jesus as being nonviolent and pacifist, which makes the two swords even more curious. The most telling detail is the specific number, two. Why would anyone arm eleven men with two swords? It can't be for the purpose of the story because only one sword is used. So the detail of the two swords must go back to something in the sources the author of Luke is using.

We can find that source in 1.15. The Gospel of Luke copies Thomas keeping the "fire," which is explained correctly as the spirit. But it does not have "sword" or "war." Instead, the author of Luke has relocated this aspect to the conflict between Jesus' disciples and the retinue of the high priest. The "three against two and two against three" has been interpreted as a prediction of this coming conflict. So the smaller party, the disciples, are given two swords. The other side comes equipped with *"swords and clubs"* (Luke 22:52). The number of swords is not specified because the author of Luke is following Mark here, but we can deduce that the author of Luke thinks they have three swords!

The idea that Jesus had come to bring the sword and war would have had enormous implications for early Christians. The Romans had zero tolerance for rebellion or troublemaking of any sort. So it was vital to tame this dangerous aspect of 1.15. The author of Luke's strategy was to relate it to the specific conflict between Jesus' followers and the Jewish authorities (not the Romans!). In this way, it could be seen as relating to a historical episode when Jesus was unfairly accused of violence rather than an incitement to rebellion.

When Christians achieved political power, these considerations no longer applied. When they looked to justify war, they turned to passages that were ultimately dependent on 1.15.

## *Thomas and scripture*

Appendix I discusses how the author of Matthew must have correctly identified a link between 1.15 and Micah 5:5-6. It would seem that 1.15 is based very loosely on the Micah passage. Such a loose use of scripture follows the pattern of other sayings in Thomas. For example, the five trees in paradise were based on the two trees in Eden. The Gospel of Thomas often seems to start with a scriptural reference, but develops it in a creative way that would have astonished the author of the original source. It is more accurate to say that Thomas is inspired by scripture than that it follows scripture.

This pattern occurs because the early Jesus movement consisted of amateurs and outsiders. The experts in scripture were the Pharisees and the scribes. These are precisely the two groups that the Gospels portray as being in conflict with Jesus. The same attitude is found in Thomas:

> *3.2 Jesus said: "The Pharisees and the scribes have taken the keys of knowledge; they have hidden them. They did not go in, and those who wanted to go in they did not allow. You, however, be as cunning as serpents and as innocent as doves." (Th. 38)*

What is fascinating about this is that it acknowledges the expertise of the Pharisees and scribes, and presents the idea that there is hidden knowledge in scripture. However, the Pharisees and scribes "did not go in" meaning that they did not use that knowledge. Neither do they allow others to enter, which suggests that they disapproved of the Jesus movement's interpretation of scripture. We know that the Jesus movement was persecuted by the Pharisees from almost the beginning.

There was one exception to this rule that the early Christians were amateurs in scripture. By chance, a Pharisee converted to the movement. He wrote many letters in which he quoted scripture extensively. Although he was to have a tremendous influence on future Christians, he was regarded with suspicion in his own lifetime. Many did not accept that he was an apostle as he claimed to be, or that he had a correct understanding of Jesus. He was not directly involved in the Gospel of Thomas, which presents a very different view of Christianity. However, he started a trend of scriptural interpretation and justification that found ultimate expression in the New Testament Gospels. We know him as St. Paul.

# 5

# Three threes, two twos, and a single one

*2.11 Jesus said: "Where there are three gods, they are gods; where there are two or one, I myself exist with him." (Th. 30)*

## *Three gods*

We have seen the evidence for the mathematical symbolism in which "three" is the father, and "two" the son, in saying 1.15. The true test of any theory is whether it can explain puzzling anomalies beyond the data used to construct it. Many of the sayings in Thomas are enigmatic, but there is one that is universally regarded as incomprehensible. Most commentators believe that the saying conventionally numbered as Thomas 30 must have been corrupted. The same saying is found in a slightly different version in a Greek papyrus fragment:

> *Jesus said: "Where there are three, they are gods. And where there is one, [I say] I am with him."*

The line *"where there are three gods, they are gods"* has puzzled everyone. As always, scholars tend to favor the earlier Greek version, although I have come to believe that the Coptic is the better copy. In this case though, the Greek, *"where there are three they are gods,"* is hardly any less incomprehensible. A conventional explanation would see this as a corruption of a similar passage in Matthew, in which Jesus says that two or three are gathered in his name he will be with them (Matthew 18:18–20). They would then explain the "three gods" in the Coptic as a further corruption resulting from the bewildered copyist trying to understand why the "three" should be gods. There are two reasons to reject this explanation:

1. If we look at the Matthew passage closely, we can see signs that it is dependent upon Thomas and not the other way around! The author of Matthew had the same problems trying to understand 2.11 as everyone else. He decides to interpret it using the one place in scripture where men appear to be called gods, which is Psalm 82. (This is explored further in Appendix II.)

2. Would a copyist really try and explain why the three are gods by changing "three" to "three gods"? The people who copied manuscripts were not stupid!

In any case, whether the original had "three gods" or just "three" both versions are perfectly explicable in the Thomas Code where "three" represents God the Father:

$$3 \cdot 2 \cdot 3 \cdot 2 \cdot 3$$

These are the three Gods! We have seen that "three" stands for the Father, that is God. But in the formula we have three threes, so we have three "gods" who are all God. The saying is another riddle reference to the Thomas Code.


**Reconstruction of 2.11**

When we come to the second half, we have the problem that the Coptic and Greek versions diverge. Which represents the original more closely? Appendix II gives the reason for favoring the Coptic although it also has been slightly changed by being abbreviated. I prefer a reconstruction of the saying as given below:

> *Where there are three (gods) they are gods; where there are two I am there; where there is one I am with him. (Reconstruction of 2.11)*

Appendix II explains how we can get very easily from this version to each of the three extant early copies (Greek, Coptic and Matthew). We also find evidence for this version of the saying in a fourth-century source, Ephrem's Commentary on the Diatessaron. As for whether the original had "three gods" or just "three," this makes no difference under the Thomas Code interpretation.

**Interpreting the reconstruction**

With the reconstruction, we can see that in the saying it is counting down:

> **Three** (gods) are gods
> **Two** is Jesus
> If there is **one**, Jesus is with him/her

The meaning of the three being the father and two being Jesus, supports what we have found from the "five in a house" saying. So 1.15 also has the countdown, involving three and two and then one. There is no "one" in the Thomas Code, so why is it included? The one stands for the disciple, the chosen, and brings him or her into the mystical symbolism. The promise of the saying is that the one will be transformed into the "two." Once becoming "two," they can enter the mystical union with the "three," God the Father. So the disciple does enter the Thomas Code through becoming Jesus. Christians believed that the ultimate God was too remote and powerful for direct contact with humans. The one whom the Jews had thought to be God was really a lesser being, the Angel of the Name, who carried the name of YHWH but who was not YHWH. But the real YHWH had taken pity on women and men. He had separated a part of himself, the "son," and sent it down into our level of reality. This one, Jesus, partook of human nature so that he could act as an intermediary between God and us. When a person becomes the "one," Jesus is with them; they become Jesus.

## *The single ones*

So what does the "one" mean? The "three gods" may have caused consternation among Thomas commentators, but at least it could be dismissed as a quirk in one saying. There could be no such comfort for the "single one," which is repeatedly used in the Gospel.

We have already covered the use of the "single one" in 1.15, so let us now look at the other references to the "single one":

> 1.3 [...] For many who are first shall become last and they will become a single one." (Th. 4)

> 2.4 Jesus said: "I shall choose you, one out of a thousand, and two out of ten thousand, and they shall stand as a single one." (Th. 23)

> 3.12 Jesus said: "Blessed are the single ones and the chosen, for you shall find the kingdom; for you came from there, and shall go there again." (Th. 49)

> 5.2 He said: "Lord, there are many around the well, but no one in the well." Jesus said: "There are many standing at the door, but the single ones are they who shall enter the bridal chamber." (Th. 74 & 75)

It is clear that the "single ones" are the same as the chosen. They are the elect, those who will enter the kingdom and who will go into the "bridal chamber." But why should they be called "single ones"?

The two basic conventional explanations are that it either means solitaries (as it is often translated) or single unmarried people. Both explanations have allowed conventional Christians to condemn the Gospel as elitist. Commentators compare the extrovert happy-clapping Christians of the "real" church, to the self-chosen, introverted solitaires of Thomas. Or, if it is taken to mean single people, then the extreme asceticism of the celebrate Thomas Christians is compared to the family based Christianity of the church, conveniently ignoring the anti-family sayings that are found in the New Testament Gospels as well as Thomas.

Under the Thomas Code, there is the completely different explanation that the "single one" means just what it says, the number one. It functions in the mathematical symbolism that leads down from three to one:

> Three threes,
> two twos,
> and a single one

However, the "single one" is not just any disciple. The neophyte is not a "one," but is aspiring to become "one." So how do we become a "single one"? Instead of imposing our meanings on the Gospel, we should look at what the Gospel says. Nowhere does it tell us that the single ones are those who are unmarried or who refrain from sex. In fact, the Gospel never mentions marriage or sex. What it does tell us is that becoming "one" is the end result of a process. We start off as "two" then we become "one," so it has nothing to do with remaining single. Nor is it about being solitary. The Jesus movement was a highly spiritual religion, and this must inevitably have involved the individual spending time in private contemplation, yet it was also very much a group religion. The movement never accepted that a disciple could isolate him or herself in a world of mysticism; there was always an imperative to go out and sow the word into others.

## Union

A disciple becomes "one" by making the two into one. The two here is not the number representing Jesus. It is a person and their spirit. Take, for example, a saying that comes immediately before the "single one" saying 3.12. It is available in two versions:

> *3.11 Jesus said: "If two make peace with one another in this house alone, they shall say to the mountain, 'Move away' and it shall move." (Th. 48)*

*6.13.1 Jesus said: "When you make the two one, you shall be sons of man, and when you say: 'Mountain, move away,' he shall be moved." (Th. 106)*

We will see later that the wording of the first version, Thomas 48, fits a very specific role that it plays in the third eighteen where it is found. So this first version must be original to the Gospel and date from the time when the Gospel was put together. However, it is likely to be a modification of a pre-existing saying. The second version, Thomas 106, is one of the four duplicates that have been deleted to give the total of 108 sayings. However, as will be discussed in Chapter 15, this saying is a case all by itself. Unlike the other duplicates, there is evidence that it is original but that we are supposed to remove it. Hence the unique numbering format of 6.13.1.

The mountain that shall be moved comes from Micah 4:1 and is an image of the kingdom of God. So we are not dealing with a physical miracle, the literal moving of a mountain. Instead, the two who become one, or who make peace in a house, are able to bring in the kingdom. The very next saying, 3.12 (Th. 49), says that the single ones will enter the kingdom.

Thomas 106 has *"make the two one,"* which is more likely to be original. If the two become one, then the disciples will become *"sons of man."* The son of man is a title of Jesus, so this implies that the disciples will become Jesus.

We find another play on "two" and "one" in Thomas 11:

*"[…] On the day when you were one, you were made two. But when you have become two, what will you do?" (Th. 11 —sub saying)*

The line *"On the day when you were one, you were made two"* may be a reference to the disciple becoming Jesus, so that the "one" becomes "two." However, the saying is complex and the line is capable of alternative meanings. The saying will be explored more fully in its context of the first eighteen.

The idea of two becoming one features in what is perhaps the key saying of the whole gospel:

*2.3 Jesus saw some little ones at the breast. He said to his disciples: "These little ones at the breast are like those who enter into the kingdom." They said to him: "Then if we be little ones, shall we enter the kingdom?" Jesus said to them: "When you make the two one, and when you make the inside as the outside, and the outside as the inside, and the upper side as the lower side; and when you make the male and the female into a single one, that the male be not male nor the female female; when you make eyes in the place of an eye, and a hand in place of a hand, and a foot in place of a foot, an image in place of an image, then you will enter into [the kingdom]." (Th. 22)*

To enter the kingdom, you must make *"the two one."* This involves making the inside as the outside, the upper as the lower, and the male and female into a "single one." A person must enter into the divine marriage, and so paradoxically become "two," in order to become "one." In this marriage, the male and female components are merged together. One of these components is outside and above, the heavenly spirit, and the other is inside and below, what we think of as the person, or more correctly the person's inner being, their soul.

I do not see how anyone can read Thomas 22 and then think that the "single one" is an unmarried person. Neither can we reject Thomas 22 as later than the rest of the Gospel. Remarkably, Stevan Davies posits that this saying lay behind a lengthy section of the Gospel of Mark.[39] But if the Gospel of Mark has used this saying then it must be earlier than that Gospel, which is believed to have been written around AD 70. Although Thomas 22 may seem "weird" to most Christians today, it is, in fact, earlier than any of the Gospels in the New Testament.

We have all the evidence to see what the "single one" really means. It is the union of the person and their spirit. Those who had undergone this union are called by Paul "the perfect." They were also called "the chosen" and "the elect." We should not think of the chosen as those who are of a certain grade or position, or who have been through the requisite initiation rituals. Rather they are those who have attained a spiritual state akin to what a Buddhist would call enlightenment. They were in the kingdom of heaven.

This concept should not be seen as elitist. Every Christian could and would aspire to become one of the perfect. It was true that the perfect were seen as being specially selected, but this selection was made by God before the beginning of time. The first and most important sign of this selection was to choose to join the church in the first place. To become one of the perfect was the natural result of a progression that started with baptism.

The union of the spirit and the person was at heart a mystical experience. Yet, the early Jesus movement also sought scriptural authority for this belief, which they found in the first creation in Genesis:

> So God created man in his own image, in the image of God
> he created him; male and female he created them. (Genesis
> 1:27 ESV)

Many Jews interpreted this passage as meaning that man, Adam, was first created spiritually as a hermaphrodite, being both male and female. However, in the second physical creation, the person becomes either male or female. This is illustrated by Eve being created from the side (or rib) of Adam; the male and female components are separated. The Jesus movement believed that although a person was physically born as either a man or a woman, they were still linked to the other component which remained in the heavenly sphere. Under this philosophy, there were actually three components to the person:

- The physical body, fashioned out of earth.

- The first half of the spiritual component, the conscious mind which the Greeks called the nous.

- The second half of the spiritual component, the soul/spirit, which remained in the heavenly sphere.

Because the original person was hermaphrodite, the soul/spirit was of the opposite sex to the body and mind. The intimate relationship between the body/mind and the soul/spirit was recognized in the language used for the soul/spirit; it was the wife/husband, sister/brother, daughter/son and mother/father. So a woman's spirit was her husband, her brother, her son and her father. These relationships all applied simultaneously, which was very confusing for those who did not realize that this was a mystic formula!

The soul and the spirit were the same thing in different states. Because mankind had been corrupted by the demons, the soul had been separated from God and was in an initial state of "death." Jesus had come to redeem the soul and transform it into a living spirit. The Jesus movement divided people into three groups depending on the state of their soul/spirit:

Those who had no contact with their soul/spirit were known as people of the flesh or body. They had no time for religion and lived completely in the material world. These were the ones the Jesus movement called "the dead" because their soul/spirit was dead and belonged to the demons.

The middle group were those who were known as the people of the soul, the psychics. They had listened to the message and had believed. As baptized Christians, their soul/spirit was partially redeemed but still slept. Because they had not fully united with their soul/spirits, these people were vulnerable. There was a danger that the soul would be "killed" and "eaten" by the demons who inhabited the middle heaven. But there was hope. The spiritual Christians would attempt to protect them until they could progress to the next stage.

The final group were known as the Christians of the spirit, the pneumatics. These were the spiritually reborn who were called the chosen or the perfect. For this group, the soul/spirit had been fully redeemed from the demons. It now was restored to its correct place with Jesus in the kingdom of heaven. The connection between the person and their soul/spirit was now conscious, and the two parts of the person had united into one whole. This merger was the "bridal chamber" that Thomas and other early sources speak about. It is this spiritual group who are the "single one" in the numerical mysticism.

Saying 2.3 is about the reunion of the person and their spirit. So the upper and the lower, the male and female, the inside and outside are all united. The result of this is a transformed hermaphrodite spiritual body; an eye in place of an eye, a hand in place of a hand, a foot in place of a foot. This spiritual body is the one that was created first before the secondary creation of the physical world. So it will survive death and the dissolution of the physical world.

The threefold classification of people into those of the flesh, the soul, and the spirit was universal to early Christians. It was very important and explicit in Paul's letters as well as being found in the Gospel of Thomas, and other works such as the Gospel of Philip. It is also hinted at within the New Testament Gospels.

However, the threefold grouping did not fit in with the interpretation of the spirit offered by the author of Luke / Acts and developed further in the Gospel of John. So the spirit, which was originally personal to the individual, became the Holy Spirit, an emanation sent by God to dwell inside people. This transformed the original concept into something impersonal and gave rise to the idea of the Trinity.

## Trinity

We have now seen that three, two, and one all have a meaning in the symbolism:

> Three = the Father, God
> Two = the Son, Jesus
> One = the union of the disciple and their redeemed spirit

This numerical mysticism survived but became transferred into the concept of the Trinity, the idea that God has a threefold nature; the Father, the Son, and the Holy Spirit. We can be sure that it is not the other way around, that the Thomas Code was not developed from the Trinity. This is because the numerical mysticism is encoded in saying 1.15, which is earlier than the Gospels of Luke (certainly) and Matthew (almost certainly). The Trinity, however, is a comparatively late development for which there is very little justification in the Gospels. At the end of Matthew, the resurrected Jesus commands

his disciples to teach the gospel to all the nations (the Gentiles): bap-
tizing them to the name of the Father, and of the Son, and of the
Holy Spirit (Matthew 28:19). The Gospel of John also talks about
the Father, the Son and the Paraclete, the Advocate or Holy Spirit,
although it does not give the formula of the Trinity. These are the
only references to what was to become the Trinity, and we can see
them as derivations from the Thomas Code.

# 6

# Dividing by two

*4.18 [A man said] to him: Speak to my brothers, that they may divide my father's possessions with me. He said to him: "O man, who made me a divider?" He turned to his disciples. He said to them: "Truly, do I exist as one who divides?" (Th. 72)*

There are two more sayings which allude to Jesus' role in the Thomas Code as the two twos. The first of these, 4.18, is in a significant position. It is the last saying in the fourth eighteen, and also the last in the middle thirty-six.

In this saying, a man asks Jesus to intercede with his brothers to divide his father's possessions. Ostensibly we have a situation where Jesus is being asked to act as executor, to divide up the property of a deceased person among his sons. It was common for teachers, that is Rabbis, to be asked to do this, so the man's request is not unreasonable. Yet Jesus refuses him. Jesus is teaching the abandonment of personal property in favor of the kingdom of God. He has not come to act as an executor. So is this saying a memory of a real event, something that actually happened to Jesus?

There are a number of clues in the saying that something is going on below the surface. First, Jesus' reply does not make sense under the interpretation of refusing the role of executor. If the purpose of the saying was that the followers of Jesus should abandon their property, then why does Jesus not say this? His reply should be something like: "Give your father's possessions to the poor and seek the riches of the kingdom God." Instead, he makes an obscure statement about not being a divider. And if the meaning of the saying is that Jesus was refusing the post of executor, it would be curiously anemic. Why would anyone even remember such a trivial event?

Some have seen this saying as a rare expression of humor in the early Jesus movement. Jesus does not reply with a straightforward answer but asks a question: *"O man, who made me a divider?"* He then turns to his disciples and repeats the question to them: *"Truly, do I exist as one who divides?"* (This is a literal translation, it will more normally be translated as *"I am not a divider, am I?"*) The key to the saying is the idea of "division." This is an obvious play on words. Anyone who had studied the Gospel of Thomas would know that Jesus comes to make whole the divisions within a person. In 2.3 (Th. 22), Jesus tells his disciples how to enter into the kingdom:

> *"When you make the two one, and when you make the inside as the outside, and the outside as the inside, and the upper side as the lower side; and when you make the male and the female into a single one, that the male be not male nor the female female;"*

We have seen how this is an allusion to returning to the spiritual state of the first creation. The separation of Eve from Adam is undone by making *"the two one"* and *"the male and the female into a single one, that the male be not male nor the female female."* Jesus has come to repair a division, and that division is spiritual. It is not just in the Gospel of Thomas that we find this concept. Jesus' reply to the man's question is very close to something that Paul writes in 1 Corinthians: *"Is Christ divided?"*[40]

Saying 4.18 plays with the different meanings of "division." A divider is an executor and also one who separates, whereas Jesus has come to make whole. Yet, we have come across another meaning for "divisions." In Thomas 16, it is applied to the Gospel as a whole, the way the Gospel is divided into sections and the way the individual sayings are divided against each other. The same Coptic word is used for divisions in Thomas 16 and Thomas 72. So we have a third, hidden, level of meaning to the saying. This third level shows another dimension to Jesus' irony. Jesus really is a divider. In Thomas 16, he says that he has come to cast divisions upon the world, meaning the divided Gospel of Thomas.

**Links to the Salome saying 4.6**

Let us look at the saying again. A man talks about dividing *"our father's possessions."* The reference to "our father" should alert us here. Does this really mean the Father, God? There is another saying in which Jesus shares in the things of the Father. This is saying 4.6 (Th. 61) when Jesus replies to Salome's question asking who he is: *"I am he who is from that which is equal; to me was given of the things of my Father."* The saying continues: *"Therefore I say, when he should be equal,[41] he will be filled with light, but when he should be divided he will be filled with darkness."* To be equal is good but to be divided is bad. So there are similarities between 4.6 and 4.18:

- Both have the concept of the father's possessions. In 4.6, Jesus has the things of the Father, whereas in 4.18 the man wants his brothers to share the father's possessions.

- Both have the concept of "division"; in 4.6, division leads to darkness, whereas being equal is to be filled with light, with Jesus coming from that which is equal. In 4.18, Jesus asks ironically if he is a divider.

These two sayings are linked. They are in the same eighteen, with saying 4.6 the last of the first six and 4.18 being the last of the third six. But if the sayings are linked, then the father in 4.18 is actually God.

**Division in the Thomas Code**

So how does this relate to the structure? In the formula, the Father is represented by the three threes. Yet they are divided up by the two twos, which are "equal," being placed each side of the central three:

$$3 \cdot 2 \cdot 3 \cdot 2 \cdot 3$$

The twos represent Jesus. So Jesus is indeed a divider! His number two divides up the threes twice. There is an allusion in 4.18 to this two-fold division because Jesus asks whether he is a divider twice. This is the only time in the Gospel that Jesus repeats a question in this way and it is this that gives the suggestion of humor. We can now see why because Jesus is a two-fold divider in the formula.

In 4.18, Jesus has come from that which is equal and, as saying 4.6 tells us, shares the possessions of the Father. To be equal implies that two things are the same. It implies twinship and the number two, the number that represents Jesus. A man and his brothers want to share in the possessions of their father, but Jesus refuses. If the Father is God, then only Jesus is the valid son, the only one who shares in what belongs to the Father. Jesus then replies with a cryptic reply that both affirms that he has not come to divide and is also an allusion to the structure of the Gospel. Jesus divides the Thomas Code because his twos split up the Father's threes.

So who is the "man" and his brothers? They believe they are entitled to share in the Father's possessions, so they must be divine beings. The early Jesus movement believed that the earth was under the control of evil powers. These powers were not the Romans although the powers controlled the Roman authorities. They were the fallen angels, the sons of God. It is the sons of God who attempt to share the Father's possessions but there is only one true Son of God, and that is Jesus.

## The wood, the stone, and the all

The Greek version of 2.11 includes the sub-saying about the stone and timber which is found in 5.4 (Th. 77) in the Coptic. In Appendix II, I suggest that this was because it replaced the line: "*where there are two I am there.*" Whoever altered 2.11 in the Greek must have believed that the stone and timber related to the "two." The full Coptic version of 5.4 is:

> *5.4 Jesus said: "I am the light that is over them all. I am the all of it, the all of it came out of me and the all of it*

*bursts up to me. Burst a timber, I am there. Raise up the
stone, and you shall find me there." (Th. 77)*

There is another saying featuring wood and stone, and that is one
of the key sayings about the Thomas Code, 1.18. In this saying, we
have both "stones that minister" and "five trees in paradise." We
have seen that the "stones" refer to the central triplet:

$$3 \cdot 2 \cdot 3 \cdot 2 \cdot 3$$

If we "raise" it out of the sequence, then Jesus is there in the form
of the two twos:

$$2 \cdot 3 \cdot 2$$

Now, suppose we equate the timber with the "five trees" which
are the five factors. We again find the two twos embedded within
the timber:

$$3 \cdot 2 \cdot 3 \cdot 2 \cdot 3$$

Note how we have to "burst" or split the timber open to find the
twos because they are not on the outside, at the beginning or end. So
we can see the mysterious phrase concerning the timber and stone
as a reference to the two twos. If so, then whoever moved this to 2.11
was quite right in believing that it related to "where there are two I
am there."

This leaves the first part of the saying:

> *Jesus said: "I am the light that is over them all. I am the
> all of it, the all of it came out of me and the all of it bursts
> up to me.*

A conventional explanation might see this as related to Gnosticism. The all is the totality of everything. So Jesus is the light over
the whole of creation, and it came out of him and attempts to "burst
up" or reach up to him. But there is a problem with this. The totality
should have come out of the Father, not the Son. It is God who created everything.

With the Thomas Code, we get a very different interpretation of
"the all of it." The clue is in the very first saying, 1.1. We will see that

this keystone saying alludes to the three thirty-sixes. But it ends with another phrase:

*...and he will become king over the all of it.*

It is the same phrase as we find in 5.4. As the keystone saying first covers the thirty-sixes, "the all of it" must be the totality of the Gospel, the full 108 sayings. So the "all of it" is the Gospel of Thomas! Let us now look at 5.4 again with this interpretation:

*I am the light that is over them all.*

Jesus is the light that is within the sayings. This is quite literal in sayings such as 2.5 (Th. 24): *"There is light within a man of light, and he becomes light to the whole world."* It is Jesus who is this light as he is also in the Gospel of John.

*I am the all of it...*

Jesus is the whole Gospel. The sayings are the stream that Jesus has measured out. As saying 6.15 (Th. 108) says: *"Whoever drinks from my mouth shall become like me; I myself will become he..."* Thomas, meaning twin, is a reference to the twin twos in the Thomas Code. So the very name, the Gospel of the Twin, refers to Jesus.

*...the all of it came out of me...*

The sayings, with their "Jesus says" statements, have literally come out of Jesus.

*...and the all of it bursts up to me.*

The word for "burst" can mean to reach up, or attain. The same word is used for bursting open the timber and also, in saying 3.10 (Th. 47), for the wineskins that are burst or split when filled with new wine. The Gospel reaches up to Jesus because it tells the disciples how to attain to Jesus.

With this explanation, we can see the unity of 5.4. It starts with the summary that Jesus is present in the Gospel as its light; the Gospel is, in fact, Jesus. It has come from him, and the sayings "burst up" to him. The saying then alludes to Jesus being the "2"s in the Thomas code, found if you lift out the "stone," the central triplet, or if you burst open the "wood," the whole Code.

## *Thomas the twin*

There is a link between the two twos and the very name of the Gospel. Thomas is not a real name but the Aramaic word for "twin." Later, Thomas became associated with Judas, not the Iscariot but the "brother" of Jesus who had the same name. However, there is no evidence that Judas and Thomas were conflated into one person until the late second century. They are different people in both the Gospel of Luke and especially in the Gospel of John where Thomas is more prominent than in the other gospels and is clearly not the same person as Judas.

The Coptic version of Thomas actually has the word for "twin" twice. It is attributed to Didymus Judas Thomas, but Didymus means twin in Greek! We cannot be sure about the name on the Greek papyrus fragments because the first word falls on a missing section. It is normally recreated as Judas Thomas but could equally be Didymus Thomas. Could it be that the very name of the Gospel reflects the formula and that the Gospel was originally attributed to the "twin twin"? If so, this must be an allusion to the two twos in the Thomas code. Normally the Gospel is seen as being named after the disciple Thomas, but I have argued that it is the other way around and that the disciple was created after the Gospel.[42] The author of Mark was looking for names for the group called the Twelve, and knowing that there was a Gospel attributed to Thomas, thought there must be a disciple of the name. Apart from the mere listing of his name, Thomas does not feature any further in Mark, Matthew or Luke. So it seems that the earliest gospel writers knew no stories about him.

# 7

# Powers of ten

*2.4 Jesus said: "I shall choose you, one out of a thousand, and two out of ten thousand, and they shall stand as a single one." (Th. 23)*

## *One out of a thousand*

One of the clues that a saying points to the Thomas Code is the presence of numbers. There are two more sayings that involve numbers, and we will see that the two are linked. The first is 2.4, which not only features numbers but which also has the chosen being called the "single one." We would expect the saying to relate to the numerical mysticism of the Thomas Code. But what does the strange formula *"one out of a thousand and two out of ten thousand"* mean? The Thomas Code is a prime factorization, so we will start by looking at the prime factorization of "one out of a thousand" and "two out of ten thousand."

**One out of a thousand**

The prime factorization of 1,000 is:

$$1000 = 2^3 \cdot 5^3 = (2 \cdot 5)^3$$

This combines the three significant numbers; 2, 3, and 5. Both 2 and 5 are raised to the power of 3, symbolizing the father. This is the first hint that we again have a countdown.

## Two out of ten thousand

The prime factorization of 10,000 is:

$$10,000 = 2^4 \cdot 5^4 = (2 \cdot 5)^4$$

We now have the power of 4, which is not a prime number. However, the formula is actually "two out of 10,000." What does it mean to take "two" out of 10,000? We might divide by two, which would give "one out of five thousand." But if so why does the formula not say "one out of five thousand"? Instead, we must work with the prime factorization. The power of 4 can be divided into two 2s enabling us to split the factorization into two:

$$(2 \cdot 5)^4 = (2 \cdot 5)^2 \cdot (2 \cdot 5)^2$$

We now have two expressions each involving a power of two. So taking "two out of ten thousand" gives us one-half of the factorization:

$$(2 \cdot 5)^2$$

So this time the factor $(2 \cdot 5)$ is raised to the power of 2, the number of the Son. We should note other clues pointing to the number of the Son; we have twin copies of the expression, just as we have twin twos in the Thomas Code, and "two" is included explicitly in the formula "two out of 10,000."

## The countdown

The saying then gives a countdown:

3) $(2 \cdot 5)^3$—indicating the Father

2) $(2 \cdot 5)^2$—repeated twice, indicating the twin twos, which is the symbol of the Son

1) The 'single one" being the chosen disciples.

We again have the Trinity!

**One out of a thousand and two out of ten thousand**

We can do one last operation with the factors. The saying includes an "and" suggesting that we might combine the "one out of a thousand" and "two out of ten thousand." Instead of summing the two numbers, we should combine their prime factorizations. This gives:

One out of a thousand $((2 \cdot 5)^3)$
and two out of ten thousand $((2 \cdot 5)^2)$

$$= (2 \cdot 5)^3 \cdot (2 \cdot 5)^2$$

$$= (2 \cdot 5)^5$$

So we have now have a power of 5, signifying the 5 factors of the Thomas code.

# Ten

There is one puzzle left in saying 2.4, and that is why it should concern factors of $(2 \cdot 5)$? We would normally write this, of course, as 10:

$$10 = 2 \cdot 5$$

Factors of 10 were important for the Jews and Romans, just as they are for us. But it is not a prime. The numerical symbolism revolves around prime numbers, so why should powers of 10 feature in saying 2.4? The answer is that 10 stands in substitution for a prime number.

We have seen how the three primes, 2, 3 and 5, involved in the Thomas Code are intimately related. In particular, 2 and 5 have a unique property:

- The numbers 2 and 5 are the only pair of prime numbers whose difference $(5 - 2)$ equals the prime number 3.

Because 3 stands for the Father, it would have had supreme importance in the mysticism of the Thomas Code. Whoever developed the mathematical symbolism has noticed that 2 and 5 uniquely indicate 3 through this property of their difference. So the combination of 2 and 5 (multiplying out to 10) is taken as symbolizing 3.

If this is correct then "one out of a thousand" = $(2 \cdot 5)^3$ indicates three threes ($3^3$). We have already seen how "two out of ten thousand" symbolizes two twos, and we end with the "single one."

This property of $(2 \cdot 5)$ substituting for 3 will prove to be very significant for the parable of the loaves and fishes. But first, we will look at another saying that involves 10.

## Sixty and one hundred and twenty

The final saying involving numbers is the parable of the sower. The culmination of this saying features a super yield from the seed that falls onto the good ground:

> ...*sixty per measure and a hundred and twenty per measure. (From 1.8, Th. 9)*

The same parable is found in the Synoptics. The Matthew and Luke versions are derivative from Mark, which has thirtyfold and sixtyfold and a hundredfold.[43] The rest of the parable is very similar so why should Thomas have different numbers? This parable is undoubtedly a pre-existing saying dating from before the Gospel of Thomas was compiled in its final form. This suggests that the numbers have been changed in the Thomas version to fit in with the numerical mysticism of the Thomas Code.

We can, in fact, see some clear links with the saying we have just considered, 2.4:

1. One concerns the chosen, the other the seed that gives "good fruit." But this fruit that comes from the sowing of the Gospel is also the chosen!

2. They both compare the numbers of the chosen in parallel format (x and y):

- One out of a thousand and two out of ten thousand

- Sixty per measure and a hundred and twenty per measure

3. In one case, the numbers involve powers of 10 ($10^3$ and 10), and in the other, the numbers are products of 10:

$$60 = 6 \cdot 10$$
$$120 = 12 \cdot 10$$

If we complete the sum, adding 60 per measure and 120 per measure, then we get 180 per measure:

$$180 = 18 \cdot 10$$

The parallelism with 2.4 suggests that in this case, we should be looking at the numbers that multiply 10, just as in 2.4, it was the powers of 10 that were significant. We have already found "12" in saying 1.18, where it is the value of the "stones that minister," the central triplet in the Thomas Code. In fact, we can get to each one of these numbers by looking at all the subsequences involving two or three factors in the Thomas code:

$$3 \cdot 2 \text{ or } 2 \cdot 3 = 6$$
$$2 \cdot 3 \cdot 2 = 12$$
$$3 \cdot 2 \cdot 3 = 18$$

We can see the numbers attached to the Thomas version of the sower as presenting a mathematical theorem. The Thomas Code is a play on the three prime numbers 2, 3, and 5. If we take the smallest prime, 2, and add it to the second smallest prime, 3, we get the next prime, 5. This is unique to these three prime numbers; in fact, there are no other two consecutive primes that will sum to give a third prime. Whoever put the numbers in the Thomas version of the parable would seem to have discovered a parallel property in the Thomas Code, as is illustrated in the table below.

| | Prime numbers | Thomas Code subsequences |
|---|---|---|
| Smallest | 2 | $3 \cdot 2 \text{ or } 2 \cdot 3 = 6$ |
| Second smallest | 3 | $2 \cdot 3 \cdot 2 = 12$ |
| Sum to: | | |
| Third smallest | 5 | $3 \cdot 2 \cdot 3 = 18$ |

This equivalence applies only to the Thomas Code ordering. It would have been seen as confirmation that the Thomas Code had been placed into the structure of mathematics by God. The use of subsequences, as found in 1.8, will be important to the miracle of the loaves and fishes to which we will now turn.

# INTERLUDE

# 8

# Five and seven loaves

The miracle of the loaves and fishes, in which Jesus feeds a multi-tude, is well known even to non-Christians. What is less well known is that there are actually two separate but almost identical miracles. Numbers are very prominent in the story, and the numbers are the only thing that substantially change between the two miracles. In the first miracle (Mark 6:34-45), Jesus divides up five loaves and two fishes to feed five thousand with twelve baskets of scraps. Then a lit-tle later (Mark 8:1-10), Jesus divides up seven loaves and a few fishes to feed four thousand with seven baskets of scraps. Unusually, the story of the loaves and fishes is included in all four gospels. It is clear that it is the Mark account that is the earliest, and Matthew follows Mark very closely (Matthew 12:13-21; 15:32-39) with two separate miracles. The authors of Luke and John must have been bothered by the oddity of two almost identical miracles and streamlined their accounts by keeping only the first and more impressive miracle (Luke 9:10-17; John 6:1-15).

If we look at the two miracles in the earliest version, that of Mark, we will see that they both start with Jesus showing compassion for the people and they both end with Jesus making a boat journey across the Sea of Galilee. So why does the author of Mark include what seems to be the same miracle twice? Did he have two slightly different accounts of a real event that happened in Galilee? But what is odd is how specific the numbers are and how they differ between the two versions. If we had two memories of an actual event, we would not have expected them to stress the numbers in this way. The numbers must mean something!

The real clincher for rejecting the idea that there were two separate versions of the same story is that the two are brought together in

Mark. When Jesus and his disciples are in a boat after the second miracle, Jesus warns his disciples to beware of the yeast of the Pharisees and Herod. His disciples are confused and begin to discuss among themselves their lack of bread. Jesus, hearing them, upbraids them and asks if they have eyes to see and ears to hear. He then poses a conundrum:

> When I broke the five loaves for the five thousand, how many baskets full of broken pieces did you take up?" They said to him, "Twelve." "And the seven for the four thousand, how many baskets full of broken pieces did you take up?" And they said to him, "Seven." And he said to them, "Do you not yet understand?" (Mark 8:19-21 ESV)

Many people have wondered if this is a mathematical puzzle. It seems that Jesus is challenging his disciples, and us, to solve something. If so, then both versions of the miracle must be involved in the solution. We should not consider them in isolation, but as two halves of a greater whole. And this provides the answer as to why the author of Mark includes the miracle twice. He does not have two separate sources, but one source which includes both versions and the summary. So he concludes that there must have been two very similar miracles, and incorporates both into his narrative.

We can feel some sympathy for the disciples, rebuked for their inability to understand an apparently insoluble problem. But we are in a more fortunate position. We have the key to the mathematical mystery that Jesus is propounding – the Thomas Code.

## The feeding of the five thousand

We will start with the first miracle, that of the feeding of the five thousand. Here it is in full:

> When he went ashore he saw a great crowd, and he had compassion on them, because they were like sheep without a shepherd. And he began to teach them many things. And when it grew late, his disciples came to him and said, "This

*is a desolate place, and the hour is now late. Send them away to go into the surrounding countryside and villages and buy themselves something to eat." But he answered them, "You give them something to eat." And they said to him, "Shall we go and buy two hundred denarii worth of bread and give it to them to eat?" And he said to them, "How many loaves do you have? Go and see." And when they had found out, they said, "Five, and two fish." Then he commanded them all to sit down in groups on the green grass. So they sat down in groups, by hundreds and by fifties. And taking the five loaves and the two fish, he looked up to heaven and said a blessing and broke the loaves and gave them to the disciples to set before the people. And he divided the two fish among them all. And they all ate and were satisfied. And they took up twelve baskets full of broken pieces and of the fish. And those who ate the loaves were five thousand men. Immediately he made his disciples get into the boat and go before him to the other side, to Bethsaida, while he dismissed the crowd. (Mark 6:34-45 ESV)*

An obvious clue here is the number of loaves and fishes; 5 and 2. The Thomas Code is a play on the three prime numbers 2, 3, and 5. We have two of them here, and we have seen how the combination of 2 and 5 represent the other number 3, the number of the father.

What first led me to the miracle, though, was what it says about organizing the multitude: "*So they sat down in groups, by hundreds and by fifties.*" One problem with the idea that Thomas was structured as a hierarchy, was the lack of any other examples of such an organizing principle in ancient texts. How could I be sure that early Christians could think in this way? To my amazement, I found what I was looking for in the way the five thousand sat down in groups.

So how is it possible to arrange 5,000 people "by hundreds and fifties"? Do we have some groups of 50 and some of 100? No, because we should note that:

$$5,000 = 50 \cdot 100$$

In fact, we can go further than this because $100 = 2 \cdot 50$, so:

$$5{,}000 = 50 \cdot 2 \cdot 50$$

But this is the same type of symmetrical factorization as we find in the Thomas Code! And just as we can generate a hierarchical ordering from the Thomas Code, so we can generate an equivalent ordering from the above formula:

- First, we must group people in fifties.
- Then we combine pairs of fifties to make groups of hundreds.

This is what is meant by grouping "by hundreds and fifties"! The groupings of fifties and hundreds apply simultaneously just as the groupings into multiple levels apply in Thomas. And just like Thomas, we can reverse the process by dividing the whole into fifty groups and then one hundred groups. So we can write the grouping in this way:

5000 groups of 1 person
100 groups of 50 people
50 groups of 100 people
1 group of 5000 people

Compare this to the Thomas grouping:

108 groups of 1 saying
36 groups of 3 sayings
18 groups of 6 sayings
6 groups of 18 sayings
3 groups of 36 sayings
1 group of 108 sayings

The Thomas Code has more levels, but the organizing principle being used is the same.

### Completing the prime factorization

The above factorization of 5,000 is not complete because 50 is not a prime number. To go further and compare the sequence with the

Thomas Code, we need to continue the factorization until it only consists of prime numbers. To do this, we must split 50 into primes:

$$50 = 2 \cdot 5^2$$

As the Thomas Code is an ordered prime factorization, we need to put the factors in order. We already have part of this order from the formula $5{,}000 = 50 \cdot 2 \cdot 50$. We can also write the factorization of 50 in a way that looks very similar:

$$50 = 5 \cdot 2 \cdot 5$$

Substituting this into the formula for 5,000 gives the complete ordered prime factorization:

$$5000 = 5 \cdot 2 \cdot 5 \cdot 2 \cdot 5 \cdot 2 \cdot 5$$

## Five loaves and two fishes

To feed the five thousand, Jesus splits five loaves and two fishes. This is clearly a reference to the prime factorization into 5s and 2s. It shows us that we are on the right track. We have already seen the significance of the 5s and 2s in indicating the number of the father, 3.

## Thomas Code and the 5,000 sequence

If we place the Thomas Code alongside the five thousand sequence, we can see the similarity:

$$3 \cdot 2 \cdot 3 \cdot 2 \cdot 3$$
$$5 \cdot 2 \cdot 5 \cdot 2 \cdot 5 \cdot 2 \cdot 5$$

- Both sequences consist of two prime numbers
- The number of factors in the sequence is equal to the next highest prime number (5 or 7)
- If we add the two prime numbers we get the number of factors:

$$3 + 2 = 5 \text{ factors}$$
$$5 + 2 = 7 \text{ factors}$$

- If we add any two consecutive numbers, we also get the number of factors.

We have seen how the Thomas sayings draw attention to precisely these features of the Thomas Code, which are also true of the five thousand sequence! In fact, there is a family of series with these properties, all of which must involve 2 as one of the prime factors. The first three members of this family are:

Five factors:
$$3 \cdot 2 \cdot 3 \cdot 2 \cdot 3 = 108$$

Seven factors:
$$5 \cdot 2 \cdot 5 \cdot 2 \cdot 5 \cdot 2 \cdot 5 = 5{,}000$$

Thirteen factors:
$$11 \cdot 2 \cdot 11 \cdot 2 \cdot 11 \cdot 2 \cdot 11 \cdot 2 \cdot 11 \cdot 2 \cdot 11 \cdot 2 \cdot 11 = 1{,}247{,}178{,}914$$

The next sequence, with 2 and 17, would have 19 factors and would be an extremely large number! Sequences giving totals of a billion or more are going to have little interest to the mystics of the Jesus movement, so we are left with basically just the first two. We could also switch the order of the factors (giving us $2 \cdot 3 \cdot 2 \cdot 3 \cdot 2$ and $2 \cdot 5 \cdot 2 \cdot 5 \cdot 2 \cdot 5 \cdot 2$), but this would involve having more occurrences of the lower factor than the higher.

The probability that by chance we should hit upon a sequence with the same properties as the Thomas Code is vanishingly small. It reduces to zero when we consider the clues supplied in the story; the hierarchy for arranging the multitude, and the two prime factors in the number of fish and loaves.

We have not explained everything yet about the first miracle— there is still the twelve basket of scraps. But to understand this feature, we need to look at the second miracle.

# The second miracle

This is the second miracle:

> *In those days, when again a great crowd had gathered, and
> they had nothing to eat, he called his disciples to him and
> said to them, "I have compassion on the crowd, because
> they have been with me now three days and have nothing
> to eat. And if I send them away hungry to their homes,
> they will faint on the way. And some of them have come
> from far away." And his disciples answered him, "How
> can one feed these people with bread here in this desolate
> place?" And he asked them, "How many loaves do you
> have?" They said, "Seven." And he directed the crowd to
> sit down on the ground. And he took the seven loaves, and
> having given thanks, he broke them and gave them to his
> disciples to set before the people; and they set them before
> the crowd. And they had a few small fish. And having
> blessed them, he said that these also should be set before
> them. And they ate and were satisfied. And they took up
> the broken pieces left over, seven baskets full. And there
> were about four thousand people. And he sent them away.
> And immediately he got into the boat with his disciples
> and went to the district of Dalmanutha. (Mark 8:1-10
> ESV)*

## A few small fish

All the numbers in the miracles of the loaves and fishes are very
precise with one exception; in the second miracle, there are "a few
small fish." This vagueness indicates that the detail of the fish has
been added by the author of Mark to make the story consistent with
the first miracle. There are a couple of clues that support this. When
Jesus asks his disciples how many loaves they have, the disciples
include "two fish" in their reply in the first miracle, but do not men-

tion fish in the second miracle. The scraps collected include fish in the first miracle, but fish are not mentioned in the second. (A more literal translation of the Greek is that in the first miracle the baskets are "full of fragments, and also of the fish," but in the second miracle they have just "fragments.")

We can conclude that the source did not mention fish in the second miracle but only had loaves. This is important because the first miracle was the expansion of the two primes 2 and 5. In the second miracle, we are only given one number, 7. Nor do we have the detail of grouping the multitude. So although the two miracles sound very similar, we cannot simply repeat the pattern of the first but must now do something completely different. So how starting with seven loaves can we feed the four thousand? Perhaps we should look to the summary that brings the elements of the two miracles together, for they must be solved as a whole.

After the second miracle, Jesus crosses the lake and has a brief argument with the Pharisees who ask for a sign, before getting into a boat again. He then gives his disciples the following summary:

> Now they had forgotten to bring bread, and they had only one loaf with them in the boat. And he cautioned them, saying, "Watch out; beware of the yeast of the Pharisees and the yeast of Herod. And they began discussing with one another the fact that they had no bread. And Jesus, aware of this, said to them, "Why are you discussing the fact that you have no bread? Do you not yet perceive or understand? Are your hearts hardened? Having eyes do you not see, and having ears do you not hear? And do you not remember? When I broke the five loaves for the five thousand, how many baskets full of broken pieces did you take up?" They said to him, "Twelve." "And the seven for the four thousand, how many baskets full of broken pieces did you take up?" And they said to him, "Seven." And he said to them, "Do you not yet understand?" (Mark 8:14-21)[44]

We should ignore the novelistic details the author of Mark has added to flesh out the story, such as the disciples not having enough bread (the detail that they had one loaf recalls the "single one," indicating the chosen disciples). Jesus repeats most of the numbers in the two miracles although missing out fish. We can represent the two miracles and the summary in the diagram.

## The two miracles of the loaves and fishes

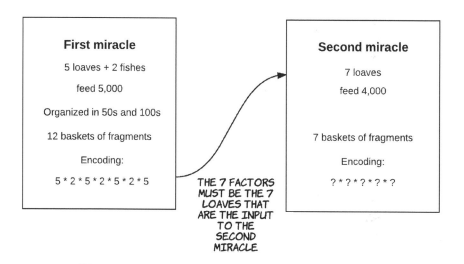

**Five and seven loaves**

We have seen that the sequence encoded by the miracle of the five thousand is the second in a series starting with the Thomas Code. The other members of this series have too many factors and multiply out to too large a value to be of interest to the Jesus movement. So if the first miracle encodes the seven-factor sequence, then we should expect the second miracle to encode the five-factor sequence of the Thomas Code. However, we know that the Thomas Code value is 108 and not 4,000! So we are looking for something that is parallel to the Thomas Code but not identical.

Now we have two sequences; one with five factors and one with seven factors. In the two miracles, we have five loaves and seven loaves with the numbers emphasized in both the summary and in Jesus' questions to the disciples. So it makes sense that the loaves represent the number of factors in the sequence. The first miracle, with five loaves, constructs the sequence of seven factors, so the second miracle, with seven loaves, should construct the five-factor sequence.

The five loaves in the first miracle do double duty because they also represent one of the two prime factors. This is because the number 5 is both the number of factors in the Thomas Code and one of the prime factors in the five thousand sequence.

**From seven loaves to five**

The second miracle starts with seven loaves, which must represent the seven-factor sequence. We now need to get from these seven loaves to a five loaves sequence.

## *Feeding the four thousand*

Our starting point then is the five thousand sequence:

$$5 \cdot 2 \cdot 5 \cdot 2 \cdot 5 \cdot 2 \cdot 5$$

From this, we must generate "five loaves," a sequence of five factors.

## Fragments

There is one prominent feature of the story that we have not so far considered, the baskets of "fragments" (*klasmata*) or broken pieces. There are 12 baskets of fragments in the first miracle and 7 baskets in the second miracle. Clearly, the numbers must be significant.

So what is a "fragment"? In mathematical terms, we might ordinarily think of it as a remainder. However, we are working with sequences of prime factorizations. This suggests the idea that the "fragment" represents a subsequence. We have seen how such subsequences are important in the Thomas sayings. For example, the "stones that minister" in 1.18 refer to the central subsequence $2 \cdot 3 \cdot 2$.

If "fragments" are subsequences, then we must break off some subsequences from our seven loaves to make the new five loaves. We are trying to create something similar to the Thomas Code:

$$3 \cdot 2 \cdot 3 \cdot 2 \cdot 3$$

So, we need a subsequence that represents the 3 and another that represents the 2. Let us now look for these.

## Three threes

The 3s occupy the beginning, middle, and end of the Thomas Code. Can we find three "threes" in the same positions in our seven loaves code? We can:

Beginning:
$$[5 \cdot 2 \cdot 5] \cdot 2 \cdot 5 \cdot 2 \cdot 5$$

Middle:
$$5 \cdot 2 \cdot [5 \cdot 2 \cdot 5] \cdot 2 \cdot 5$$

End:
$$5 \cdot 2 \cdot 5 \cdot 2 \cdot [5 \cdot 2 \cdot 5]$$

So, the fragment [5 · 2 · 5] will represent the 3s.

## Two twos

In the Thomas Code, the 2s occupy positions similar to the two fillings in a double decker sandwich:

$$3 \cdot 2 \cdot 3 \cdot 2 \cdot 3$$

We can find two sequences of two factors positioned in this way in the "seven loaves":

$$5 \cdot [2 \cdot 5] \cdot 2 \cdot [5 \cdot 2] \cdot 5$$

Our two subsequences are not identical but are mirror images of each other, giving the same value. So we must break off these two fragments of [2 · 5] and [5 · 2].

## The number of baskets

The number of baskets of fragments is 12 and 7. We can equate these to the subsequences representing "3" and "2" if we add the factors in each subsequence:

[5 · 2 · 5] gives: 5 + 2 + 5 = **12**

[2 · 5] and [5 · 2] both give: 2 + 5 = **7**

So the numbers in our "fragments" add up to the right number of baskets. This shows we are on the right track!

## Five loaves

We can now put together our "five loaves" from the fragments we have broken off the seven loaves:

$$[5 \cdot 2 \cdot 5] \cdot [2 \cdot 5] \cdot [5 \cdot 2 \cdot 5] \cdot [5 \cdot 2] \cdot [5 \cdot 2 \cdot 5]$$

This is complex and unattractive, which is a sign that we are not quite there yet. If we were to multiply out the sequence as it stands we would get the following answer:

$$5 \cdot 2 \cdot 5 \cdot 2 \cdot 5 \cdot 5 \cdot 2 \cdot 5 \cdot 5 \cdot 2 \cdot 5 \cdot 2 \cdot 5 = 12{,}500{,}000$$

There are three problems with this:

- We have thirteen factors and not five.
- The two prime numbers do not alternate as we would expect—we have too many factors of 5.
- The value of the sequence, 12.5 million, is far too high.

The sequence is not right yet. We are not finished baking our loaves!

## The yeast of the Pharisees and Herod

We must turn to another clue in the account of the two miracles. When Jesus is in the boat after the second miracle he gives this warning:

> *"Watch out; beware of the yeast of the Pharisees and the yeast of Herod."*

We have assembled five loaves from the fragments of the seven:

$$[5 \cdot 2 \cdot 5] \cdot [2 \cdot 5] \cdot [5 \cdot 2 \cdot 5] \cdot [5 \cdot 2] \cdot [5 \cdot 2 \cdot 5]$$

The role of yeast is to make loaves of bread swell up, and our loaves are too big! So we must take out the yeast put into the loaves by those malign forces, the Pharisees and Herod. The Gospel of Matthew interprets the yeast as being the teachings of the Pharisees and Sadducees,[45] but this cannot be right. The author of Matthew is forced to substitute the Sadducees for Herod to support this interpretation because Herod did not have any teachings.[46] In any case, the yeast must be a number because Jesus gives us a numerical calculation:

> *When I broke the five loaves for the five thousand, how many baskets full of broken pieces did you take up?"* They

*said to him, "Twelve." "And the seven for the four thou-*
*sand, how many baskets full of broken pieces did you take*
*up?" And they said to him, "Seven."*

So the "yeast" is given by the numbers 12 and 7. We have seen that these are the sums of the factors in our loaves. But we are now looking for a factor or factors to eliminate from the loaves. If we multiply out the values of the loaves, we get $5 \cdot 2 \cdot 5 = 50$ and $2 \cdot 5 = 10$. So we are looking for something that divides 50 or 10. These are the possibilities:

- We might try and use **both** 12 and 7 as the yeast. This does not work because neither 10 or 50 is divisible by either 12 or 7.
- If we were to **multiply** 12 and 7, we would get 84, which is not correct because it is larger than any of our loaves.
- We cannot **divide** 7 into 12 or 12 into 7.
- If we were to **add** 12 and 7, we get 19, which does not divide either 10 or 50.

There is only one option left:

- We must **subtract** one number from the other: 12 - 7 = 5

This works very well because 5 is a factor in all of our loaves. So:

Yeast = 5

This conclusion is supported by the fact that the word for yeast, *zymes*, has 5 letters.

### Feeding the four thousand

We can now remove the yeast by eliminating one of the 5s from each one of the loaves:

$$[5 \cdot 2 \cdot 5] \cdot [2 \cdot 5] \cdot [5 \cdot 2 \cdot 5] \cdot [5 \cdot 2] \cdot [5 \cdot 2 \cdot 5]$$
$$=$$
$$[2 \cdot 5] \cdot 2 \cdot [2 \cdot 5] \cdot 2 \cdot [2 \cdot 5]$$

This is now much better! First, there are two twos in the correct place:

$$[2 \cdot 5\} \cdot \mathbf{2} \cdot [2 \cdot 5] \cdot \mathbf{2} \cdot [2 \cdot 5]$$

Then, we have the factors [2 · 5] in the same place as 3s in the Thomas Code:

$$\mathbf{[2 \cdot 5]} \cdot 2 \cdot \mathbf{[2 \cdot 5]} \cdot 2 \cdot \mathbf{[2 \cdot 5]}$$

As we have seen, the factors [2 · 5] =10 are alternatives to 3 because 2 and 5 are the only prime numbers whose difference equals 3. If we write the sequence with 10 instead of [2 · 5], then we get an alternative version of the Thomas Code:

$$10 \cdot 2 \cdot 10 \cdot 2 \cdot 10$$

This is equivalent to the Thomas Code as both 10 and 3 stand for the Father. If we multiply it out we get:

$$10 \cdot 2 \cdot 10 \cdot 2 \cdot 10 = 4{,}000$$

So starting with the seven loaves, we have fed the four thousand!

## *Jesus and the fish*

The fish is, of course, a well-known symbol for Jesus. It dates from the earliest years of the Jesus movement and has been found in the Catacombs of Rome. Yet nowhere in the New Testament is Jesus called a fish. When Jesus appoints Simon and Andrew as his disciples and says that he will make them *"fishers of men."*[47] But this implies that it is the potential converts who are fish and not Jesus.

However, in the miracle of the feeding five thousand, the two fishes represent the number 2, the number which is Jesus. Jesus breaks the bread and gives it to the disciples, and then he takes the two fish: *"And he divided the two fish among them all."* (Mark 6:41) The bread is a symbol for the spiritual substance of Jesus, as in the Eucharist. This is the only place in which the fish is also a symbol for Jesus. The miracle is describing the sequence of seven, but this is also an allusion to the Thomas sequence, where the two twos are divided on each side of the three: $3 \cdot 2 \cdot 3 \cdot 2 \cdot 3$.

So the numeric symbolism explains why Jesus should be represented by the sign of the fish, just as it explains how the concept of the Trinity arose.

# PART TWO

# 9

# The structure of Thomas

We have seen how the Thomas Code is alluded to in the sayings. We will now look at how the structure is reflected in the Gospel. The first problem is to recreate the Gospel in its original form. We will take as our starting point the Coptic version of Thomas found at Nag Hammadi. Given the age of this copy, some 1,600 years old, it is remarkable that it is both complete and in relatively good condition. There are some lacunae through insect and other damage, but most of these are minor. Usually, it is possible to reconstruct the few words of lost text in these lacunae. We also have the Greek papyrus fragments, and the tendency is to see these as better copies than the Coptic because they are earlier. However, it is by no means true that an earlier manuscript is always better than a latter manuscript, and in this case, I believe that the Coptic is a better representation of the original Gospel.

The first problem is to recreate the individual saying structure of the original Gospel. The modern Gospel numbering is not always reliable, and we will have to eliminate some sayings because we have too many.

The first key indicator of a separate saying is the presence of a "Jesus said." Indeed, the existence of this label shows that whoever composed Thomas thought that it was important to distinguish individual sayings. This is necessary if there is structure to Thomas, but completely unnecessary if there is no structure. Unfortunately, we cannot use "Jesus said" as our only criteria. A number of sayings do not have "Jesus said" but "he said." These often involve a dialogue between Jesus and his disciples. In a few cases, there is no distinguishing indicator. The problem is that any structure to Thomas was quickly forgotten and the Gospel has been transmitted through

113

scribes who were not aware of the structure. The "Jesus said" statements seem to serve no purpose, so it is not surprising that they have become degraded over time as scribes made mistakes in leaving out a "Jesus said."

One of the surprising features of the Coptic is the existence of a number of duplicate sayings. These are not exact duplicates, but two variations of basically the same saying. Although the first instance of each pair can appear anywhere in the Gospel, the second instance always occurs near the end. How do we account for these duplicates and this pattern? If the Gospel were used for divination, as Stevan Davies believed, they could have been added to make the number of sayings up to exactly 108. However, we have seen evidence of a very carefully crafted Gospel. Would the mind behind it have resorted to anything so crude as introducing variations of other sayings just to make up numbers? It was more likely that the duplicates have arisen in transmission when two or more copies of the Gospel have been combined into one.

We know that the Egyptian monastery that produced the Coptic translation had an excellent library of Greek manuscripts because of the range of works found at Nag Hammadi, so it was very likely that they had multiple Greek copies of Thomas. If so, we would expect these copies to differ in places. Now suppose that the monastery is consolidating these multiple copies into one new copy. Most obviously this would arise when the Gospel was being translated into Coptic. The very existence of the Coptic library shows most of the brothers could not read Greek. So the translators had the responsibility of ensuring that the Coptic Thomas reflected the source material as closely as possible. But if that source material were two or more copies with variations they would have to make difficult choices. They could either decide that one manuscript was better and copy that. Or they could try and combine the multiple versions into one consolidated copy. Modern translators of the New Testament are faced with a similar problem. There are many ancient manuscripts of the books of the New Testament in existence, and they all vary from each other! Most translations take the second of the two approaches and produce what is called an eclectic version. This does not follow a single manuscript but attempts to get back to the original by combining features from multiple manuscripts. Scholars have sophisticated techniques to help them decide on the original version, but even with these techniques, the final text will depend on some subjective judgment.

Those working in the monastery copying Thomas did not have the benefits of modern scholarship. For most sayings, the multiple versions would be close to each other. The copyist would either take the version they preferred or combine two or more versions together. But what if there were two different variations that might even be separate sayings? Our copyist would then have to choose between two approaches; (i) copy one version and discard the other or (ii) keep both versions. The pattern we observe in Thomas suggests that our copyist started with the approach (i). As they worked through the Gospel, they kept one of the two copies in its original place. It would, after all, be very odd to read two versions of a saying one after the other. However, as they neared the end of the Gospel, they became concerned about losing the duplicate versions. So they decided to slot in these duplicates rather than lose them. This would give the observed pattern with the duplicates concentrated towards the end.

As the copyist approached the end of the Gospel, we can see a sense of panic take hold. It is very clear that something has gone wrong around saying 111. Here there is evidence that an insertion has been made into the saying itself with the "smoking gun" of a comment, "because Jesus said: ..." This is followed by a variation of a saying found in two other places in Thomas. It is also significant that this saying is sandwiched between two other duplicates, 110 and 112. And this is the very last place in the Gospel where sayings could be added without disrupting the end.

All these duplicates occur in the last eighteen. It appears that the copyist or translator of the Coptic version had destroyed the structure of this eighteen not because they were careless, but because they were scrupulous. Unwilling to throw away the alternative versions, they disrupted the last section and the sayings count. It would have been very easy to add all the duplicates after the end of the Gospel, but they did not do this. This tells us that the copyist who made the insertions did not understand the significance of the Gospel having 108 sayings. Knowledge of the structure must have long been lost. They were, however, very keen to preserve the original ending.

To recover the original Gospel, we have to remove these duplicates. The approach adopted is not so much to delete sayings, as to reposition the duplicates that appear in the later section of the Gospel as alternatives for the original occurrence of the saying. The additional comment in Thomas 111 has been removed, and the sayings on either side treated as duplicates. With these changes, the remainder of Thomas 111 makes sense when combined with Thomas 113. This was originally a single dialogue between Jesus and his disciples which had been disrupted by the additions. So this effectively eliminates three sayings. There are another two duplicates in the last eighteen; eliminating these also give the desired total of 18 sayings in the last section and 108 for the Gospel as a whole.

In total, four sayings were removed; all duplicates and all in the final eighteen. Three of these are deleted because they are believed to have been added by copyists. However, one, Thomas 106, may have been original. The Gospel itself contains clues that we are to delete this extra saying. The motivation of adding such a saying can only have been to disguise the fact that the original sayings count was 108. This is typical of the tricks that the Gospel plays to hide its secrets. In addition to the duplicates, we have had to make a few other judgments concerning what constitutes a separate saying. The following table summarizes how we get from the conventional 114 sayings to 108 sayings:

| | |
|---|---|
| Conventional no of sayings | 114 |
| Thomas 1 is part of the Incipit | -1 |
| Thomas 69 is two sayings | +1 |
| Thomas 74 and 75 are one saying | -1 |
| Thomas 94, 110 and 112 are duplicates | -3 |
| Thomas 106 is to be removed | -1 |
| Thomas 111 and 113 are one saying | -1 |
| Recreated no of sayings | 108 |

We can break down the 108 sayings by the indicator as follows.

| | |
|---|---|
| "Jesus said" | 92 |
| "He said" | 10 |
| Other | 6 |
| Total sayings | 108 |

In the Coptic manuscript, there are 97 "Jesus said" statements. In one case, Thomas 111, an extra "Jesus said" has clearly been added by a redactor. An additional 4 "Jesus said" statements are eliminated through the four duplicate sayings, giving a total of 92 in the final 108 sayings. The "Jesus said" sayings account for 85% of the total, with the other 15% divided between "He said" and the other category.

In his own analysis, Stevan Davies eliminated the "other" category by assuming that all sayings must have had either a "Jesus said" or a "He said" marker. Any saying without one of these two indicators, he combined with the previous saying. In this way, he was able to get to a total of 108 sayings without eliminating any duplicates. However, the basis of his analysis was that the Gospel had continued to be used for divination right up to the time it was copied in the Nag Hammadi codices. To function as a divination tool, the separation of sayings had to be preserved in some objective way. This differs from our analysis where it is assumed that the original rationale for the separation into individual sayings was soon lost, so that the extant Coptic copy does not exactly replicate the original structure. There is no evidence that the Gospel of Thomas was used for divination, and I believe that the assumption that the original markers would all have been maintained is artificial.

## Using triplets as a guide

In the reconstruction, I have been guided by the presence of triplets of sayings. The first level of the hierarchy is to group sayings into three. Sometimes it is obvious why three sayings have been placed in a group together, although other times this is much less clear! If a saying is wrongly included or excluded, then all the subsequent triplets will be out of sync. So where triplets can be discerned they provide a powerful clue as to the structure before that group.

The triplets provided the reason why one saying, Thomas 69, has been split into two. Although the second part of Thomas 69 does not have a "Jesus said" phrase, it constitutes a group of three with Thomas 68 and the first part of Thomas 69:

> 4.13 *Jesus said: "Blessed are you when they hate you, and persecute you, and they do not find a place in the place where they persecuted you." (Th. 68)*

> 4.14 *Jesus said: Blessed are they who have been persecuted in their mind; they are those who have known the father in truth. (Th. 69a)*

> 4.15 *Blessed are those who are hungry, that they may fill the belly of he who desires. (Th. 69b)*

In this case, the triplet is obvious, indicated by "Blessed are" statements. But some of the triplets are more subjective.

## *The role of the keystone sayings*

It was Stevan Davies who drew attention to certain key sayings involving searching and finding and who proposed that they may have a role in the structure of the Gospel. In an appendix to *The Gospel of Thomas and Christian Wisdom*, he proposed a structure dividing the Gospel of Thomas into four sections. At the start of each section was one of the sayings about searching and finding. The sections varied in length and did not tie in with his divination idea. But the idea of starting sections with a saying about searching and finding was interesting.

When I began to sketch out in pencil the structure on a copy of the Gospel, it became clear that most of these sayings were going to fall at the start of an eighteen. This was exciting! Was each eighteen going to be marked by a similar saying? However, although three of the four fell precisely at the start of an eighteen, one did not. Had the Gospel been shuffled at some point to lose the structure? No, because the three which were placed correctly were very similar to each other. The one that did not start a section was the oddball and was not a key saying at all. Rejecting it gave three "keystone" sayings, each of which fell within one of the three thirty-sixes. These keystone sayings did not mark the groups of eighteen but the groups of thirty-six.

The first two keystone sayings were the first sayings in the first and second thirty-sixes. If the same pattern had been followed, the third should have been placed at the start of the fifth eighteen, but it was actually the first saying of the sixth and final eighteen. Given the importance of the "first and last," it was not surprising that the last eighteen should be marked by the presence of a keystone saying. But it was still a little disappointing that the placing did not follow the expected pattern.

While working on Thomas, I have often found that progress starts with frustration at something "wrong," which then leads to a new insight. So it was in this case. When I placed the last two keystone sayings side by side, not only was it obvious how similar they were, with one having "some days will come" and the other "in those days," but something else clicked. The one that occurred in the first eighteen of the thirty-six talked about the present and the future. The one that was placed in the second eighteen talked about the past and the present. The keystone sayings were not just marking the thirty-sixes, they were also alluding to the eighteens!

It also became clear that the first keystone saying did double duty. Not only did it stand at the head of the first thirty-six, and allude to the two eighteens within this thirty-six, it also stood at the head of the whole Gospel. So it acted as keystone to the whole, and alluded to the three thirty-sixes that made up the whole.

The content matched the keystone sayings. For example, the first keystone saying implies that the middle thirty-six should be about being "troubled." This thirty-six is indeed the most negative section of the whole Gospel. The keystone saying in this thirty-six then says that the first eighteen should be about rejecting teachers other than

Jesus, and the second eighteen is about not finding Jesus. When we look at the sayings within each eighteen, we find exactly these themes predominating.

## *The keystone sayings*

The keystone sayings start with the very first saying proper:

> *1.1 Jesus said: "Let him who seeks not stop seeking until he finds, and when he finds he will be troubled, and if he is troubled he will become amazed, and he will become king over the all of it." (Th. 2)*

The second keystone saying occurs at the start of the third eighteen, which is also the start of the second thirty-six:

> *3.1 Jesus said: "Many times have you desired to hear these words which I speak to you, and you have none other from whom to hear them. Some days will come when you will seek after me, and you will not find me." (Th. 38)*

The final keystone saying occurs at the start of the last eighteen:

> *6.1 Jesus said: "Seek, and you shall find; but those things you asked me in those days, I did not tell you then. Now I wish to tell them, and you seek not after them." (Th. 92)*

Each of the keystone sayings occurs at the head of a group of eighteen. The position of the keystone sayings is included in the diagram in Chapter 2, and the relevant part of that diagram is shown below.

**Position of keystone sayings**

| Keystone sayings |
| --- |

| 1st thirty-six | | 2nd thirty-six | | 3rd thirty-six | |
| --- | --- | --- | --- | --- | --- |
| 1st eighteen | 2nd eighteen | 3rd eighteen | 4th eighteen | 5th eighteen | 6th eighteen |
| 1.1 | 2.1 | 3.1 | 4.1 | 5.1 | 6.1 |
| 1.2 | 2.2 | 3.2 | 4.2 | 5.2 | 6.2 |
| 1.3 | 2.3 | 3.3 | 4.3 | 5.3 | 6.3 |

All the keystone sayings are linked by the concepts of seeking and finding that occur in each one. In the first and last, the seeking and finding are successful, but in the middle saying it is unsuccessful. The last two of these sayings have a similar form. The first starts with a reference to the present and then to the future ("some days will come"). The second refers to the past ("those things you asked in those days") and then the present. And if we look at how these two sayings are placed, it explains why we have this pattern.

The saying situated on the first eighteen in the thirty-six talks about the present and then the future. The saying on the second eighteen of the thirty-six talks about the past and then the present. In each case, the two parts of the saying must relate to the two different eighteens within the thirty-six.

Although the first saying does not naturally split into two parts like the other two keystone sayings, it does have a three-fold or perhaps four-fold structure. This is shown below:

> *Let him who seeks not stop seeking until he finds,*
> *and when he finds he will be troubled,*
> *and if he is troubled he will become amazed*
> *and he will become king over the all of it.*

The first three parts each consist of two pairs, in which the last element of the pair forms the first element of the next pair:

[seek and find]
[find then troubled]
[troubled then amazed]

The last element "and he will become king over the all of it" does not take the pair form and so must be the summary of the whole. We can interpret this as a sequence:

Seek and find
then troubled
then amazed

=

King over all

The first saying does not just head up the first thirty-six but is also the first of the whole Gospel. So we can relate the sequence of three to the three thirty-sixes. In this case, the saying does double-duty, relating to both the first thirty-six and the whole Gospel. With this structure, we can see the elements that relate to each thirty-six and eighteen below:

| Thirty-six | | Eighteen | |
|---|---|---|---|
| **Ruling principle:** | | **Ruling principle:** | |
| 1 | *Let him who seeks not stop seeking until he finds,* | 1 | *Let him who seeks not stop seeking until he finds…[and he will become king over the all of it.]* |
| | | 2 | *…and when he finds he will be troubled, and if he is troubled he will become amazed, and he will become king over the all of it.* |
| 2 | *and when he finds he will be troubled,* | 3 | *Many times have you desired to hear these words which I speak to you, and you have none other from whom to hear them.* |
| | | 4 | *Some days will come when you will seek after me, and you will not find me.* |
| 3 | *and if he is troubled he will become amazed* | 5 | *Seek, and you shall find; but those things you asked me in those days, I did not tell you then.* |
| | | 6 | *[Seek and you shall find…] Now I wish to tell them, and you seek not after them.* |

Immediately, we can see a correspondence between the parts of the first saying relating to the three thirty-sixes and the sayings relating to the eighteens. The first thirty-six is ruled by the principle of "seeking and finding." This is the overall subject of the first saying which rules over both the eighteens. The second thirty-six is ruled by "being troubled," whereas the eighteens are about having none other than Jesus to hear his words from, and about seeking and not finding him. The third thirty-six are about "being amazed," and the eighteens are about a question that is not answered and a revelation that is not asked for.

The Gospel as a whole would then be ruled by the conclusion of 1.1, that "he will become king over the all of it," meaning to enter the kingdom of heaven. This is the same as is promised by the beginning of the Gospel, before 1.1, that those who understand the meaning of the words "will not taste death."

The searching and finding sayings give us the clue to the structure of the Gospel. They specify certain themes that the various sections of the Gospel use. We must now look at the evidence for those themes in the Gospel sayings.

## DeConick's kernel speeches

Other people have also seen hints of a structure in Thomas. One interesting attempt is that of April DeConick who believes that the original Gospel was structured as five speeches. Her technique involves identifying a kernel Gospel by removing all those elements she sees as having been added later. When she analyses the remaining kernel sayings, she sees themes running through them that suggest to her that the Gospel was organized into separate speeches. What is fascinating is how well her division of the Gospel into these speeches corresponds to the structure of eighteens. This is shown in the table below.[48]

|  | Start | End |
|---|---|---|
| Kernel speech one | Th. 2 | Th. 16 |
| *First eighteen* | *Th. 2* | *Th. 19* |
|  |  |  |
| Kernel speech two | Th. 17 | Th. 36 |
| *Second eighteen* | *Th. 20* | *Th. 37* |
|  |  |  |
| Kernel speech three | Th. 38 | Th. 61 |
| *Third eighteen* | *Th. 38* | *Th. 55* |

| Kernel speech four | Th. 62 | Th. 91 |
| *Fourth and fifth eighteens* | *Th. 56* | *Th. 91* |
| | | |
| Kernel speech five | Th. 92 | Th. 111 |
| *Sixth eighteen* | *Th. 92* | *Th. 114* |

The correspondence between the two is not perfect, but it is close. The main divergence arises in the fourth kernel speech. The division between the third and fourth speech comes part way through the fourth eighteen, and the speech then continues for the remainder of the fourth and the whole of the fifth eighteen. Because the fourth speech effectively combines two eighteens we are left with five and not six divisions. Another more minor difference is that one saying in the first eighteen (Thomas 17) is included in the second and not the first speech. Otherwise, the first, second and fifth speeches correspond perfectly with the first, second and sixth eighteens, allowing for the fact that DeConick's method eliminates many sayings.

One reason for the close correspondence is that she identifies five sayings that start and set the tone for each speech.[49] Of these five, three are the keystone sayings. Only where there is no keystone saying to mark the boundaries between the eighteens, do her divisions wander from the eighteens.

The fact that DeConick has independently divided up the Gospel in a way that is surprisingly close to the eighteens is a strong piece of evidence in favor of the eighteens. It shows that there are themes that run through the eighteens and tie them together. These themes are apparent to a sensitive reader even though that person is working with a completely different theoretical framework.

# 10

# The first eighteen

## Ruling principle

The first eighteen is in the first thirty-six. The ruling principle of this thirty-six is:

> let him who seeks not stop seeking until he finds

The ruling principle of the eighteen is:

> let him who seeks not stop seeking until he finds ...and he
> will become king over the all of it.

## Seeking and finding

The first eighteen starts with the first and most important keystone saying:

> 1.18 Jesus said: "Let him who seeks not stop seeking until
> he finds, and when he finds he will be troubled, and if he is
> troubled he will become amazed, and he will become king
> over the all of it." (Th. 2)

This does double duty for the whole Gospel and the first thirty-six. It is necessary to split the saying between the first two eighteens, and in this split, we have assumed the first part applies to the first eighteen and that the end ("...and he will become king over the all of it") applies to both eighteens.

It has long been obvious to commentators that the first part of the Gospel of Thomas is about seeking and finding. Among the first thirty-six sayings are some of the most dynamic in the whole Gospel. It includes key sayings such as Thomas 11, Thomas 13 and, most significant of all, Thomas 22. These seeking and finding sayings are particularly concentrated in the first eighteen. As well as 1.1, some of the main seeking and finding sayings are:

1.2 (Th. 3) The Kingdom is not to be found in the heaven or under the sea but *"inside you and outside you."*

1.3 (Th. 4) The man aged in days should ask the child of seven days *"about the place of life"* and will live.

1.4 (Th. 5) Know what is in front of you and what is hidden will be revealed.

1.5 (Th. 6) There is nothing hidden or covered that will not be revealed.

1.7 (Th. 8) Man is like a fisherman casting his net in the sea. He catches a large fish (the kingdom) and throws back the little fish (the things of the world).

1.8 (Th.9) The sower casts the seed which yields an abundant harvest (the kingdom) when it falls on good soil.

1.10 (Th. 11) A complex saying about the living and the dead and about becoming one and two.

1.12 (Th. 13) A complex saying about the nature of Jesus and the transformation of the disciple by drinking from the stream that Jesus has measured out.

1.14 (Th. 15) When you find he who was not born of woman.

1.16 (Th. 17) Jesus will give what eye has not seen and ear has not heard.

1.17 (Th. 18) Look for the end in the beginning.

1.18 (Th. 19) The five trees in paradise as the culmination of the search.

It is clear that seeking and finding is a major theme of this eighteen, just as the ruling principles tell us. Equally, not every single saying fits in with the theme and we will see this is very typical. Most of the sayings will be earlier than the structure of the Gospel, and there will always be sayings that need to be slotted in somewhere.

## *The first shall be last*

We have covered some of the structure of the first eighteen in Chapter 3. The most important structural elements are the way the eighteen clearly comes to an end at saying 1.18 with chiastic links between the beginning and end. The last saying, about the five trees in paradise, is symmetrical with the first keystone saying and also links back to the Incipit at the very start of the Gospel. The penultimate saying, 1.17, about standing in the beginning to know the end, is symmetrical with the second saying 1.2, that the kingdom is not in the sky or the sea but is inside you and outside you. Saying 1.15, which specifies the structure of Thomas better than any other saying, is symmetrical to 1.4, which is about knowing what is in front of your face so that the hidden will be revealed. All of these links concern sayings in the first and last sixes. But there is a mystery in these sixes, two sayings that we would certainly expect to be linked but which are not in symmetrical positions.

The mystery revolves around saying 1.5 (Th. 6) in which the disciples ask Jesus how they should fast, pray, and give alms. Jesus, however, does not answer this question until saying 1.13 (Th. 14). Why are the question and answer split into two halves that are separated by several intervening sayings? Some commentators take the normal "Thomas must be wrong" approach. Perhaps the scribe was not paying attention while copying 1.5 and simply missed out the answer. Certainly, the end of 1.5 seems to repeat material in 1.4 that could indicate a tired scribe. If so then the scribe, or his supervisor, noticed the mistake a little later and slotted the missed ending of 1.5 into a convenient place at the beginning of 1.13. We have seen, however, that believing that Thomas is right rather than wrong has proved a much more fruitful approach to understanding the Gospel. So we should start by assuming that the placing of the answer to 1.5 at 1.13 is deliberate and not a scribal error.

Is there any link between the placing of these two sayings in the first eighteen? The answer might seem to be no; one is the middle saying of the second three, the other is the first saying of the fifth three. There is nothing special about these two positions. But perhaps we should not look at 1.5 but at the saying that comes after. This saying, 1.6, is symmetrical with 1.13. Moreover, one is the end of a three and the other the beginning of a three. We have seen the links between the first sayings in each of the threes in the first six, and the symmetrical last sayings in the threes in the last six. Could it be that the last sayings in the first six are linked to the first sayings in the last six?

If this were the case, it is not enough to just make a connection. We would actually have to move sayings. At first sight, this seems a crazy idea. It would suggest that the authors of Thomas have quite deliberately resorted to tricks to scramble the message of the Gospel. But this is consistent with the idea that the meaning of the words is hidden or secret. And we will find strong evidence that we are indeed supposed to switch sayings.

The first piece of evidence lies in clues in the sayings themselves. Let us look at the first saying that would be affected by a move, the last in the first three:

> *1.3 Jesus said: "The man aged in days will not hesitate to ask a little child of seven days about the place of life, and he will live. **For many who are first shall become last and they will become a single one.**" (Th. 4)*

This is currently situated in the first three of the eighteen and would have to move to the last three. And we find a phrase that suggests just this: *"for many who are first shall become last."* In its new place, it is followed by 1.17. This saying, positioned almost at the end of the eighteen, does not itself move, but hints at the opposite move, from the end to the beginning:

> *Have you discovered then the beginning, that you seek after the end? **For where the beginning is, the end will be also.***

# The First Eighteen - swaps

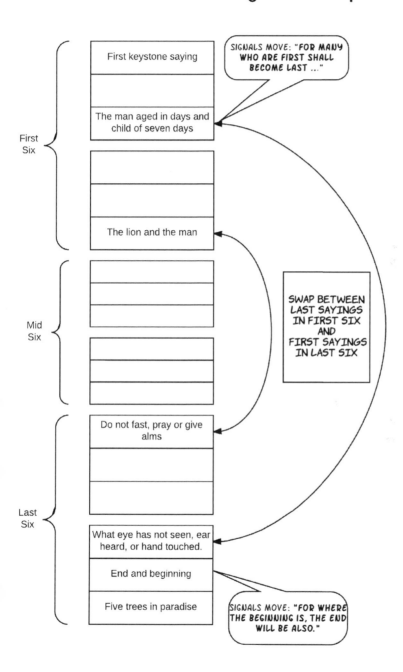

If these sayings are telling us about the move, then this move involves "many" sayings. So let us look at the results of switching the two pairs of sayings, starting with 1.3 in its new position:

> 1.16R Jesus said: "The man aged in days will not hesitate to ask a little child of seven days about the place of life, and he will live. For many who are first shall become last and they will become a single one." (Th. 4)

> 1.17 The disciples said to Jesus: "Tell us how our end shall be." Jesus said: "Have you discovered then the beginning, that you seek after the end? For where the beginning is, the end will be also. Blessed is he who will stand in the beginning, and he will know the end and not taste of death." (Th. 18)

To reflect the reordering, we will change the numbering of 1.3 to 1.16R, where the "R" indicates that the saying has been reordered and moved. If we use a number without the "R," then it will refer to the saying in its original position. The two sayings above are obviously linked. We have the "first becoming last" compared to "where the beginning is, the end will be also." We also have the theme of the man "aged in days" (representing the end) learning the place of life from the child of seven days (the beginning). These two sayings belong together!

The counter move is that the old 1.16 becomes the new 1.3R:

> 1.2 Jesus said: "If those who lead you say to you: 'Behold, the kingdom is in the sky' then the birds of the sky will become first before you. If they say to you: 'It is in the sea' then the fish will become first before you. Rather the kingdom is inside you and outside you. When you should know yourselves, then you shall be known, and you shall realize that you are the sons of the living Father. But if, however, you do not know yourselves, then you are in poverty, and you are poverty. (Th. 3)

*1.3R Jesus said: I will give you what eye did not see, what ear did not hear, and hand did not touch, and which did not enter into the heart of man. (Th. 17)*

Again this new positioning makes perfect sense! Saying 1.2 is about the kingdom not being found in a particular place, discernible with the normal senses, but "inside you and outside you." Saying 1.3R is about giving something that is not perceptible to the senses (eye, ear, and hand) and which has not entered into the heart of man. Both are about finding the kingdom, and they also are linked by a common theme.

The next pair to be moved would involve switching 1.6 (about a lion which a man will eat, and a man which a lion would eat) to immediately before 1.14 (about the one who was not born of woman). There is nothing immediately obvious connecting these sayings but that does not mean that this juxtaposition is wrong! (In my book *The Rock and the Tower*, I suggested a new interpretation of the man and the lion.[50] This interpretation would cast new light on "the one not born of woman.")

The final move is where we started. Saying 1.13 would become the new 1.6R:

*1.5 His disciples asked him and said to him: "Do you want us to fast? And how shall we pray? Shall we give alms? And what rules for what we should not eat?" Jesus said: "Do not lie; and that which you hate, do not do. For all things are revealed before heaven. For there is nothing hidden which shall not appear forth, and there is nothing covered which shall not be revealed." (Th. 6)*

*1.6R Jesus said to them: "If you fast, you will beget a sin for yourselves; and if you pray, you will be condemned; and if you give alms, you will do evil to your spirits. And if you go into any land and walk in its regions, if they should receive you, eat what they set before you. Heal the sick among them. For that which goes into your mouth*

*will not defile you. Rather that which comes out of your*
*mouth, is that which will defile you." (Th. 14)*

The placing of the two sayings now makes perfect sense with the previous 1.13 continuing 1.5. So out of the four new combinations, at least three make immediate sense. This gives confidence that we are really meant to reorder the Gospel in this way.

We have only applied this reordering to the first and last six but not to the middle six. This reflects the theme of interchanging the beginning and end. If we were to apply the reordering to the middle six, then sayings would only move around within the six and not between the sixes. In fact, all we would be doing is swapping sayings 1.9 and 1.10, which are already next to each other.

Are we supposed to reorder the rest of the Gospel in the same way? Saying 1.3 tells us that "many who are first shall become last," but so far we have only moved two sayings from the first to the last six. We will see that switching the same pairs makes excellent sense in the second eighteen. However, reordering the remainder of the Gospel does not make sense and would destroy some existing patterns. So we conclude that this reordering is intended to apply to the first thirty-six only, which is the domain of the first keystone saying. We will see that a very similar reordering does also apply to the third eighteen, and it also involves switching two pairs of saying. But they are not the same pairs. And this reordering of the third eighteen is marked by its own internal clues.

The diagram illustrates the links between sayings after the move.

# The First Eighteen reordered

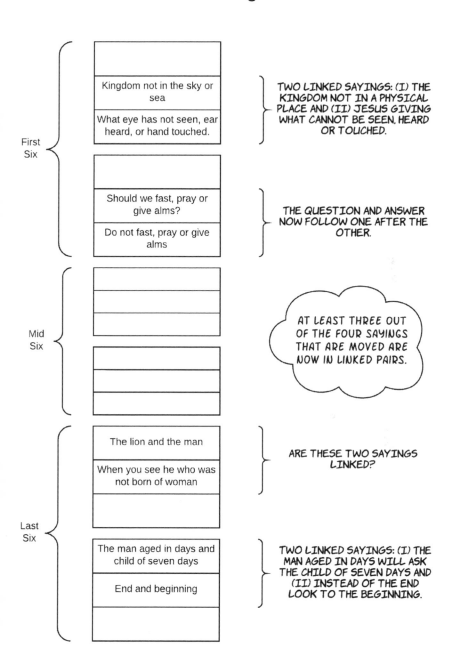

**First Six**

- Kingdom not in the sky or sea
- What eye has not seen, ear heard, or hand touched.

TWO LINKED SAYINGS: (I) THE KINGDOM NOT IN A PHYSICAL PLACE AND (II) JESUS GIVING WHAT CANNOT BE SEEN, HEARD OR TOUCHED.

- Should we fast, pray or give alms?
- Do not fast, pray or give alms

THE QUESTION AND ANSWER NOW FOLLOW ONE AFTER THE OTHER.

**Mid Six**

AT LEAST THREE OUT OF THE FOUR SAYINGS THAT ARE MOVED ARE NOW IN LINKED PAIRS.

**Last Six**

- The lion and the man
- When you see he who was not born of woman

ARE THESE TWO SAYINGS LINKED?

- The man aged in days and child of seven days
- End and beginning

TWO LINKED SAYINGS: (I) THE MAN AGED IN DAYS WILL ASK THE CHILD OF SEVEN DAYS AND (II) INSTEAD OF THE END LOOK TO THE BEGINNING.

# 11

# The second eighteen

## Ruling principle

The second eighteen is in the first thirty-six. The ruling principle of this thirty-six is:

> *let him who seeks not stop seeking until he finds*

The ruling principle of the eighteen is:

> *when he finds he will be troubled, and if he is troubled he will become amazed, and he will become king over the all of it.*

## Being troubled and amazed

The second eighteen gives effect to the second part of the keystone saying: "*...and when he finds he will be troubled, and if he is troubled he will become amazed....*" The continuation, "*and he will become king over the all of it*" applies to the whole thirty-six rather than just the second eighteen. So although the second eighteen continues to give effect to the theme of the thirty-six "searching and finding," it turns more negative in emphasizing some of the problems the disciple will encounter and how to overcome them.

Before we can look at the structure in detail, we must first look at the reordering of the eighteen.

## *Reordering the second eighteen*

The reordering follows the same pattern as in the first eighteen; switching the last saying in the first and second threes, with the first saying in the last and second last threes. We will now see why the new order makes sense.

The new first three would involve moving the old 2.16 to 2.3R:

> *2.2 (…) "If the Lord of the house knows that the thief is coming, he will keep watch before he comes, and will not let him dig into his house of his kingdom to carry off his vessels. You, then, keep watch from the beginning of the world. Gird up your loins with great strength, that the robbers may not find a way to come at you, since the help you will look for, they will find." (…) (Th. 21)*

> *2.3R Jesus said: "No one can go into the strong man's house and take it/him by force, unless he bind his hands; then he will rob his house." (Th. 35)*

Only the middle of saying 2.2 is shown above because it is long. There is clearly a strong likeness between the two, with both sayings about robbing a house! The next three is changed by switching sayings 2.6 and 2.13. This gives the following pair in the second three:

> *2.5. His disciples said: "Show us the place where you are, for it is necessary for us to seek after it." He said to them: "He that has ears, let him hear. There is light within a man of light, and he becomes light to the whole world. If he does not become light, he is darkness." (Th. 24)*

> *2.6R Jesus said: "A city that is built on a high mountain and fortified cannot fall, nor can it be hidden." (Th. 32)*

The "city" in saying 2.6R is the disciple; if his or her faith is sufficiently strong enough to survive attack, then it is too strong to be hidden from others. This obviously ties in with 2.5, which says that there is light within a man of light, a light that is visible to the whole world.

The saying which 2.6R replaces has now moved to the second from last three, which is shown below:

> *2.13R Jesus said: "Love your brother as your soul; guard him as the pupil of your eye." (Th. 25)*

> *2.14 Jesus said: "What you shall hear in your ear, proclaim to the other ear on your housetops. For no man lights a lamp and puts it under a bushel, nor does he put it in a hidden place; but he puts it upon the lamp-stand, that all who go in and come out may see its light." (Th. 33)*

> *2.15 Jesus said: "If a blind man leads a blind man, they both fall into a pit." (Th. 34)*

This group form a triplet concerned with sight and, in the middle saying only, hearing. The new 2.13R ties in with the last saying, 2.15. You should guard your Christian brothers (and sisters) as if they were the pupil of your eye (2.13R), whereas if both are blind, they will fall into a pit (2.15). The central saying emphasizes the light which should be placed where all can see and ties back to saying 2.5 that there is a light within a man of light.

The last three is also affected by the move. This involves the important saying 2.3 which becomes 2.16R. We will leave the discussion of this new position, and why it makes sense, to later.

## *The reordered second eighteen*

The diagram shows how the reordered second eighteen reflects the ruling principle of being troubled, being amazed, and reigning over it all.

The first section is about the troubles that come upon the disciple after he or she has entered into the spiritual union that is the kingdom. This is symmetrical with the last section, which is about

# The Second Eighteen reordered

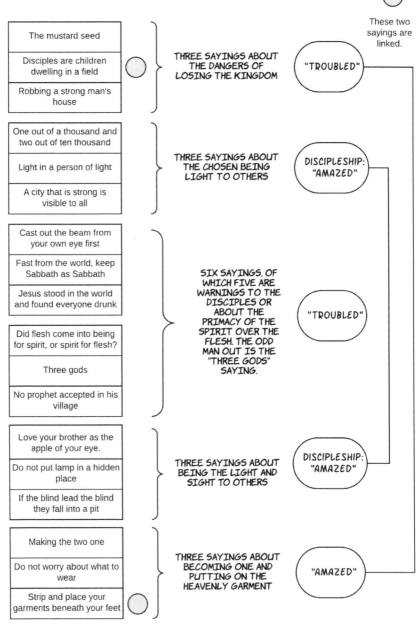

These two sayings are linked.

The mustard seed

Disciples are children dwelling in a field

Robbing a strong man's house

THREE SAYINGS ABOUT THE DANGERS OF LOSING THE KINGDOM

"TROUBLED"

One out of a thousand and two out of ten thousand

Light in a person of light

A city that is strong is visible to all

THREE SAYINGS ABOUT THE CHOSEN BEING LIGHT TO OTHERS

DISCIPLESHIP: "AMAZED"

Cast out the beam from your own eye first

Fast from the world, keep Sabbath as Sabbath

Jesus stood in the world and found everyone drunk

Did flesh come into being for spirit, or spirit for flesh?

Three gods

No prophet accepted in his village

SIX SAYINGS, OF WHICH FIVE ARE WARNINGS TO THE DISCIPLES OR ABOUT THE PRIMACY OF THE SPIRIT OVER THE FLESH. THE ODD MAN OUT IS THE "THREE GODS" SAYING.

"TROUBLED"

Love your brother as the apple of your eye.

Do not put lamp in a hidden place

If the blind lead the blind they fall into a pit

THREE SAYINGS ABOUT BEING THE LIGHT AND SIGHT TO OTHERS

DISCIPLESHIP: "AMAZED"

Making the two one

Do not worry about what to wear

Strip and place your garments beneath your feet

THREE SAYINGS ABOUT BECOMING ONE AND PUTTING ON THE HEAVENLY GARMENT

"AMAZED"

achieving the kingdom; that is "being amazed" and becoming king. These two themes flow through the rest of the eighteen. The chiastic structure is very evident in the second and fifth threes, which are both concerned with the chosen and with light. The second three is very positive, whereas the emphasis on the fifth three is about using the inner light in the disciple for the benefit of others. The middle six is much more downbeat. It is largely about the conflict between the spirit and the world, but it is also a bit of a miscellany.

We will start a more detailed look with the first three that are summarized below:

2.1 The kingdom is like a mustard seed.
2.2 The disciples are like children in a field that is not their own. Beware of the robbers. A man of understanding will reap the fruit.
2.3R To rob a strong man you must bind his hands.

At first sight, the odd man out of this list is the first saying about the mustard seed. This has long been taken as a beautiful metaphor for finding the kingdom of heaven. However, the chiastic structure above shows that the first three sayings are about losing the kingdom after it has been found. Is the parable of the mustard seed an exception to this pattern? Or is the conventional explanation of the mustard seed all wrong?

## The evil mustard seed

Here is the mustard seed parable in its Thomas version:

> 2.1 *The disciples said to Jesus: "Tell us what the kingdom of heaven is like." He said to them: "It is like a grain of mustard, smaller than all seeds; when, however, it falls onto tilled earth, it sends out a great branch, and becomes shelter for the birds of the sky." (Th. 20)*

The same parable is found in all three of the synoptic Gospels, starting with Mark:

*And he said, "With what can we compare the kingdom of God, or what parable shall we use for it? It is like a grain of mustard seed, which, when sown on the ground, is the smallest of all the seeds on earth, yet when it is sown it grows up and becomes larger than all the garden plants and puts out large branches, so that the birds of the air can make nests in its shade." (Mark 4:30-32 ESV)*

It is very similar to Thomas except that the mustard plant has been made more impressive so that it "puts out large branches" rather than "a great branch." Another subtle difference is that in Mark the seed is sown, so the planting of the mustard bush is deliberate. In Thomas, it falls onto cultivated ground, which gives the possibility that it is actually a weed. Matthew develops the parable further:

*He put another parable before them, saying, "The kingdom of heaven is like a grain of mustard seed that a man took and sowed in his field. It is the smallest of all seeds, but when it has grown it is larger than all the garden plants and becomes a tree, so that the birds of the air come and make nests in its branches." (Matthew 13:31-32)*

In Matthew, the mustard plant has now become a tree so that birds can make nests in its branches. Most people, I am sure, will prefer this Matthew version. It makes a better parable. The kingdom of heaven, like a mustard seed, will start as something tiny and insignificant, but it will grow huge and impressive. And this demonstrates what is wrong with the mustard seed parable. It will only work if the mustard plant is impressive. This is why the author of Matthew makes it into a tree. Yet the mustard plant is no tree, nor even a bush. It is a fast growing scrubby annual that can grow to several feet high. It completes its life cycle, growing and dying, in a single year. There is absolutely no way that birds can make their nests in its branches. The Thomas version, in which it puts out a branch under which birds can shelter, is more realistic. Writing in the first century AD, Pliny says this about the mustard plant:

*This last, though it will grow without cultivation, is considerably improved by being transplanted; though, on the other hand, it is extremely difficult to rid the soil of it when once sown there, the seed when it falls germinating immediately. (Pliny the Elder, Natural History 19:54)[51]*

He tells us that the mustard plant grows wild. However, if you want to grow it for food then, like almost any other plant, you are best cultivating it, giving it space and light and water to grow. Most interesting is what he says about it being a weed. Once it has grown in a piece of cultivated ground, it is very difficult to get rid of because the seeds germinate very quickly and easily. Any gardener will understand this. There is an English gardening proverb that one year's annuals give seven years' weeds. Before herbicides, such annual weeds were very difficult to eliminate from cornfields. They would have to be pulled out by hand, but the seeds would remain in the soil to germinate again and again.

So the mustard plant, far from being a great tree, is something that will infest cultivated ground. Some modern commentators have seen the parable as an ironic comment on the kingdom that will spread like a weed, but this is surely projecting modern tastes on the past. No one in the first century would think like this. The weed-like nature of the mustard plant shows that there is something wrong with the conventional understanding of the parable.

It is not just the mustard plant that is wrong; there are also the birds. Commentators have long wondered what the birds in the parable stand for. We might see "birds of the sky" as a poetic metaphor for the kingdom of heaven, yet the Gospel of Thomas explicitly rejects this. Thomas 3 says that if the kingdom is in the sky, then the birds *"will be before you,"* implying a negative view of our feathered friends. Another saying with birds is Thomas 86: *"[The foxes have] the[ir dens] and the birds have [their] nests, but the son of man has no place to lay his head and to rest."* The foxes are certainly intended to be negative; for example, in the Song of Songs, they are destroyers of vineyards,[52] and in the Gospel of Luke, Herod is compared to a fox.[53]

So we should read the birds as being negative also. Most significantly, the birds that occur in the parable of the sower (Thomas 9):

> *Behold, the sower came out, he filled his hand, he cast.*
> *Some indeed fell upon the road; the birds came and gath-*
> *ered them.*

The birds are clearly malevolent forces that rob the potential convert of the kingdom of God. In Mark, Jesus offers this explanation for the birds:

> *"And these are the ones along the road, where the word is*
> *sown: when they hear, Satan immediately comes and takes*
> *away the word that is sown in them." (Mark 4:15)*

So the author of Mark thinks that the birds represent Satan! In reality, they were probably intended to represent demons who stop a person from properly listening to the word. In the parable of the sower, cultivated ground represents those whose nature can accept the word, so that it can grow within them and yield fruit. The mustard plant is a weed that thrives on cultivated ground, taking away light, water, and nutrients from the crop and giving shelter to the birds that eat the crop and the seed. Birds would not have been popular on farms in the ancient world. Most peasant farmers were close to subsistence level with starvation a real and constant threat. The birds are literally taking food from the mouths of the farmer's children.

The parable of the mustard seed does not mean what people have long thought it to mean. The mustard seed does not stand for the kingdom but for a fragment of sinful weakness that enters the heart of one who is already in the kingdom. This weakness might relate to sexuality, or a love of riches, or anger and hate. If allowed to grow then it will become a large weed that infests the cultivated soil and gives shelter to the birds, the demons. The demons will gradually gain control of the person and divert them from the kingdom of heaven.

We know from Pliny that once the mustard plant was established, it was difficult to eliminate because it germinated from seed so easily. The moral of the parable then is that a person must be alert to any weakness in their own nature, no matter how small. They must deal with it while it is small and not allow it to grow and set seed.

There is one feature of the saying that may seem to go against this interpretation, and that is that Jesus compares the kingdom to a mustard seed. However, the formula "the kingdom is like X" introduces a story that illustrates some aspect of the kingdom. It does not mean that X necessarily stands for the kingdom in the story. When a person entered the spiritual state of the kingdom, they did not always stay in the state permanently. Disciples, even the chosen, would often fall away. There are many sayings in Thomas that warn against such a loss. So we find a negative form of the kingdom parable, where the kingdom is compared to something that illustrates the dangers of losing the kingdom. The mustard seed parable is of this type, and it is not alone in Thomas. Consider, for example, a saying in the last eighteen:

> 6.5 *Jesus said: "The kingdom of the [Father] is like a woman carrying a jar full of meal; walking on a road a long way the handle of the jar broke; the meal poured out behind her on the road. She did not know, she did not realize her loss. When she came into her house, she put the jar down; she found it empty." (Th. 97)*

It is amusing to see the efforts that some commentators go through to cast a positive light on this saying because it is introduced by the words "the kingdom ... is like." The saying will not bear such a positive interpretation. The real meaning is obvious and straightforward. It is about the loss of the kingdom. The meal in the jar relates to the grain in the parable of the sower. The woman with the jar is one of the chosen and the meal represents her spiritual treasure. She should guard it and sow it, but she treats it with neglect. She is too preoccupied with her journey on the road to notice it leaking away. The road stands for the world and its many distractions. Without even knowing what is happening, she loses the kingdom bit by bit. Until one day, in a moment of quietness, she realizes it is gone.

There is a close similarity between the parable of the mustard seed and the parable of the woman and the jar. In the one, the kingdom is lost by allowing a minuscule sinful weakness to grow unchecked; in the other, it is lost through becoming distracted by the things of the world. Both are warnings for the chosen.

Thomas 97 is not the only negative kingdom saying in the last eighteen. The very next saying, Thomas 98, compares the kingdom to an assassin:

> 6.6 *Jesus said: "The kingdom of the Father is like a man wanting to kill a powerful one. He drew the sword in his house and drove it into the wall, that he might know that his hand would be strong. Then he slew the powerful one."*
> (Th. 98)

Once again commentators search for a positive interpretation of this saying. Perhaps it is a trial of strength necessary before the coming of the kingdom. Yet the kingdom would never be compared to a murderer. I believe that it is a universal rule in Thomas that malefactors of all kinds represent demons, which would make the assassin stand for a demon. What then about the "powerful one" who is the assassin's target? The same word is used for the powerful ones in soft raiment who are despised in Thomas 78. But we have seen how the Gospel of Thomas loves contradiction and frequently uses the same word in both a negative, literal meaning and a positive, spiritual meaning. Power is negative when used to describe the powerful ones of this world, but is also used positively to describe those who reign in their kingdom. The "powerful one" in Thomas 98 must be the person/spirit, the single one who is chosen. The demon wishes to rob the person of their kingdom by destroying their spirit. But he is too weak to attack the spirit directly, so he will first run the sword through the wall of his own house. What does the house stand for? The early Jesus movement believed that the body belonged to the demons, and it is the body that is the house. In Luke 11:24-26 there is a story about a demon that is cast out of a person, and wanders the wilderness before it decides to *"return to my house from which I came."*

Finding the house empty and ready, it enters with *"seven other spirits more evil than itself."*

Thomas 98 is telling the disciples that the first attack of a demon will be through their bodies. If the demon succeeds in this trial of strength, then it will go on to slay the spirit. In the New Testament Gospels, demons are shown as causing all manner of psychological and psychosomatic conditions. The people they possessed would harm themselves, like the demon-possessed man in the country of the Gerasenes: *"Night and day among the tombs and on the mountains he was always crying out and cutting himself with stones"* (Mark 5:5). Even bodily disease could be caused by demons. When Jesus appoints his disciples, he gives them power to cure disease and cast out demons, and it would seem there was little distinction between the two.[54]

The demon's trial blow will damage his own house, the body. As well as mental illness and perhaps physical disease, this would also include addictions such as gluttony and drunkenness, as well as going with prostitutes which could lead to venereal disease. So the body was seen as a battleground in which the chosen fought the demons who were attempting to gain control. We find similar concepts in Paul's letters. He describes how he is tough on his body so that it obeys him. He talks about a "thorn in his flesh" that made him stronger[55], some affliction which he fought; and he says that the moral failings of the Corinthians had caused some of them to become sick.[56]

Is it significant that neither Thomas 97 nor Thomas 98 is found in the Gospels? Most likely the Gospel writers rejected these sayings because they could not understand why the kingdom should be compared to something negative. The mustard seed parable was included because it was misunderstood, with the gospel writers thinking the mustard plant was a positive image of the kingdom. We go back to that small detail; in Mark, the seed is sown, whereas in Thomas it falls onto the ground. In Mark and the other Synoptics, the mustard plant is a crop. Only in Thomas do we see the truth, that the mustard plant is a weed, and the tiny mustard seed is evil.

## The first three

If the mustard seed parable is about the dangers of losing the kingdom, it can take its place coherently within the first three of the second eighteen. Let us now look at the other two sayings in the three, starting with 2.2 (Th. 21). This saying consists of three parts that were probably originally three standalone sayings. The first part is about children dwelling in a field:

> Mary said to Jesus: "Whom are your disciples like?" He said: "They are like children dwelling in a field which is not theirs. When the Lords of the field come, they will say: 'Give our field back to us.' They strip naked in their presence to give it back to them, and they give their field to them."

The field here stands for the physical universe, including the disciple's own body. The Lords of the field are the fallen angels and their servants/progeny, the demons. The Jesus movement believed that the world was under the control of these evil forces. We have already seen how the body was regarded as the house and dwelling of the demons. The disciples live in the physical world in a physical body, but neither body nor world belongs to them. When the Lords of the field ask for its return, the disciples are told to strip naked in their presence to give the field back. Why should the disciples have to take off their clothes to give a field back to its owners? The answer is found in the metaphor of the "garment" that occurs time and again in the early Jesus movement. The garment meant the "body" in two different senses; it stood for both the physical body and the spiritual body. The early Jesus movement believed that humans could only travel to heaven in spiritual form, which involved putting aside their physical garment (the body) and assuming a spiritual garment (the soul/spirit). This was true whether the journey to heaven was made after death or in life through mystic ascent. If the later, then the body would only be put aside temporarily, to be reoccupied when the mystic returned to the world. So if they are to stop living in the field (the physical world), the disciples have to take off their garment (the body) and give it back to its rightful owners (the fallen angels and demonic powers).

The saying is an instruction to accept martyrdom without resistance. The evil powers do not rule in their own form but through their human avatars and intermediaries, the kings and rulers of the world. In a greater sense, the entire physical world is under their power until the apocalypse, so the disciple's body belongs to them, and they can demand it back. The disciple must offer non-resistance to evil in evil's rightful domain. There is a similarity here with the saying about money and taxes; one should give to Caesar what belongs to Caesar. Money is inherently evil and belongs to Caesar, so it should be returned to him when he asks for it. The next part of the saying is about robbers:

> *"Therefore I say this: If the Lord of the house knows that the thief is coming, he will keep watch before he comes, and will not let him dig into his house of his kingdom to carry off his vessels. You, then, keep watch from the beginning of the world. Gird up your loins with great strength, that the robbers may not find a way to come at you, since the help you will look for, they will find."*

Robbers are malefactors and so stand for demons. We have just seen the demonic powers called "lords of the field" so why are they now robbers? The reason is that the first part of the saying concerned the physical world and this part concerns the kingdom of heaven. The demons are now attempting to take what does not belong to them, to rob the disciples' of their kingdom. The "Lord of the house" is a person in the kingdom, and the vessels in "the house of his kingdom" stand for the spiritual treasures of the kingdom of heaven. The meaning is straightforward; the chosen must be vigilant and alert for demonic incursions into their own nature. The last part of the saying is about the harvest:

> *"May there be among you a man of understanding; when the fruit was ripe, he came quickly, his sickle in his hand, and reaped it. He that has ears to hear, let him hear."*

The fruit is the fruit of the kingdom. It is the end result of the process that starts with the sowing of the seed. The chosen yield fruit to God through their behavior. This saying is inducing a sense of urgency into the disciples. The best way to repel the demons is through harvesting the fruit as soon as it is ready rather than letting it wither on the vine. The disciple must live in their everyday lives the kingdom of God while they are able, for who knows when their body will be required of them? And they must be alert to the moment when others have completed their own spiritual development and are ripe to be "harvested," to be initiated into the kingdom. The disciple must not delay.

The final saying in the three is as short as the previous saying was long:

> 2.3R *Jesus said: "No one can go into the strong man's house and take it/him by force, unless he bind his hands; then he will rob his house." (Th. 35)*

The one who would rob the house is a demon, the "strong man" is one of the chosen (male or female), and their house is the kingdom. The demons want to take the "strong man's" house, meaning to deprive them of the kingdom. But they are too weak to attack the "strong man" directly. This is similar to the parable of the assassin. However, in this saying, the demon weakens the strong person not with a trial of strength but by binding. This can only mean the "cares that bind." The chosen are weakened by anxiety and by the worries of the world. Many of these cares came from being married and having children. Paul tells his readers that it is better to be unmarried because being married will bring many troubles to the Christian.[57] As the church developed this was to become a moral difference, with the married being regarded as weaker than those who remained single and "pure." But originally this was simply a matter of practicalities. If you had children, you would have to spend your time working to feed them. You could not obey the instruction to *"become passersby"* (Thomas 42). Commitments drag you into the world and threaten to make you part of the world; if you become obsessed with worldly worries, you will lose the kingdom. This is a warning rather than a rule, and most members of the early church would still have been married.

This leaves the mystery of the three disparate parts of 2.2. Many of the sayings that make up Thomas must have circulated for decades before the Gospel was assembled as a whole. So it is likely that the three parts of 2.2 were originally separate sayings that the compiler of Thomas has conjoined. The three do form a natural sequence, starting with a warning that the demonic powers can at any time claim back the disciple's body, followed by a warning about the same powers attempting to rob the disciple of their spirit, and finishing with the urgency of yielding the fruit of the kingdom. Yet the combination still gives a rather odd, disjointed feel due to the different metaphors in the three sections.

The motivation for combining multiple sayings into one may have been to give the correct total sayings count of 108 or to implement the desired structure of the Gospel, or both of these at once. In the case of 2.2, the combination enables the saying to link into other parts of the Gospel in three different ways:

Part 1: Links in with the symmetrical last three, which are all about the "garment."

Part 2: Ties in with the other two sayings in the first three. All are about the dangers of demonic attack, and they form a symmetrical threesome:

- 2.1 is a warning about not allowing any sinful weakness to become established, no matter how small, because this will give shelter to the birds/demons.
- 2.2 is a warning be on your guard and to be strong against demonic attack.
- 2.3R is a warning not to allow yourself to be weakened by the "cares that bind."

Part 3: Links to the first three of the symmetrical fifth eighteen, which starts with a saying about the need for laborers for the harvest.

So the saying is not a random amalgamation of the parts but a carefully crafted whole. The last point, about the link with the fifth eighteen, is significant because both of these eighteens have a theme of discipleship. The discipleship theme is present in the first three, with the sayings warning of the dangers facing the chosen, but becomes more developed in the following three, which we will look at now.

## The second and fifth threes

Like the first three, the second three are also about the chosen, but they are much more positive in tone. The three sayings are shown below:

> 2.4 Jesus said: "I shall choose you, one out of a thousand, and two out of ten thousand, and they shall stand as a single one." (Th. 23)

> 2.5. His disciples said: "Show us the place where you are, for it is necessary for us to seek after it." He said to them: "He that has ears, let him hear. There is light within a man of light, and he becomes light to the whole world. If he does not become light, he is darkness." (Th. 24)

> 2.6R Jesus said: "A city that is built on a high mountain and fortified cannot fall, nor can it be hidden." (Th. 32)

It starts with those who are chosen. We have seen the symbolism beneath the numbers "one in a thousand and two out of ten thousand" and the significance of the "single one." Thomas sayings carry multiple meanings, and we should not forget the simple literal understanding that the chosen are very few in number.

In the second saying, the disciples ask where Jesus is because they must seek after him. He does not answer directly but says there is *"light within a man (person) of light."* If a person does not become light, then he, or she, will be darkness. Jesus is not in a physical place but is spiritual in nature. He is the light within which transforms the nature of a person until that person becomes a light to the whole world. (We find the same idea that Jesus is light in the Gospel of

John.) The idea that Jesus is the light within the disciple ties in with the numeric symbolism of the previous saying. We have seen this represents God (three), Jesus (two) and the disciple (one). Jesus is with the "one" to make it "two," a concept which is found in the "three Gods" saying, which is positioned in the identical location to 2.5 in the following six.

The last saying builds on the idea of the disciple as a light to the world. It uses a metaphor that to be defensible against invaders a city must be situated on a "high mountain." However, it is then visible for many miles around and cannot be hidden. In the same way, if the disciple is fortified against demonic invasion, their faith must be so strong that it is visible to all.

The sayings in the three have a coherent message. We start with the chosen who are few in number, and who are the single ones in the sequence three, two, one. Then we have Jesus as the light within a person of light which is visible to the whole world. The disciples must become a person of light, or they will be filled with darkness. If they are a person of light, then they will be like a city on a mountain which is impregnable but which cannot be hidden. If the mood of the first three is to become troubled, then the mood of this second three is to be amazed.

In the central six, the "troubled" theme will emerge again, but we will jump ahead to the fifth three. This is symmetrical with the second three, and the two form a chiastic whole. The emphasis in the second three was the disciples becoming chosen and becoming light. The fifth three is all about using that light to become the light for others. We have the same pattern as the second three with the first and last saying being short, and the middle saying a little longer:

> 2.13R Jesus said: "Love your brother as your soul [psyche]; guard him as the pupil of your eye." (Th. 25)

> 2.14 Jesus said: "What you shall hear in your ear, proclaim to the other ear on your housetops. For no man lights a lamp and puts it under a bushel, nor does he put it in a hidden place; but he puts it upon the lamp-stand, that all who go in and come out may see its light." (Th. 33)

*2.15 Jesus said: "If a blind man leads a blind man, they
both fall into a pit." (Th. 34)*

The first mentions the "eye," the second the "ear" and the third
implies the eye (through "blind"). The central saying is about pro-
claiming what is heard, and about not hiding the light under a bushel, but placing it where all can see. This saying is symmetrical with
2.5 where there is light within a person of light, and it lights the
whole world. The first saying tells the disciple to love their brothers
(and sisters!) and guard them as the *"pupil (apple) of your eye."* This
is using a traditional Jewish expression to imply that the disciple
should be the eye of their brothers and sisters in the Jesus movement. The last saying is about what happens if the blind are led by
the blind; they both fall into a pit.

The meaning of the whole is that those with light should guide
those who would otherwise be blind. It is not, of course, literal blind-
ness that is intended. The early Jesus movement had two grades of
followers; the "chosen" or "pneumatics" and the "called" or "psychics." The pneumatic are those of the spirit and the psychic those
of the soul. The movement started out as being elitist in a spiritual
sense, appealing to the pneumatic alone. This limited its growth, and
it began to offer water baptism to appeal to the non-spiritual majority. Very quickly the church became dominated by the psychics,
the Christians of belief rather than gnosis, and it is these psychics
who are called "the blind." The sayings in the fifth three are about
the love and guidance the pneumatics should give to their psychic
brothers and sisters. Left to themselves (as they were soon to be), the
psychics will *"fall into a pit."* So the pneumatics must act as their eyes
and share with them their light.

Each of the two threes is a coherent whole in its own right, and yet
also ties in beautifully with the other three. In terms of the individual
sayings, we have seen how 2.5 is linked with the symmetrical 2.14,
and how 2.6 and 2.13 are switched. The remaining symmetrical pair
is the chosen saying, 2.4, whose subject is the pneumatics, and the
blind saying, 2.15, whose subject is the psychics. These two sayings
represent the two wings of the church, which are called elsewhere
the right and the left.

## *The middle six*

The middle six section goes back to the principle of being "troubled." The section starts and ends with two sayings that give warnings to the disciples. The first is a saying that is familiar from the Synoptics:

> *2.7 Jesus said: "The mote which is in your brother's eye, you see; the beam, however, in your eye, you do not see. When you cast out the beam from your own eye, then you will see to cast out the mote from your brother's eye." (Th. 26)*

This links in with the theme of light in the previous section, but the joyful nature of that section is now gone. This saying warns the disciple about criticizing their fellow brother and sisters if they themselves cannot see. (In the original ordering this saying is next to the saying about the blind leading the blind, which also makes sense.) This saying is addressed not to the chosen, but to those who have not yet reached the chosen state. Only when they achieve the ability to see clearly can they lead the blind. The last saying in the section is a warning about the disciple remaining in their hometown:

> *2.12 Jesus said: "No prophet is accepted in his own village; a physician does not heal those who know him." (Th. 31)*

This saying is telling the disciple to leave their familiar environment and *"become passersby."* So both the first and last saying in the six are concerned with situations where the disciple cannot help others.

The second saying in the six is about fasting from the world:

> *2.8 Jesus said: If you do not fast from the world, you will not find the kingdom; if you do not keep the Sabbath as Sabbath, you will not see the father. (Th. 27)*

The Gospel of Thomas loves contradiction, and this saying seems to contradict other sayings. The disciples are told to fast, although 1.5 & 1.6R have already told them not to fast! In this case, the contradiction is easily resolved; the disciples are not to fast in the tra-

ditional Jewish sense, but to "fast from the world." This reflects the
new spiritual law that supersedes the traditional Jewish law. Traditional fasting is linked to Sabbath observance, which is mentioned
next. The disciples are now told to "keep the Sabbath as Sabbath."
The conventional explanation is that this means that the disciples
must observe the Jewish Sabbath. Such an emphasis on Sabbath
observance contradicts many other sayings in the Gospel, such as
3.16 (Th. 53) which rejects circumcision. To resolve this contradiction, many conventional commentators take their usual approach
of assuming that Thomas is wrong. They see this saying as a later
addition, perhaps from a group of Jewish Gnostics. We shall take
the contrary approach of assuming that the Gospel is right and that
the contradiction is deliberate. It is encouraging that we can see just
such a deliberate contradiction in the first part of the saying, along
with its resolution, that "fasting" is interpreted in a way that under-
mines traditional Jewish observance.

If the contradiction is deliberate, then the two "Sabbaths" are two
different Sabbaths. The saying is not a defense of traditional Jewish
Sabbath observance, but a rejection of such observance. We know
that the Christians did abandon the traditional Jewish Sabbath, the
last day of the week (Saturday), in favor of the first day of the week
(Sunday). So the obvious conclusion is that this is what is intended
here. This change in Sabbath is puzzling on the conventional view.
If Christians had started by observing the Jewish Sabbath, then
this practice would have continued. To change the day of Christian
observance once it had become established would be all but impossible. As the Sabbath did change, this change must have occurred
at the beginning of the movement. There are, in fact, clues that the
Christians did not keep the Jewish Sabbath; in the Gospel of Mark,
the disciples are accused of eating ears of corn on the Sabbath, and
Jesus replies that the Son of Man is Lord of the Sabbath. The implication is that Jesus had ordered a change in the way the Sabbath was
interpreted.

We should note that this change of Sabbath, from the first to the
last, is consistent with the chiastic structure and reversal of the last
and first in the Gospel of Thomas. We have seen how four sayings

in each of the first two eighteens have to be switched so that the end becomes the beginning and the beginning the end. So perhaps the change of Sabbath, from the end of the week to the beginning of the week, is also indicated by 1.17: "*Have you discovered then the beginning, that you seek after the end? For where the beginning is, the end will be also.*"

The conventional explanation is that the Sabbath was changed to celebrate the resurrection of Jesus which, according to the Gospels, occurred on the first day the week. But this is to confuse cause and effect based on a literal interpretation of the resurrection stories. Instead, we can see both the relocation of the new Sabbath to the first day of the week and Jesus' resurrection occurring on the same day as indicating a single underlying cause.

The "fasting from the world" theme is developed in the next two sayings:

> 2.9 Jesus said: "I stood in the midst of the world, and I appeared to them in the flesh. I found them all drunk, I found none among them thirsting; and my soul was afflicted for the sons of men, for they are blind in their mind and do not see, for they came into the world empty; they seek also to depart from the world empty, but now they are drunk. When they have thrown off their wine, then they will repent." (Th. 28)

> 2.10 Jesus said: "If the flesh came into being because of the spirit, it is a marvel; but if the spirit because of the body, it is a marvel of marvels. But as for me, I marvel at this, how this great wealth has settled in this poverty." (Th. 29)

These are followed by the "three Gods" saying which we have already covered. The central point of the second eighteen comes between these two sayings, so they are symmetrical with each other. The first has the vocabulary associated with the psychics. Jesus' soul (psyche) is afflicted for the "sons of man" who are "blind in their mind." The terminology links this saying to the fifth three. Those of the soul are drunk, not with literal drink, but with the things of the world. This contrasts with the spiritual drunkenness in saying 1.12 where Jesus says that Thomas (representing the pneumatic) is drunk with the spring (the spirit) he has measured out. We have a similar imagery towards the end of the Gospel in saying 6.15, where if the disciples drink from the mouth of Jesus (meaning to listen to his words) the hidden things become visible.

The two sayings are linked by the theme of the flesh against the soul/spirit. In the first saying, Jesus appears in the flesh, standing in the midst of the world. He sees that the psychics have become drunk by the flesh/world, although they came into the world with nothing and must depart with nothing. They are drunk, yet there is a message also of hope, for they will repent.

The second saying is about the relationship between the flesh and the spirit. Did the body come into existence because of the spirit or did the spirit come into existence because of the body? The first represents the primacy of the spirit, the second the primacy of the body/flesh. The saying depreciates the body and indicates that it was the spirit that came first; if the body was created to hold the spirit it would be a marvel, meaning that it is unlikely, but it would be a marvel of marvels if it were the other way around.

These central two sayings summarize the two themes of the second eighteen, being troubled and then amazed. The soul exists between the two poles of the body (being troubled) and the spirit (being amazed). It is corrupted by its thirst for the things of the world, yet it contains the seed and promise of redemption. The proper role of the body is as the container for the spirit; the spirit does not exist for the purpose of the body. It is the spirit that is the subject of the final climatic three of the eighteen.

## The last three

The last three of the second eighteen are also the last three of the first thirty-six. We would expect this section to end with a bang and it does! This is where the first thirty-six reaches its climax of being amazed and becoming king over everything. In the reordered version, it starts with one of the most important sayings in the whole of Thomas:

> *2.16R Jesus saw some little ones at the breast. He said to his disciples: "These little ones at the breast are like those who enter into the kingdom." They said to him: "Then if we be little ones, shall we enter the kingdom?" Jesus said to them: "When you make the two one, and when you make the inside as the outside, and the outside as the inside, and the upper side as the lower side; and when you make the male and the female into a single one, that the male be not male nor the female female; when you make eyes in the place of an eye, and a hand in place of a hand, and a foot in place of a foot, an image in place of an image, then you will enter into [the kingdom]." (Th. 22)*

To call this enigmatic would be an understatement! It starts by Jesus and his disciples seeing some babies breastfeeding. Jesus says that those who enter the kingdom are like these babies. The disciples ask, quite reasonably, whether if they become little ones they will enter the kingdom. But instead of a simple answer, Jesus gives them a formula;

> Make the two one;
> The inside as the outside
> The upper as the lower;
> The male and female into a single one
> Eye / hand / foot in place of an eye / hand / foot;
> Image in place of an image

This is a formula of twinship, where the two twins are mirror-like images of each other that merge into a single whole. One of the twins is male and the other female so the whole is hermaphrodite. One of these twins is the body / soul and the other the spirit. The spirit is above and outside, the body is below and the soul inside it. The early Jesus movement believed that a person's spirit was of the opposite sex, so the combination of the body / soul and the spirit becomes the divine marriage. If the disciple was to ascend to heaven, they must leave their fleshy body behind and put on their spirit body. As we have seen from the first three of the second eighteen, the physical and spiritual bodies were both called "garments." It is this garment analogy that we find in the final saying of the eighteen:

> *2.18 His disciples said: "On what day will you appear to us, and on what day will we look upon you?" Jesus said: "When you strip naked and are not ashamed, and take your garments and put them beneath your feet like little children and trample them, then [you will see] the son of the living one and you shall not fear." (Th. 37)*

In order to see Jesus, the disciples must take off their garments, which means the body. In the first three, putting off the garment meant accepting martyrdom, but in this final three, it is about the mystic ascent in which the body must be put aside to see Jesus. Another theme that appears in this saying is that of the child; those who take off their garments are like little children. This ties back to the first saying in the three where those who enter the kingdom are like babies. In one of the two middle sayings, Jesus says that those who were drunk "came into the world empty; they seek also to depart from the world empty." It would seem that "being empty" means not being filled with worldly desires, possessions, and fears. Those who are full of the things of the world are weighed down and cannot ascend to heaven.

There is another link to the child theme. Saying 2.16R is in the same place in the second eighteen as saying 1.16R in the first eighteen: *"The man aged in days will not hesitate to ask a little child of seven days about the place of life, and he will live."* A little child of seven days is a baby before circumcision on the eighth day. So in a literal sense, both 1.16R and 2.16R say that you must become like a baby to enter the kingdom. This only leaves the middle saying of the last three, which is also about garments:

> *2.17 Jesus said: "Do not be anxious from morning to evening and from evening to morning about what you shall put on." (Th. 36)*

This seems to be comparatively mundane, warning the disciples about attaching too much importance to clothes. However, the Greek papyrus has a much longer version:

> *Jesus said: Do not fret from morning until evening and from evening until morning, about your food and what you will eat, nor about your clothing and what you will wear. You are far better than the lilies that neither card nor spin. As for you, when you have no garment what will you put on? Who shall add to your stature? He will give you your garment. (Th. 36—Papyrus)*

DeConick suggests that this longer version was shortened in the Coptic because of the apparent inconsistency with the following saying; Thomas 36 tells the disciples that they will be given a garment whereas Thomas 37 says that they should put off their garment. A very similar saying to the long version is found in the Gospels of Matthew and Luke.

> *"Therefore I tell you, do not be anxious about your life, what you will eat or what you will drink, nor about your body, what you will put on. Is not life more than food, and the body more than clothing? Look at the birds of the air: they neither sow nor reap nor gather into barns, and yet your heavenly Father feeds them. Are you not of more value than they? And which of you by being anxious can add a single hour to his span of life? And why are you anxious about clothing? Consider the lilies of the field, how they grow: they neither toil nor spin, yet I tell you, even Solomon in all his glory was not arrayed like one of these. But if God so clothes the grass of the field, which today is alive and tomorrow is thrown into the oven, will he not much more clothe you, O you of little faith? Therefore do not be anxious, saying, 'What shall we eat?' or 'What shall we drink?' or 'What shall we wear?' For the Gentiles seek after all these things, and your heavenly Father knows that you need them all. But seek first the kingdom of God and his righteousness, and all these things will be*

*added to you. Therefore do not be anxious about tomorrow,*
*for tomorrow will be anxious for itself. Sufficient for the*
*day is its own trouble. (Matthew 6:25-34 ESV)*

The meaning from Matthew is very obvious. The disciples should not worry about food or clothing because God will provide. The lilies of the valley neither card nor spin, yet are clothed better than Solomon in all his glory. Does God not care for people more than plants? Anyone familiar with the Matthew and Luke versions will tend to regard Thomas as being inferior. This is the "Sunday school" effect whereby people always think that the version they have been familiar with since Sunday school must be right.

In his recent book, *Thomas and the Gospels*, Mark Goodacre argues that the Thomas version must be dependent upon the Matthew and Luke versions because it shows a phenomenon that he calls the missing middle.[58] His argument is that the Matthew version makes perfect sense as a well-developed story. However, the Thomas version does not make sense unless we were already familiar with Matthew or Luke, because it has extracted certain elements from Matthew but excluded others. So in Thomas, we have the detail that the lilies do not card or spin, but without any explanation. However, what Mark Goodacre never considers is that the Matthew version does not actually make sense, any more than the synoptic version of the mustard seed makes sense.

Matthew has two parallel themes; eating/drinking and clothing. The eating/drinking theme uses the metaphor of the birds that do not sow or reap and yet God provides for them. The clothing theme uses the example of the lilies. And it is here that the saying goes wrong. Consider what Jesus says about the lilies:

*"...even Solomon in all his glory was not arrayed like one*
*of these. But if God so clothes the grass of the field, which*
*today is alive and tomorrow is thrown into the oven, will*
*he not much more clothe you, ..."*

So the lilies of the valley are better clothed than Solomon who is used as the supreme example of the well-dressed man. Jesus then promises that the disciples will be even better clothed than these lilies of the valley. But this means that the disciples are to be better clothed than anyone in history! Yet the Jesus movement depreciated the things of the world, and the disciples were vagabonds who would have gone about in rags. How then could they be more gorgeous even than Solomon? Clearly, it is not literal garments that are intended, but the spiritual garment. This is the obvious meaning of the ending of the Thomas saying: *"As for you, when you have no garment what will you put on? Who might add to your stature? He will give you your garment."* Here there is a switch from the literal garment, to the garment of the body. This is the meaning of the odd expression *"who shall add to your stature?"* which means "who can make your body bigger?" God has power over the physical body; he could even make your body taller, yet he will do better and clothe you spiritually.

This is the only meaning that makes sense of the metaphor of the lilies of the valley. But the Matthew version cannot support this interpretation because of the parallel structure between eating and clothing. In the Matthew version, eating is literal eating, so clothing must be literal clothing. We also find eating at the beginning of the Thomas Greek version, but it is not developed in the same way as in Matthew. The eating theme is not present at all in the Coptic. It seems likely that several different versions of this saying were in circulation, and that neither the surviving Greek nor Coptic exactly represent the original saying. We can attempt to reconstruct this original using both versions:

> *2.17 Jesus said: "Do not be anxious from morning to evening and from evening to morning about what you shall put on. You are far better than the lilies that neither card nor spin. As for you, when you have no garment what will you put on? Who might add to your stature? He will give you your garment." (Th. 36—reconstruction)*

This would make perfect sense. The whole is a play on the literal garment of clothes, the physical garment of the body, and the spiritual garment. The saying then ties in with 2.2 where the physical garment, meaning the body, has to be discarded, and the other sayings in the last three, where the body is replaced by the spiritual garment.

What has happened is that the author of Matthew has struggled with the meaning of this saying. He has understood the first part and has developed this into his story, incorporating the elements of the continuation but distorting their meaning in the process. So the best explanation is that Thomas came first and Matthew second.

# 12

# The third eighteen

## Ruling principle

The third eighteen is in the second thirty-six. The ruling principle of this thirty-six is:

> *and when he finds he will be troubled*

The ruling principle of the eighteen is:

> *Many times have you desired to hear these words which I speak to you, and you have none other from whom to hear them.*

## None other from whom to hear them

We must now turn to the middle thirty-six, which consists of the third and fourth eighteens. The second part of keystone saying 1.1 tells us that this thirty-six is all about being troubled. As we would expect, this central thirty-six is the most negative in the Gospel. It starts with another keystone saying:

> *3.1 Jesus said: "Many times have you desired to hear these words which I speak to you, and you have none other from whom to hear them. Some days will come when you will seek after me, and you will not find me." (Th. 38)*

The first part of this saying relates to the first group of eighteen in the thirty-six and the second part, in the future tense, to the next eighteen. The third eighteen then is about the words of Jesus as compared to the words of other teachers who lack the power of Jesus. When we look at the eighteen, we see a large number of sayings that conform to this theme. We will take these saying by saying below, starting with the second saying in the eighteen:

> *3.2 Jesus said: "The Pharisees and the scribes have taken the keys of knowledge; they have hidden them. They did not go in, and those who wanted to go in they did not allow. You, however, be as cunning as serpents and as innocent as doves." (Th. 38)*

This is directed against the Pharisees and scribes who were the experts on Jewish scripture. Although "the keys of knowledge" are contained in these scriptures, the Pharisees have not understood the keys nor allowed others to find them.

> *3.3 Jesus said: "A vine was planted apart from the Father, and since it is not established it will be pulled up by its roots and destroyed."*

The vine represents false teachers, probably the Pharisees and the scribes who are the subject of the previous saying.

> *3.6 His disciples said to him: "Who are you, that you speak these things to us?" "From what I say to you, you do not understand who I am, but you have become as the Jews; for they love the tree and hate its fruit, and they love the fruit and hate the tree." (Th. 43)*

This contrasts the teachings of Jesus (the tree that yields the fruit of life) with the teachings of the Jews (the tree that yields only death). The Jews hate the tree, the teachings of Jesus, but would love its fruit, meaning eternal life.

> *3.9 Jesus said: "From Adam to John the Baptist there is none born of woman who is higher than John the Baptist, so as to lower his eyes. I spoke however this: He who shall*

> *be among you as a little one shall know the kingdom, and*
> *shall be raised up above John." (Th. 46)*

Saying 3.9 contrasts John the Baptist with those in the Jesus movement. Unlike the Pharisees and the scribes, John is praised extrava-
gantly. Between Adam and John, there have been none higher than
John—we should not take this too literally; it is a praise formula.
Today, we might say something like "John is the best person ever!"
to convey the same meaning. (Saying 1.11 says something similar
about James.) However, the sting in the tail is that anyone in the
kingdom will be above John. So although John is highly praised in
comparison with all others, he is lower than the lowest of Jesus' chosen followers. So Jesus must give his disciples something that is far
beyond anything that John could have taught them.

> *3.15 His disciples said to him: "Twenty-four prophets*
> *spoke in Israel, and they all spoke of you." He said to them:*
> *"You have left out the living one in your presence and*
> *have spoken about the dead." (Th. 52)*

The twenty-four prophets were those who were supposed to have
written the Jewish scripture, what we call the Old Testament. This
saying depreciates scripture itself and all those (such as the Pharisees) who spent their days studying the scripture. The source of
true knowledge is not the dead prophets of Israel but the living one
(Jesus) in their presence.

> *3.18 Jesus said: "Whoever does not hate his father and his*
> *mother cannot be my disciple, and whoever does not hate*
> *his brothers and his sisters and take up his cross like me,*
> *he shall not be worthy of me." (Th. 55)*

The eighteen ends with an attack on one final authority, the disciple's own family. In Aramaic the same word was used for "hate"
and "put aside," and it is the later meaning that is probably intended
here. The disciple must put aside mother, father, sisters, and brothers. They must leave their home and not listen to the counsel of those
who have been closest to them. The word of Jesus trumps even the
word of a father or mother.

All of the above sayings target a particular group or individual. These targets are not necessary condemned; John is praised highly, and nothing negative is said about the prophets except that they are dead. However, they are all compared unfavorably to Jesus or those in the Jesus movement.

There is something special about the placing of these six sayings. All of them except the first, 3.2, are the last saying of a three. The only last saying of a three that is not included is saying 3.12, which says that the single ones and chosen will find the kingdom. Before we consider the significance of this exception, we will first look at some of the other sayings in the third eighteen.

## Accepted and rejected

The sayings in the previous section were aimed at particular groups. But there are other sayings in the eighteen that involve rejection in a less specific sense. These are in the form:

A is rejected and B accepted

The first such saying is 3.4:

> 3.4 Jesus said: "He who has in his hand, to him shall be given; and he who has not, from him shall be taken even the little that he has." (Th. 41)

The one who has shall be given more (accepted), whereas the one who has not will lose what little they have (rejected).

> 3.7 Jesus said: "Whoever blasphemes against the Father will be forgiven, and whoever blasphemes against the Son will be forgiven but whoever blasphemes against the holy spirit will not be forgiven, either on earth or in heaven." (Th. 44)

In this saying, those who blaspheme the Father or Son will be forgiven (accepted), whereas those who blaspheme the Holy Spirit will never be forgiven (rejected).

> *3.8 Jesus said: "They do not harvest grapes from thorns, nor gather figs from thistles; they do not yield fruit. A good man brings forth a good thing from his treasure; a bad man bring forth evil things from his evil treasure which is in his heart, and he says evil things; for out of the abundance of his heart he brings forth evil things." (Th. 45)*

This saying is about a bad man (rejected) who is like thorns or thistles that do not yield good fruit. In contrast, a good man (accepted) brings forth good things from his treasure.

> *3.10 Jesus said: "A man cannot ride two horses or draw two bows, and nor can a servant serve two masters; or he will honour the one and despise the other. A man does not drink old wine and immediately desire to drink new wine; and they do not pour new wine into old wineskins, lest they burst, nor do they pour old wine into new wineskins, lest it spoil. They do not sew an old patch on a new garment, because a split will come." (Th. 47)*

This saying sets up a whole series of dualities. A man cannot ride two horses or draw two bows nor can he have two masters (in each case one must be accepted and one rejected). In a similar way "old wine" is accepted and "new wine" rejected.

> *3.16 His disciples said to him: "Is circumcision beneficial or not?" He said to them: "Were it beneficial, their father would beget them from their mother circumcised. But the true circumcision in spirit is entirely profitable." (Th. 53)*

In this case, physical circumcision (rejected) is compared to the superior spiritual circumcision (accepted). The circumcision of a baby boy was the moment he was brought into Judaism, with all its benefits and obligations. To be circumcised was to be under the law. So the repudiation of circumcision is equivalent to the repudiation of the Jewish law. Jesus' new spiritual law is represented by a spiritual circumcision, a fasting from the world.

There are five of these accept/reject sayings in the third eighteen, and four of these five are the first saying of a three. We can make this five out of six if we include the first part of the keystone saying: the disciples have desired to hear Jesus' words (accepted) and have none other to hear them from (all others rejected). The one exception to this pattern is saying 3.8, which should be positioned at 3.13.

So we have six sayings aimed at particular teachers/authorities that are positioned as the last saying of a three with one exception, and six other accept/reject sayings that are positioned as the first saying of a three with one exception. We must now consider how to make sense of these exceptions.

## *Moving the mountain*

The diagram shows the positions of these sayings, where either an authority other than Jesus is rejected, or one thing is rejected and the other accepted.

In the first two eighteens, we had to make two switches of sayings. The arrows in the above diagram show that if we move two pairs of sayings in this eighteen will have a perfect pattern. The two sayings that would have to be moved are 3.2 and 3.8 in the center of the first and third threes. They would have to switch with the two consecutive sayings, the last of the fourth and first of the fifth sixes. Are there any clues that would support such a move? The two consecutive sayings are preceded by this saying:

> 3.11 Jesus said: "If **two make peace with one anoth-**
> **er in this house alone**, *they shall say to the mountain,*
> **'Move away' and it shall move."** (Th. 48)

We have a clear signaling of the impending move: the mountain is told to move away, and it shall move! Moreover, we are told that two make peace with each other implying that it is two sayings that must be moved. The two are in this "house alone" so the move will

# The Third Eighteen

Key
 An authority other than Jesus rejected

 Accepted/rejected pattern

| | |
|---|---|
| Second keystone saying |  |
| Pharisees, scribes and the keys of knowledge |  |
| Vine planted apart from the father |  |

THIS IS THE ONLY REJECTED AUTHORITY SAYING THAT IS NOT THE LAST IN A THREE

| | |
|---|---|
| He who has and he who has not | 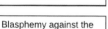 |
| Become passers-by | |
| The Jews and the fruit and the tree |  |

| | |
|---|---|
| Blasphemy against the father, son and holy spirit |  |
| Bringing forth good or evil things |  |
| John the Baptist |  |

THIS IS THE ONLY ACCEPTED/REJECTED SAYING THAT IS NOT THE FIRST IN A THREE

| | |
|---|---|
| Cannot serve two masters |  |
| The mountain shall be moved | |
| Single-ones are blessed | |
| From where have you come? | |
| When will the rest of the dead come? | |
| Twenty-four prophets in Israel |  |

THESE ARE THE TWO PLACES THAT THE SAYINGS MUST BE MOVED TO.

| | |
|---|---|
| Is circumcision beneficial? |  |
| Blessed are the poor | |
| Hate father and mother | |

only affect this eighteen. Consider now the first of the two sayings that must be moved:

> *3.12 Jesus said: "Blessed are the single-ones and the cho-sen, for you shall find the kingdom; **for you came from there, and shall go there again." (Th. 49)***

So the saying contains the clue that it is to be moved back to where it belongs: *"you came from there, and shall go there again."* Now look at the second saying that must be moved:

> *3.13 Jesus said: "If they say to you, '**From where have you come?**' Tell them, 'We have come from the light, the place where the light came into being by his hand him-self. He [stood], and he revealed himself in their image.' If they say to you: 'Are you him?' say, 'We are his sons, and we are the chosen of the living father.' If they ask you, 'What is the sign of your Father in you?' tell them, '**It is a movement and a rest.'" (Th. 50)***

This saying is also signaling that it must be moved! Like 3.12, it includes a formula to show that it belongs in a different place: *"From where have you come?"* implies that the saying has been moved. The saying ends with a reply *"It is a movement and a rest."* We are to move the saying to the place from whence it came where it will rest.

Let us look again at saying 3.11, which tells us that the mountain will be moved if two in a house make peace with each other. How should we interpret making peace? The same word for peace is found in the key saying 1.15, which specifies the structure of the Gospel. In this saying, the peace that people expect is contrasted with the divi-sions and war that Jesus will cast upon the world. We have seen how this refers to the Gospel itself, and that it is the individual sayings that are at "war" with each other. By "war" is meant the paradox and contradiction that is so typical of the Gospel. So two making peace must mean two sayings that are not contradictory and opposed, but harmonious and mutually supporting. All of which indicates say-ings 3.12 and 3.13.

These two sayings are indeed harmonious because they link in beautifully together. Saying 3.12 starts by blessing the single ones and the chosen who will find the kingdom: *"for you came from there, and shall go there again."* Saying 3.13 starts: *"If they say to you, 'From where have you come?' Tell them, 'We have come from the light, the place where the light came into being...'"* The place where the light came into being is the kingdom. The saying continues with the disciples saying *"we are the chosen of the living father,"* a line which links back to the *"chosen"* of 3.12. In fact, saying 3.13 is virtually a continuation of 3.12.

All of this shows that the third eighteen, like the first and second eighteens, has two pairs of sayings which must be switched. This reordering is shown in the copy of the Gospel at the end of the book. We have continued the practice of labeling the reordered sayings as "R" so that 3.12, for example, becomes 3.2R. Following this reordering, each three now starts with an accept/reject saying and ends with a saying rejecting an alternative authority to Jesus. This structure, of course, ties in with the keystone theme.

As well as the perfected pattern, there are a few other features that make more sense in the reordered eighteen. Saying 3.13 becomes 3.8R and now follows 3.7, which is about those who blaspheme the Father, Son and Spirit. These two sayings together have a chiastic structure. Saying 3.7 has a threefold structure dealing with blasphemy against Father, Son, and Holy Spirit. Saying 3.8R also has a threefold structure, consisting of three question and answer pairs; the first has the disciples coming from the light; the second being the "sons" of Jesus, and the third with the disciples as chosen of the Father and showing the signs of the Father. If we equate the light with the spirit (remembering there is light within a person of light), then 3.8R symmetrically reverses 3.7.

One thing that might be thought to be lost in the reordering is the way saying 3.13 follows on from saying 3.12, as these two sayings are now in different positions. In fact, we could add 3.14 to the sequence. Saying 3.13 ends with "a movement and a rest" and saying 3.14 starts with "on what day will the rest of the dead come?" However, the reordering of the Gospel results in each of these sayings being in

# The Third Eighteen - reordering

PATTERN IS NOW COMPLETE

Before

After

| Before | After | |
|---|---|---|
| | Second keystone saying | ◐ |
| Pharisees,scribes and the keys of knowledge | Single-ones are blessed | |
| | Vine planted apart from the father | ⊗ |
| | He who has and he who has not | ◐ |
| | Become passers-by | |
| | The Jews and the fruit and the tree | ⊗ |
| | Blasphemy against the father, son and holy spirit | ◐ |
| Bringing forth good or evil things | From where have you come? | |
| | John the Baptist | ⊗ |
| | Cannot serve two masters | ◐ |
| The mountain shall be moved | The mountain shall be moved | |
| Single-ones are blessed | Pharisees,scribes and the keys of knowledge | ⊗ |
| From where have you come? | Bringing forth good or evil things | ◐ |
| | When will the rest of the dead come? | |
| | Twenty-four prophets in Israel | ⊗ |
| | Is circumcision beneficial? | ◐ |
| | Blessed are the poor | |
| | Hate father and mother | ⊗ |

an equivalent place in the three sixes. If we read the second saying of each six, we recover the sequence:

> *"Blessed are the single-ones and the chosen, for you shall find the kingdom; for you came from there, and shall go there again."*

> *"If they say to you, 'From where have you come?' Tell them, 'We have come from the light, the place where the light came into being by his hand himself. He [stood], and he revealed himself in their image.' If they say to you: 'Are you him?' say, 'We are his sons, and we are the chosen of the living father.' If they ask you, 'What is the sign of your Father in you?' tell them, 'It is a movement and a rest.'"*

> *His disciples said to him: "On what day will the rest of the dead come? And on what day will the new world come?" He said to them, "That which you look for has come, but you know it not."*

It is interesting that this echoes the meaning of the chiastic structure of the two bookend sayings that stand as the second saying, and second from last saying, in the Gospel as a whole. We should remember that the keystone saying for this eighteen is not wholly negative, for it starts with *"Many times have you desired to hear these words which I speak to you."* It is the central sayings of the sixes that give effect to this more positive message.

## *Is the pattern random?*

The pattern of this third eighteen lends itself to a probability calculation. Not only will this rule out any realistic possibility that the pattern could be random, it also provides strong evidence in favor of the Thomas Code. The calculation involves 2.5 million stochastic simulations in which sayings are randomly allocated to the eighteen places. We can then count those simulations that show a similar pattern to that found in the eighteen and express this as a probability.

Before we move any sayings, we find the following pattern: five out of six sayings rejecting an alternative authority are the last saying of a three, and five out of six rejecting/accepting sayings are the first saying of a three. If we have two groups of six sayings, then the probability that five of each will occur in the same position within a three is 1 in 1,700.[59]

This calculation assumes that we include the keystone saying in the rejecting/accepting group. This is perhaps less clear-cut than for the other sayings. If we were to exclude it, we would have only four out of five in this group as the first in the three. This would increase the probability of a random result to 1 in 500.[60]

These probabilities do not allow for the fact that there are clear signs that two sayings should be moved, and these two sayings occur in precisely the two places that are exceptions to the pattern. This turns out to be very significant. Taking it into account results in a reduction in the probability that the result could be random to just 1 in 120,000.[61]

To put these probabilities in perspective, the standard for determining whether a scientific result is statistically significant enough for publication is that the probability of it being random should be no greater than 5% (1 in 20). All the above probabilities are far more significant than this.

Is it possible that subjective judgments or "data mining" has contributed to these low probabilities? A degree of subjectivity is inevitable when dealing with an ancient document. We do not have the luxury of being able to generate any new data to test a hypothesis! However, we should note two features that limit the amount of subjectivity. First, the third eighteen was placed in its final form before it was analyzed to find the pattern. The eighteen has not been adjusted in any way to fit the pattern. Second, the themes of the two groups gel perfectly with the keystone saying about rejecting teachers other than Jesus. We have not data mined to find some exotic theme that fits a pattern. The analysis started by isolating those sayings that developed the keystone theme and noting the coincidence that they were occurring in the same positions.

The most important conclusion comes from the observation that the pattern makes no sense unless the Gospel is put into the Thomas Code structure. If the Thomas Code structure were not real, then placing the Gospel into this structure would simply add a random element. So the fact that we find a pattern valid at the 1 in 120,000 level is strong evidence for the reality of the Thomas Code.

# 13

# The fourth eighteen

## *Ruling principle*

The fourth eighteen is in the second thirty-six. The ruling principle of this thirty-six is:

> *and when he finds he will be troubled*

The ruling principle of the eighteen is:

> *Some days will come when you will seek after me, and you will not find me.*

## *Losing Jesus*

The concept of "being troubled" reaches its climax in the fourth eighteen, which is the most negative part of the whole Gospel. The keystone saying 3.1 stands at the head of the second thirty-six. The phrase *"Some days will come…"* signifies the fourth eighteen, which is the second part of the thirty-six. This sets the tone of the eighteen, many of whose sayings are about not being able to find Jesus. It is concerned with the attributes, or lack of attributes, that may cause a person not to find Jesus or to lose Jesus once found. It is also concerned with the angelic and demonic forces that are arrayed against humankind. But there is also a deep message of hope, the promise that the obstacles can and will be overcome. In this fourth eighteen, the structure of the threes is significant, so we will look at each of these in turn.

## The first three

The first three introduces the eighteen, and it starts on an appropriately downbeat note:

> 4.1 Jesus said: "He who has known the world has found
> a corpse, and he who has found a corpse, the world is not
> worthy of him." (Th. 56)

The world is compared to a corpse; a place of death that lacks the true life of the spirit. Yet a person who finds a corpse can overcome the world. To understand why the world is a corpse we must look at the second saying:

> 4.2 Jesus said: "The kingdom of the Father is like a man
> who had [good] seed. His enemy came by night, he sowed
> a weed among the good seed. The man did not allow them
> to pull up the weed. He said to them: 'So that you do not
> go to pull up the weed, and pull up the grain with it.' For
> on the day of harvest the weeds will be visible and will be
> pulled up and burned." (Th. 57)

The first good creation has been corrupted by an adversary (the devil) who has sown weeds among the good seed. In the myth of the Garden of Eden, the fall of Adam and Eve is due to the eating of the fruit from the forbidden tree of knowledge. It is Eve who is tempted by the snake to eat the apple. The story of the Garden of Eden is well known, but what is less well known is that there was an alternative story of the corruption of humankind, which is found in the Book of Enoch. In this alternative, the corruption is not due to Eve eating an apple, but to fallen angels who descended to earth to take human women as wives. These angels bring forbidden knowledge to people, teaching them all the arts and technologies. The early Jesus movement has inherited both myths and combined them into one; in this combined version, the eating of the apple becomes a metaphor for Eve having sex with the "snake."

The Jesus movement believed that the angels had quite literally sown their seed among people. Although humans were originally made in the image of God, the human line has been corrupted by the sin of Eve and the other women who took angels as husbands. As a result, every person alive is infected within by the progeny of the angels, the demons. God could destroy the demons by wiping out humanity, but if he did so he would also destroy what is good in humankind. So he has patience until the "harvest." The same saying is found in the Gospels, and traditional commentators follow the interpretation in Matthew where the "harvest" is the apocalypse. However, the Gospel of Thomas reveals a more complex view of the apocalypse; in God, all time is complete as a whole, so the apocalypse has in a sense already happened. Applied to an individual, the harvest is the state known as the kingdom of heaven, in which the individual yields fruit for God. Applied collectively, the time for harvest has already come, and people will instinctively either accept or reject Jesus according to whether their own inner nature more closely resembles the good or bad seed.

The last saying in the opening three gives the promise that although there are troubles and suffering awaiting the disciples, these will lead to life:

> 4.3 Jesus said: "Blessed is the man who has been troubled. He has found life." (Th. 58)

In fact, this is a theme that runs throughout this opening three. In each of the three sayings, there is a promise of redemption.

## The second three

The first three starts with a comparison of the world with a corpse and the second three is all about death. It starts with a warning:

> *4.4 Jesus said: "Look upon he who lives while you are liv-*
> *ing, lest you die, and seek to see him, and you are not able*
> *to." (Th. 59)*

Conventional Christians believe that you see Jesus after you die and go to heaven. Yet the view in the Gospel of Thomas is very different. The living one ("he who lives") is Jesus. A person must look upon Jesus while alive or they will not be able to find him when dead. In this saying, we have the first clear statement of the theme of not finding Jesus. Those who wrote Thomas were mystics who believed in the direct spiritual experience of Jesus. The theme of death is continued in the second saying of the three:

> *4.5 They saw a Samaritan carrying a lamb going into*
> *Judaea. He said to his disciples: "That one is around the*
> *lamb." They said to him: "That he may kill it and eat it."*
> *He said to them: "While it is living he will not eat it. Only*
> *if he kill it and it becomes a corpse." They said: "Other-*
> *wise he cannot do it." He said to them: "You also, seek for*
> *yourselves a place within rest, so that you do not become*
> *corpses and be eaten." (Th. 60)*

In this saying, a man is carrying a lamb that he will kill and eat. The disciples are warned not to become like the lamb. To understand this saying, we must understand that the fallen angels who were believed to rule the world were also called "shepherds," which was a metaphor for rulers. The angels were bad shepherds who abused and killed the flock in contrast to the good shepherd, Jesus. In Thomas, "life" is spiritual life. The angels seek to kill men and women by depriving them of their spirit. Jesus is called the living one, and if the spirit is killed, then that person can no longer see or experience Jesus. The angels and their demonic offspring will then consume that person body and soul. To avoid this fate, the disciples should seek "a place within rest," meaning the kingdom. This saying is parallel to the previous one; both are about finding the place of rest/the living one while alive, in case you die.

The last saying in the three is a complex discourse between Jesus and "Salome," which takes place on a couch or bed upon which diners would recline at meals. It starts with a declaration by Jesus: *"Two shall rest upon a bed; one shall die, the other live,"* which ties in with the living and dead theme of the three. It ends with another declaration of warning: *"Therefore I say, when he should be equal he will be filled with light, but when he should be divided he will be filled with darkness."* The one who is divided will not have "the light within a man if light," he will not know Jesus.

The sayings in the second three all contain warnings: to look upon Jesus while living, to find a place in rest, and to be equal rather than divided.

## The third and fourth threes

The fourth three opens with a saying concerning Jesus' mysteries:

> *4.7 Jesus said: "I tell my mysteries to those [who are wor-*
> *thy] of my mysteries. What your right hand shall do, let*
> *not your left hand know what it does." (Th. 62)*

We can equate the right hand to the chosen, pneumatic Christians and the left with the called, psychic Christians. The saying then is a command to keep the mysteries secret and, in particular, to keep them from those Christians who have yet to progress to the spiritual state of the "chosen." The mysteries should only be revealed when a person is ready. After this comes the Thomas version of a familiar parable, that of the rich man who dies after storing up a treasure:

> *4.8 Jesus said: "There was a wealthy man who had many*
> *riches. He said: 'I will use my riches that I may sow and*
> *reap and plant, and fill my treasure house with fruit, that*
> *I may have need of nothing.' These were his thoughts in*
> *his heart. And in that night he died. He that has ears, let*
> *him hear." (Th. 63)*

The same parable occurs in Luke, where the rich man builds larger barns to store the abundant fruit of his land. As in Thomas, he thinks he will want for nothing: *"And I will say to my soul, 'Soul, you have ample goods laid up for many years; relax, eat, drink, be merry'" (Luke 12:19 ESV)*. But the same night he dies. In Luke, the meaning is crystal clear because the Gospel spells it out: *"But God said to him, 'Fool! This night your soul is required of you, and the things you have prepared, whose will they be?' So is the one who lays up treasure for himself and is not rich toward God" (Luke 12:20-21 ESV)*. The difference between Thomas, which uses paradox and contradiction to hide its meaning, and the lack of ambiguity in Luke is stark. But if the sayings were intended to hide as much as reveal, then has the author of Luke got it wrong? There is one crucial difference between Thomas and the Luke version. In Luke, the rich fool tears down his old barns to make new ones to store the abundant produce of his land. In doing this, he is a responsible farmer, making sure that his barns are large enough to hold the crop. Yet in the story, the rich man is planning to live off his crop indefinitely. This is completely unrealistic. A real farmer would use his crop to feed his household over the following year and sell the excess at market. Next year there will be a new crop to go into his barns.

If we look at the Thomas version, then it also has features that do not look realistic. The man is rich and is using his riches to "sow, reap and plant" to fill his "treasure house" with fruit. It does not explain how he is going to use his riches to accomplish this. Is he going to buy a farm? Or is he going to upgrade an existing farm, as in Luke? He dies before he is able to "sow, reap and plant." We are not sure from the Thomas version what he has done wrong. The saying ends with the formula "He that has ears, let him hear," which is telling us that we need "ears" to "hear" the saying and that those without "ears" will not be able to understand it. This is a clue that the meaning is metaphorical and not obvious.

In fact, the saying uses a system of metaphors that runs through Thomas. In Thomas, "riches" is usually interpreted in a spiritual sense, as the wealth of the kingdom of heaven. So for example, 5.8 (Th. 81) has *"Whoever has become rich, let him become king..."* and 1.2 (Th. 3) says about one who is not in the kingdom because they do not know themselves: *"you are in poverty, and you are poverty."* Like other such terms in Thomas, it can, however, also be used in a literal sense, which gives a rich vein of the paradoxes and contradictions that the Gospel loves. So 6.3 (Th. 95) is against lending money at interest (literal sense of wealth), whereas 6.16 (Th. 109) approves of this (spiritual sense of wealth).

The process of sowing, planting, and reaping is a consistent metaphor for the spreading of the kingdom to others. This is perfectly clear from the parable of the sower, 1.8 (Th. 9), but is also found elsewhere, such as the call for reaping in 2.2 (Th. 21) and the call for workers for the harvest in 5.1 (Th. 73). The idea of using riches to derive fruit comes in 3.8 (Th. 45), where a good person yields fruit from the good treasure of their heart.

Put all this together, and a completely different interpretation of the parable of the rich man becomes visible. The rich man is spiritually rich with the wealth of the kingdom of heaven. He should use his riches to *"sow and reap and plant"* that he may fill his treasure house with fruit. The concept is that by using our spiritual riches to sow the seed in others, we yield fruit for God, and our own spiritual riches are increased. We find the same meaning in 6.16 (Th. 109), where a man finds a hidden treasure, representing the kingdom, and can then lend money at interest. By using his treasure, he increases it in value.

The rich man does not, however, do what he intends because he dies that very night. The moral of the story is not that what he wants to do is wrong, but that he delays doing it until too late. One who is in the kingdom should not hesitate for even a day before sowing and reaping. The first saying of the three warned the pneumatics (the right hand) not to share all the mysteries with the psychics (the left hand). So it is fitting that the very next saying reverses this advice. It is against those spiritual Christians who revel in their spiritual riches without doing the hard work of spreading the gospel. It warns the pneumatics not to waste a single day before preaching to the psychics. Although spiritual Christians must keep the mysteries secret from the left-hand Christians of the soul for now, they must sow, plant, and harvest so as to bring these soul Christians into spiritual fruition, so that they too become the right-hand. And we find just this situation in 1 Corinthians. Paul says he has fed the Corinthians on milk and not strong food because they were not yet ready for the mysteries.[62]

The author of Luke has got it wrong. The rich man is not someone who focuses on the wealth of this world rather than on heavenly treasure. The detail of the barns being rebuilt has been added to the original to conform to this false reading. The Thomas version supports the correct understanding and must be earlier.

The final saying in the three, 4.9, is the parable of the feast. A man invites his guests to a feast, but they all give excuses; one has business dealings with some merchants, one is buying a house, a third attending a wedding, and another collecting rent from a village. Because the intended guests refuse his invite, the man tells his servants to go out into the roads and bring in anyone they can find. The saying ends with the statement: *"The buyers and the merchants will not enter the places of my Father."*

It is likely that this ending is not original but has been added to give the saying a more pronounced anti-mercantile cast. Although three of the excuses concern the type of transactions that wealthy merchants would engage in, one of them, the wedding, breaks this pattern suggesting that the saying was not originally aimed exclusively at merchants. The same story is found in both Matthew and Luke, but neither has the conclusion rejecting merchants and buyers. In the Matthew version, a king is holding a wedding feast for his son.[63] The invited guests do not just refuse the invitations, but some beat or kill the messengers. The king takes revenge by killing them and burning their city. This Mathew version seems to have been influenced by the parable which precedes the feast in Matthew and follows it in Thomas, that of the tenant farmers. The Luke version is much closer to Thomas, but has three invitations; one guest is purchasing some land, another some oxen, and the third has just been married.[64]

If we assume that the last line was a later addition, then the original Thomas saying ended without a conclusion. However, the meaning of the saying is clear enough. The feast is the kingdom of heaven. The intended guests, the establishment Jews, have refused the invitation, so the feast has now been made open to the poor and the Gentiles. This is certainly the conclusion of the parable in Matthew and Luke. The city that is destroyed in Matthew is probably intended to represent Jerusalem, which was sacked by the Romans.

The original target of the Thomas saying cannot be the merchants because they were not, as a group, invited to the feast. Instead, the target must be the establishment Jews who were seen by the Jesus movement as having become obsessed with worldly matters. Although the temple priesthood was supported by the tithe, other religious authorities were forbidden from taking money in exchange for teaching and preaching the word of God. So to provide for their families they would be forced to engage in trade. Inevitably, many became much richer than those they were supposed to be serving. The Jesus movement reversed this, insisting that those who preached the gospel should be dependent on their flock and remain poor. The emphasis in saying 4.9 on buying and selling can be seen as a criticism of the way in which the Jewish religious establishment, and Jews in general, had been corrupted by the things of the world. When the Gospel of Thomas circulated in a non-Jewish environment, it was reinterpreted as a condemnation of merchants, and the last line added. The fact that the saying has four invited guests rather than the expected pattern of three like Luke suggests that it has been edited at some time, perhaps by combining two versions of the saying.

To summarize, the third three is about three different groups who cannot find or may lose Jesus:

- 4.7—the psychic "soul" Christians who cannot share in the mysteries
- 4.8—the pneumatic, "spirit" Christians who indulge in their spiritual wealth and do not immediately sow and reap
- 4.9—those Jews who have become obsessed by the world, and so reject the invitation to the kingdom

The fourth three continues the theme of not finding Jesus. Saying 4.10 is about a man who lets out his vineyard to tenants. He sends two servants to get the fruit of the vineyard, yet they are both beaten. He then sends his own son hoping that he will be honored by the tenants; but they, knowing he is the heir to the vineyard, kill him. This saying is one of the most important in Thomas, but we do not have space here to explore its full meaning. Suffice to say that the Son represents Jesus and the tenants the sons of God, the fallen angels. The tenant saying is followed by the "cornerstone" saying:

> 4.11 Jesus said: "Show me the stone which the builders rejected; it is the cornerstone." (Th. 66)

The building will not be built on the expected stone, but on the stone that has been rejected. There is a similarity to the parable of the feast, where the guests at the feast are those who were in the streets, rather than those who were invited. The final saying in the fourth three is about those who know everything:

> 4.12 Jesus said: "He who knows everything, but lacks himself, lacks everything." (Th. 67)

This is a saying that attacks those who are proud of their knowledge. A person who knows everything, but who lacks himself (or herself) will lack everything. It is not knowledge that is important, but the spirit. This is an ironic counterpoint to saying 4.7 about knowledge of the mysteries.

The sayings in the fourth three echo the themes in the third three but give those themes a different emphasis. The bleak center of the eighteen is the pair of sayings 4.9 and 4.10; the first about the Jews rejecting Jesus, and the second about the death of Jesus.

## The fifth three

In contrast to the rest of the fourth eighteen, the next group of three blesses those who will find Jesus. However, it fits in with the overall theme because all those who are blessed are also troubled:

> 4.13 Jesus said: "Blessed are you when they hate you, and persecute you, and they do not find a place in the place where they persecuted you." (Th. 68)

*4.14 Jesus said: "Blessed are they who have been persecut-
ed in their mind; they are those who have known the father
in truth." (Th. 69a)*

*4.15 "Blessed are those who are hungry, that they may fill
the belly of he who desires." (Th. 69b)*

Saying 4.14 is about those "persecuted in their mind" meaning
those who were thought to be possessed by demons, the ones we
might call mentally ill. Although they suffer inside, the very nature of
their illness gives them a special insight of God. Saying 4.15 is about
those who go without food so that others might be fed. Although the
meaning may seem obvious, we should remember that food had a
spiritual significance to the movement. So the real meaning might be
to bless those who have gone physically hungry so as to spiritually
feed others. The life of an itinerant apostle and preacher was full of
hardships, and they would have often been cold and hungry. We can
see this saying as a counterpart to 4.8 about the man who was spiritually rich and wanted to fill his barns with fruit so that he lacked
nothing, but who put off the task of sowing the Gospel.

The most difficult saying of this group is 4.13, which blesses those
who have been persecuted and hated but then adds: "*they do not find
a place in the place where they persecuted you.*" The key to this saying
is that word used for the first occurrence of "place" is used elsewhere in Thomas to mean the kingdom. So the saying is a play on
two meanings of "place," one spiritual and one literal. The second
"place," that "where they persecuted you," is a house, village or
town where the disciples have been attacked and driven out. Those
who have persecuted the disciples in such a place will not find a
spiritual "place" (the kingdom). Like the son of man who has no
place to lay his head in Thomas 86, the disciples do not belong to this
world but live in an unseen kingdom. If those who have power in
the physical world expel the disciples, they will, in turn, be expelled
from this spiritual kingdom.

## *The sixth three*

The final three of the eighteen starts with another warning:

> *4.16 Jesus said: "When you begat that one in yourselves,*
> *he who you have will save you. If you do not have that one*
> *in you, he that you do not have will kill you." (Th. 70)*

This saying is closely related to 4.12, where he who *"lacks himself,*
*lacks everything."* This time the disciple must *"begat the one in your-*
*selves"* and if they do not have such a one, this lack will kill them.
There is something within a person that they must give birth to, but
they can only do this if it is, in a sense, already there. Paul uses similar phrasing to this in his letter to the Galatians, where he says they
are *"my little children, of whom again I travail in birth, till Christ may*
*be formed in you" (Galatians 4:19).* In the Gospel of John, Jesus tells
Nicodemus about the necessity of being reborn: *"Verily, verily, I say*
*to thee, If any one may not be born from above, he is not able to see the reign*
*of God" (John 3:3).* When Nicodemus asks incredulously how one can
be reborn from the mother's womb a second time, Jesus explains:
*"that which hath been born of the flesh is flesh, and that which hath been*
*born of the Spirit is spirit" (John 3:6).* The thing that has to be begotten
is the spirit, so that the disciple-spirit is then a "single one" and can
see Jesus. If they do not possess the spirit, then they will not find life.
     The next saying is even more provocative:

> *4.17 Jesus said: "I will des[troy this] house, and none shall*
> *be able to build it [again]." (Th. 71)*

The "house" was a common Jewish way of referring to the temple.
Jesus says he will destroy the temple and it will not be rebuilt. This
destruction is symbolic of the removal of God from traditional Jewish worship. The idea of Jesus destroying the temple so shocked the
author of Mark that he placed a similar saying in the mouth of false
witnesses.[65]

The last saying in the eighteen is the man who asks Jesus to speak to his brothers to divide his father's possessions. We have seen that this saying is an allusion to the Thomas formula, where the twos divide the threes. The father is God, and the brothers the "sons of God," the fallen angels. We can, in fact, find the "sons of God" running like a malignant stream through the fourth eighteen:

- They sow the weed among the good seed in 4.2.
- They are the evil shepherds who eat the sheep in 4.5.
- They are the tenants who kill the son in 4.10.
- They are behind the demonic persecution in 4.14.
- Finally, they are the brothers in 4.18.

In this list, there is a saying about the "sons of God" in every group of three with the exception of the third three. Is there also a saying about the fallen angels in the third three? If so this can only be the first part of saying 4.7: "*I tell my mysteries to those [who are worthy] of my mysteries.*" In 1 Corinthians, Paul talks about the hidden mysteries that are kept for the spiritual Christians, whom he calls the perfect:

> *Yet we speak wisdom among the perfect, but not the wisdom of this age or of the rulers [archonton] of this age, who are becoming useless. Yet we speak in a mystery the hidden wisdom of God, which God foreordained before the ages for our glory. None of the rulers [archonton] of this age understood this, for if they had, they would not have crucified the Lord of glory. (1 Corinthians 2:6-8)*

The archons, "the rulers of the age," are the fallen angels, the ones who killed the "the Lord of glory," the Son. Paul tells us that the archons did not know the hidden wisdom, although the perfect, those of the right hand, know it. We can see a number of connections between this passage in Paul and saying 4.7. It provides the clue as to why the left hand is not to know what the right may do. The "left hand" must not be told the mysteries to keep them secret from the archons.

As well as being about the sons of God, the final saying 4.18 alludes to the divisions of the Gospel. The joke is that the number representing Jesus, two, does divide the formula. And since the formula provides for the divisions of the Gospel, it is fitting that this saying marks the end of second thirty-six.

# 14

# The fifth eighteen

## *Ruling principle*

The fifth eighteen is in the third thirty-six. The ruling principle of
this thirty-six is:

> *and if he is troubled he will become amazed*

The ruling principle of the eighteen is:

> *Seek, and you shall find; but those things you asked me in
> those days, I did not tell you then.*

## *Being amazed*

In this thirty-six, we leave behind the near total negativity of the
second thirty-six. Instead, there is some secret that will be revealed,
causing amazement. Unlike the other two thirty-sixes, the third does
not start with a keystone saying as it is positioned at the head of the
final eighteen:

> *6.1 Jesus said: "Seek, and you shall find; but those things
> you asked me in those days, I did not tell you then. Now
> I wish to tell them, and you seek not after them." (Th. 92)*

The first part of this, "Seek and you will find," applies to both the
fifth and sixth eighteens. The second part starts with the phrase in
the past tense: *"but those things you asked me in those days, I did not tell*

*you then.*" This applies to the fifth eighteen only. The last part, in the present tense, "*Now I wish to tell them, and you seek not after them,*" will apply to the sixth eighteen. So the final revelation will not occur in the fifth eighteen. Instead, what we must look for are "*those things you asked me,*" which will give us the clue to the revelation.

For the first four eighteens, the keynote saying sets the theme. This is partially true of the fifth and sixth eighteens, as seeking and finding are important, as they are in the first and second eighteens. Yet the keystone saying is mainly about a mystery contained within the thirty-six, rather than the theme of the whole thirty-six. The nature of the mystery is alluded to within the fifth eighteen, and the answer must lie in the sixth eighteen.

A major theme in the fifth eighteen is actually discipleship, which also features in the symmetrical second eighteen. This theme is introduced by the very first saying:

> 5.1 Jesus said: "The harvest indeed is great, but the labor-
> ers are few; but pray to the Lord, so he might send laborers
> into the harvest." (Th. 73)

In the fifth eighteen, we will find entwined the hidden mystery and the theme of discipleship in a strong pattern of threes.

## *The first three*

After the laborers for the harvest saying, the first three continues to expand upon the "few" who will be laborers:

> 5.2 He said: "Lord, there are many around the well, but no
> one in the well." Jesus said: "There are many standing at
> the door, but the single ones are they who shall enter the
> bridal chamber." (Th. 74 & 75)

In the standard numbering, this is two sayings. However, the first speaker is addressing Jesus (who is "Lord" here), so the saying should be considered as one.[66] The two parts are clearly linked. The first speaker, a disciple, makes a comment that there are many

# The Fifth Eighteen

| | |
|---|---|
| Send labourers for the harvest | |
| The well and the bridal chamber | THREE SAYINGS ABOUT THE CALL TO DISCIPLESHIP |
| The merchant and the pearl | |

| | |
|---|---|
| Jesus and the all | |
| You have not come to see a reed shaken by the wind | THREE SAYINGS ABOUT THE MYSTERIOUS NATURE OF JESUS |
| The wombs that bore and did not conceive | |

| | |
|---|---|
| The world and the body | |
| The rich become king, those with power renounce | THREE SAYINGS IN SIMILAR PARADOXICAL FORM |
| Close to Jesus and the fire | |

| | |
|---|---|
| Images hidden in the light of the father | |
| The likeness and the image | THREE SAYINGS ABOUT THE CREATION OF HUMANS (ADAM) IN THE IMAGE OF GOD |
| Adam came out of a great power but was unworthy | |

| | |
|---|---|
| The son of man has no place to rest | |
| Woe to the flesh that depends on the soul | THREE SAYINGS ABOUT THE TRIALS OF DISCIPLESHIP |
| The angels and prophets come to you | |

| | |
|---|---|
| Why wash the outside of the cup? | POSITIVE SAYING FINISHES DISCIPLESHIP THEME |
| Jesus' yoke is easy and his lordship gentle | |
| **Disciples ask Jesus who he is** | |

THIS IS THE QUESTION ASKED THAT JESUS DOES NOT ANSWER

standing around the cistern or well, but only one person in the well drawing up water. Jesus replies with reference to the marriage custom that the guests stand around the door of the bridal chamber, but it is the single ones, the bridegroom, who will enter. This identifies the "laborers for the harvest" as the chosen, the ones who have been through the divine marriage and become single-ones. This saying echoes the more familiar *"for many are called and few chosen" (Matthew 20:16)*.

The final saying in the three concerns a merchant who finds a pearl:

> *5.3 Jesus said: "The kingdom of the Father is like a merchant who had some goods; he found a pearl. That merchant was wise. He sold the goods, and bought for himself the pearl alone. You also, seek after his treasure which does not perish but endures, where moth does not enter to eat, nor does worm destroy." (Th. 76)*

The connection with the previous saying is that a Jewish wife was known as a "pearl." The second part of this saying, which explains the first, may have been added later. The saying is part of the call to discipleship. It tells the would-be disciple to be like the merchant and exchange all their other "goods" for the sake of the one pearl. In the early Jesus movement, discipleship was uncompromising; the disciple would give up all the comforts and security of their old life for a new existence of hardship, poverty, and danger. The pearl, representing the spirit and the kingdom of heaven, was the reward.

We can see also in this three the strong presence of "seeking and finding."

## *The second three*

Having stated the theme of discipleship in the first three, the second three is all about "amazement" and the mysterious nature of Jesus. It starts with 5.4:

> *5.4 Jesus said: "I am the light that is over them all. I am the all of it, the all of it came out of me and the all of it*

> *bursts up to me. Split a timber, I am there. Raise up the*
> *stone, and you shall find me there." (Th. 77)*

This has been dealt with in Chapter 6 where we have offered the explanation that it is about Jesus in the Gospel of Thomas and the Thomas Code. The next saying is also found in Matthew, where it is applied to John the Baptist:

> *5.5 Jesus said: "Why did you come out to the field? To see*
> *a reed shaken by the wind? And to see a man clothed in*
> *soft garments [like your] kings and your powerful ones?*
> *These are clothed in soft garments and they cannot know*
> *the truth." (Th. 78)*

The people have come in the field to see someone who is not like the rich rulers, "*the reed shaken by the wind*." There is nothing in this Thomas version of the saying to link it to John. Instead, we can see it as a saying about the nature of Jesus himself. The last saying in the three starts with woman blessing the mother of Jesus:

> *5.6 A woman in the crowd said to him: "Blessed is the*
> *womb which bore you, and the breasts which nourished*
> *you." He said to her: "Blessed are they who have heard the*
> *word of the Father and have truly kept it. For there shall*
> *be days when you will say: Blessed is the womb which has*
> *not conceived, and the breasts which have not given suck."*
> *(Th. 79)*

This saying shows similarities with two sayings in Luke (11:27-28 & 23:27-29). In *The Rock and the Tower*, I argued that the Thomas version is original and was split into two separate sayings by the author of Luke. The words "*For there shall be days when you will say…*" appear in the second saying in Luke, when Jesus is being led to crucifixion and warns his lamenting female followers of the coming apocalypse. In *The Rock and the Tower*, I thought that these words had been added to Thomas at a later stage by someone who was familiar with this Luke version. However, with the discovery of the structure of Thomas, these words take on an unexpected new meaning. The same phrase appears in the keystone saying 3.1, "*Some days will come when you will seek after me ....*" Indeed, in the Coptic, the two expressions are virtually identical. The phrase is also very similar to the expression in the past tense in the keystone saying 6.1: "*...those things you asked me in those days....*" In the keystone sayings "days" means an eighteen, "*some days will come...*" means the following eighteen, and "*those days*" means the previous eighteen. So the phrase "*For there shall be days...*" in 5.6 is talking about the next, and last, eighteen! We know that there will be a revelation in this eighteen, and this gives us a hint of what is about to be revealed.

Most likely, 5.6 was a saying that was in circulation before the Gospel of Thomas was put into its final form, and which was edited to fit in with the hierarchical structure of the Gospel. If so, then the words "*For there shall be days...*" are not original to the initial form of the saying, but allude to the structure. The author of Luke was aware of this final form of the saying but did not appreciate the structure of eighteens. So the author decided to divide it into two and position each part where it made sense in the narrative. "The days that were to come" was taken, quite reasonably, as a reference to the apocalypse. This is further evidence that Thomas is earlier than the New Testament Gospels.

Saying 5.6 brings to a climax three sayings about the mysterious nature of Jesus. It gives us an enigmatic clue as to the nature of the revelation in the last eighteen; the disciples will say, "*Blessed is the womb which has not conceived, and the breasts which have not given suck.*" We will consider what this means when we attempt to answer the final puzzle of the Gospel.

## *The third three*

The eighteen returns to the theme of discipleship in the third three. The sayings are all short and share an identical structure of two opposed halves. Let us take them in turn.

> *5.7 Jesus said: "Whoever has known the world has found the body, and whoever has found the body, the world is not worthy of him." (Th. 80)*

This involves the contradiction that knowing/finding the world leads to denial of the world:

A (the world) leads to B (the body);
B (the body) leads to the opposite of A (denial of the world)

The Gospel of Thomas loves contradiction, and each of the three sayings in this section involves an element of paradox.

> *5.8 Jesus said: "Whoever has become rich, let him become king, and he who has power let him renounce it." (Th. 81)*

Here the contradiction is that being wealthy and becoming king leads to renunciation of power, and hence a rejection of wealth. The paradox is resolved by interpreting the first half spiritually and the second half literally:

> *"Whoever has become rich, let him become king"*—the person who is spiritually wealthy will enter the kingdom.

> *"he who has power let him renounce it"*- one in the kingdom will renounce worldly power and wealth.

> *5.9 Jesus said: "He who is close to me is close to the fire, and he who is far from me is far from the kingdom." (Th. 82)*

This time two states are juxtaposed; being close to Jesus and being far from Jesus. We might expect the saying to tell the disciple to get close to Jesus, but instead it shocks the reader by warning both about the consequences of getting close, and the consequence of not being close:

> *He who is close to me is close to the fire...* (A dangerous and potentially undesirable place.)

> *... and he who is far from me is far from the kingdom.* (A far worse place.)

Fire is both destructive and life-giving. The fire that Jesus casts upon the world spreads and consumes, destroying the disciples' previous lives as they are caught up in enthusiasm for Jesus. But if they seek to avoid the fire, they will never know the kingdom. The sayings in this three have an obvious similarity in form and content, and this similarity is further evidence supporting the structure.

## *The fourth three*

The next three sayings are about "the images" of the disciples and about Adam. We shall take them all together:

> *5.10 Jesus said: "The images are revealed to the man, and the light which is in them is hidden in the image of the light of the father. He will be revealed forth, and his image is hidden by his light." (Th. 83)*

> *5.11 Jesus said: "The days you look upon your likeness, you rejoice; but when you look upon your images which came to be before you, they neither die nor become manifest, how much will you bear?" (Th. 84)*

> *5.12 Jesus said: "Adam came into being out of a great power and a great richness, and he was not worthy of you. For if he had been worthy, he [would] not [have tasted of death]." (Th. 85)*

The key to understanding these sayings is the story of the creation of man in the Book of Genesis:

> *Then God said, "Let us make man in our image, after our likeness. And let them have dominion over the fish of the sea and over the birds of the heavens and over the livestock and over all the earth and over every creeping thing that creeps on the earth." So God created man in his own image, in the image of God he created him; male and female he created them. (Genesis 1:26-27 ESV)*

We have already come across this passage in the union of the "single one"; the merger of the person and their spirit. In this first creation, God makes Adam in his own image and creates him "male and female." In Genesis, this is followed by a second account of the creation of Adam where YHWH fashions him out of earth (Genesis 2:7) and breathes life into his nostrils. The Jesus movement believed that the first creation was spiritual and the second creation physical. In the first creation, humans were made as a male-female pair so that there was no differentiation between the sexes. In the second creation, when people took physical bodies, they were born as either male or female. The Jesus movement believed that the other part of the original spiritual male-female combination remained in the heavenly sphere where it was in danger of corruption by the demons. So every woman had a male "angel" or spirit, and every man a female "angel" or spirit. A person has to be born again in a spiritual sense to recombine the two elements. This recombination is the subject of 2.16R (Th. 22).

The results of the first spiritual creation are the "images" in the Thomas sayings. These images came into existence before the physical person and will remain in existence after the physical person dies (5.11). Because they were made in the image of God, the spiritual images are naturally so bright that they are hidden in the light of the Father (5.10). However, as people have become obsessed with the world and take delight in their bodily form, their spiritual images have become corrupted (5.11). Adam came into existence out "of a great power and richness," being made in the image of God, but when he took a body, he was corrupted and became mortal (5.12). By returning to their original spiritual state, the chosen would return to the initial state of eternal life. The three sayings, like other threes in this eighteen, form a coherent whole.

## *The fifth three*

The fifth three is about the hardships of being a disciple. It starts with a saying about the homeless life of the traveling teacher:

> 5.13 Jesus said: "[The foxes have] the[ir dens] and the birds have [their] nests, but the son of man has no place to lay his head and to rest." (Th. 86)

The "son of man" was a title of Jesus but could also just mean "man." In this case, we would take it as meaning the chosen, those who have Jesus within. The foxes and birds stand for the forces of evil, those who own the world. This saying is linked to the saying in the identical place in the fourth eighteen (4.13) that those who persecute the disciples will be excluded from their "place."

The next saying is about the flesh and the spirit:

> 5.14 *Jesus said: "Woe to the flesh which depends upon the soul; woe to the soul which depends upon the flesh." (Th. 112)*

This saying is found in two duplicate versions, Thomas 87 and 112. Although Thomas 87 appears in sequence, it seems to have been corrupted in transmission. So I have taken Thomas 112 as better representing the original 5.14. The meaning of the saying is straightforward. Both the flesh that depends upon the soul and the soul that depends upon the flesh are to be pitied. The first group is comprised of those of the Jesus movement who are ruled by the soul. Their "flesh" is to be pitied because to follow Jesus involves renunciation and physical privation. The second group is made up of those people who are ruled by the flesh, and who are spiritually dead.

The final saying in the three is not so straightforward. To be consistent with the other two sayings in the three, it should also be about the hardships faced by the disciples.

> 5.15 *Jesus said: "The angels come to you, and the prophets, and they give to you what is yours; and you also, give what you have and say to yourselves: On which day do they come and take what is theirs?" (Th. 88)*

The saying is complex. To bring out its structure, we can write it symbolically as transactions between two groups:

Group 1 = the angels and the prophets.
Group 2 = those addressed as "you," the audience of the saying.

The saying then has three different steps:

Group 1 gives to Group 2 something that belongs to Group 2.

Group 2 are to give (to whom?) something that belongs to Group 2.

Group 1 will take from Group 2 something that belongs to Group 1.

When it is put in this form, the symmetry is obvious. In the first and last step, Group 1 give to and take from Group 2. Normally, if you give something, you give what belongs to you; and if you take something, you take what belongs to the other party. But in both the first and last steps these expectations are reversed. Only in the middle do we have normal giving, and only Group 2 give that which belongs to them to give.

In the structure, the roles of Group 1 are negative. The giving of Group 1 is not true giving because their gift already belongs to the recipient. They attempt to take but only succeed in taking what is already theirs. It might be surprising that Group 1 is negative because they are the angels and the prophets, the bringers of the Jewish law. However, the Gospel of Thomas is against the law! And we find a very similar notion in Paul. He compares mankind to children who are heirs to an estate. While young, they are under the control of guardians whom Paul calls "the elements of the kosmos." But when they reach maturity, they are no longer under guardians but receive the inheritance of sons and daughters. The children under their guardians represent the Jews under the law. The sons and daughters who have come into their inheritance, are the Christians who are now beyond the law. Although the elements have brought the law, Paul is very negative about them. What increases the identification of Group 1 with Paul's "elements of the cosmos" is that a guardian gives to his wards what already belongs to those wards because they are the inheritors of the estate. The only explanation that makes sense of Paul's argument is that the "elements" are the angels who were believed to rule the world and who had brought the Jewish law.[67]

We can now make sense of the three steps.

In step 1, Group 2 represents the children and Group 1 their angelic guardians. The angels give the children the law so that they might please God. But they are giving something, the promised love of God, that already belongs to the children by inheritance.

In step 2, the children have come into their inheritance as sons and daughters. They have the wealth of the kingdom of God and are instructed to give that wealth to others.

In step 3, the angels are jealous of the spiritual wealth of the children and desire to take it from them. But they can only take what is already theirs, the body.

The final step is also the subject of 2.2 (Th. 21). In this saying, the disciples are like children in a field that does not belong to them. When the Lords of the field request it back, they must strip naked to give it back to them. We have seen how this saying is about martyrdom. The body belongs to the elements of the kosmos, the powers who rule the world. It is a "garment" that should be returned to those powers should they demand it. It is likely that saying 5.15 specifically alludes to 2.2 through the phrase *"On which day...."* We have seen that in the keystone sayings a reference to "days" is code for another eighteen. So *"On which day..."* could be telling us that there is a saying in another eighteen where *"...they come and take what is theirs."*

The interpretation of the saying then is that the angels who rule the world brought the law through the prophets. But they were only giving to humankind what already belonged to humankind. Now, those in the Jesus movement, becoming sons and daughters, have come into their wealth directly and must now give it to others. But the rulers will return, this time to take what is theirs, the disciples' bodies, meaning martyrdom. With this explanation, the saying ties in with the theme of the three, the hardships of being a disciple.[68]

## *The sixth three*

The last three brings the eighteen to a climax. It starts with a saying about washing a cup:

> 5.16 Jesus said: "Why do you wash the outside of the cup?
> Do you not understand that whoever made the inside is
> also he who made the outside?" (Th. 89)

We find something very similar to this in both Matthew and Luke, where it concerns the Jews washing their cups for ritual purity. However, instead of looking at the saying in the light of the Gospels, we should first look at the version in Thomas without preconceptions. The key to understanding the saying is the idea that the one who made the inside also made the outside. This makes no sense in relation to the purity of physical cups. So we must understand it metaphorically. In the scriptures, God is described as a potter and humans as the pot he has made:

> *You turn things upside down! Shall the potter be regarded as the clay, that the thing made should say of its maker, "He did not make me"; or the thing formed say of him who formed it, "He has no understanding"? (Isaiah 29:16 ESV)*

The cup is a person, and the maker of the cup is God. The saying is aimed at those who would cleanse the outside of the cup, by washing the outside of a person. It is aimed at water baptism! The person who was most renowned for practicing water baptism was John the Baptist. Instead of cleaning the outside, the Jesus movement purified the inside. Although the movement did come to practice water baptism, it seems that this was not the case in the beginning when it was in rivalry to John's movement. Even when water baptism was adopted, it was an outer ceremony, for the left hand psychic Christians, rather than the right hand spiritual Christians. The saying is telling the disciples that it is the spiritual baptism that is the true cleansing rather than the superficial water baptism.

Now look at how the saying is applied in Matthew and Luke against the scribes and Pharisees. First Matthew:

> *"Woe to you, scribes and Pharisees, hypocrites! For you clean the outside of the cup and the plate, but inside they are full of greed and self-indulgence. You blind Pharisee! First clean the inside of the cup and the plate, that the outside also may be clean." (Matthew 23:25-26 ESV)*

Note how the metaphor goes all wrong here:

- The cup and plate start as literal.

- The inside of the Scribe/Pharisees are full of greed and self-indulgence.
- They should clean the inside of the cup and plate, so that the outside may be clean also.

The author of Matthew has an understanding that the inside of the cup concerns the inner purity of the person, but by combining literal and metaphorical cleansing makes a mess of the whole saying. Cleaning the inside does not clean the outside! The author of Luke must have both the Gospel of Matthew and access to the original saying. Unlike Matthew, Luke preserves the idea that the maker of the outside was the maker of the inside:

> While Jesus was speaking, a Pharisee asked him to dine with him, so he went in and reclined at table. The Pharisee was astonished to see that he did not first wash before dinner. And the Lord said to him, "Now you Pharisees cleanse the outside of the cup and of the dish, but inside you are full of greed and wickedness. You fools! Did not he who made the outside make the inside also? But give as alms those things that are within, and behold, everything is clean for you. (Luke 11:37-41 ESV)

This attempts to sort out the metaphorical confusion of Matthew, but it is not completely successful. The cup and the plate still start as literal, but they then become a metaphor for the Pharisees who must cleanse the inner person through almsgiving.

Saying 5.16, denying water baptism, is one of the most provocative in the whole Gospel. It is consistent with those sayings that depreciate almsgiving, prayer, and fasting, all things that were also practiced by Christians. In each case, it is the things done by the outer, psychic members of the movement that are attacked. This is all one with Thomas. The Gospel that Jesus casts upon the world is intended to disrupt; it is not a gospel of peace, but of contradiction and paradox. It continually pushes away from the literal and physical and into the spiritual domain. The placing of this saying at the start of the final three is significant because it links to the two themes of the eighteen, discipleship and the mysterious nature of Jesus. The movement is not what it appears to those on the outside. The next saying completes the theme of discipleship:

> *5.17 Jesus said: "Come to me, for easy is my yoke and my lordship is gentle, and you shall find rest for yourselves."* (Th. 90)

If we remember that "to rest" meant to enter into the kingdom of heaven, then the saying is perfectly clear. It is a counterpart to those sayings that emphasized the hardships of being a disciple. It promises that the load is yet easy to bear and that Jesus is a gentle Lord.

The keystone saying has promised that in the eighteen is a question that is not answered. Yet in the whole of the eighteen so far, no one has asked Jesus a question. In 5.2 and 5.6, people make statements to which Jesus responds, but neither is a question aimed at Jesus. Only with the last, climatic saying in the eighteen do we get the question.

## The question not answered

The keystone saying for the eighteen is: *"but those things you asked me in those days, I did not tell you then."* So we need a saying that is not answered. We find it in 5.18:

> *5.18 They said to him: "Tell us who you are so that we may believe in you." He said to them: "You examine the face of the heavens and the earth, but he who is in your presence you do not know, and you do not know how to examine this moment." (Th. 91)*

This gives us one-half of the puzzle; the question that will be answered in the last eighteen and which will cause the disciples to "be amazed." The question is deceptively simple: *"Tell us who you are so that we may believe in you."* We can see now why one of the themes of the eighteen is the mysterious nature of Jesus, with the other theme being discipleship (*"...that we may believe in you."*).

Jesus does not answer the question, but he gives us some hints. He tells the disciples that are looking for a physical answer: *"You examine the face of the heavens and the earth."* Yet the answer is not physical: *"he who is in your presence you do not know."* He adds *"you do not know how to examine this moment."* In Thomas, "days" that are to come or which have past means the other eighteens. So "this moment" suggests the saying we are reading now: Jesus is telling us to examine saying 5.18 and that the meaning is non-obvious. We will examine the saying further later, for we can only understand it in relation to the last eighteen, and indeed the whole Gospel.

# 15

# The sixth eighteen

## *Ruling principle*

The sixth eighteen is in the third thirty-six. The ruling principle of this thirty-six is:

> *and if he is troubled he will become amazed*

The ruling principle of the eighteen is:

> *Seek, and you shall find; ... Now I wish to tell them, and*
> *you seek not after them.*

## *The answers not asked for*

The last eighteen starts with the keystone saying we have already considered:

> *6.1 Jesus said: "Seek, and you shall find; but those things*
> *you asked me in those days, I did not tell you then. Now*
> *I wish to tell them, and you seek not after them." (Th. 92)*

It is the second half that applies to this eighteen. Somewhere in the final eighteen is the answer to the question that was asked in saying 5.18, which comes immediately before 6.1.

Given the importance of the revelations in the last eighteen, it is frustrating that it is this eighteen that is the least certain. We have eliminated three sayings as duplicates: Thomas 94, 110, and 112. As well as this elimination of duplicates we have combined two sayings, 111 and 113, into one. The reasons behind these decisions are discussed in the Appendix IV: Reconstructing the last eighteen.

A fourth duplicate, Thomas 106, is also disregarded. However, as discussed later in this chapter, there is evidence that this saying is original. The Gospel contains clues that it is to be moved but not to another position – effectively it is to be deleted. If so then the eighteen originally had 19 sayings and the Gospel as a whole 109 sayings. It would seem that this was an attempt to disguise the sayings total to protect the secrets of the Gospel.

## *The structure of the first half*

The final eighteen has a structure of two halves. The first half is eclectic. Although the structure of threes is visible in places, there is no single dominating theme. Instead, we have four separate themes interweaved into the half:

Two of the sayings (6.2 and 6.4) are about keeping the secrets of the movement and the Gospel (S).

Two of the sayings (6.3 and 6.8) are about rejecting money (M).

Two of the sayings (6.7 and 6.9) are about the family to be rejected and the family to be accepted (F).

Two of the sayings (6.5 and 6.6) are about losing the kingdom. (L)

This leaves one other saying—the keystone 6.1. Is this pattern of a pair of sayings on each theme deliberate? If we place them in order and exclude the keystone we get:

S M S LL F M F

There is some evidence of symmetry here. The two halves are mirror images of each other with the central point coming between the two Ls—except that one side has S (secrecy) and the other F (family). One thing supporting this structure is that it divides this group of sayings into two halves. This pattern of "halves" is prominent in the final eighteen but is not found in the rest of the Gospel.

The strongest structure among the groups of three is in the second group where each of the sayings starts with "The kingdom of the father is like…" The first saying of the three, about a woman hiding yeast in loaves, is covered later in this chapter. The other two, with a woman carrying a jar and an assassin driving the sword into his own house, are negative sayings about losing the kingdom and are covered in Chapter 11.

The third three also has a structure. The first and last sayings reject one family and accept another.[69] Sandwiched between the two is the saying about paying a gold coin to Caesar.

There is one other important structural feature in the first half. The last saying of the first three (6.3) is linked to the symmetrical saying in the eighteen (6.16). Both talk about lending money at interest.

## The structure of the second half

It is when we get to the second half of the last eighteen that we find evidence for a more remarkable structure. This half of the eighteen is linked symmetrically to the first half of the Gospel. Within each three, the successive links step closer to the beginning of the Gospel. The threes descend through the levels, starting with the eighteens, moving to the sixes and then the individual sayings of the first three:

- The fourth three is linked to the first three eighteens.
- The fifth three is linked to the three sixes of the first eighteen
- The sixth three is linked to the individual sayings of the first three.

The final structure actually applies to the last four sayings, which are linked to first four. Before we go through these levels of linkages, we must deal with the fact that at the moment we have nineteen sayings and not eighteen.

## *The lost saying*

In each of the first three eighteens, two pairs of sayings had to be moved. In the last eighteen, there is evidence of something even more radical: an extra saying has been added to make a total of nineteen. We are then given clues to tell us to remove this saying. The saying in question is Thomas 106, and I have numbered it 6.13.1. It is shown along with the preceding saying 6.13 below:

> *6.13 Jesus said: "He who shall **know father and mother** shall be called the **son of a whore**." (Th. 105)*

> *6.13.1 Jesus said: "When you **make the two one**, you shall be **sons of man**, and when you say: 'Mountain, move away,' he shall be moved." (Th. 106)*

Because the saying is very close to 3.11, I initially regarded 6.13.1 as a duplicate added by a copyist. But there were a few things that bothered me with this solution. For a start, this was the only duplicate that was positioned by itself. The other sayings to be deleted were either in a group immediately before the end (Thomas 110, the interpolation in Thomas 111, and Thomas 112) or close to the saying that they duplicated (Thomas 94). The saying also fits in very well with the previous saying 6.13 (Thomas 105) as can be seen above.

Saying 6.13 is a play on the myth of Adam and Eve.[70] In the version of the myth in Genesis, the serpent persuades Eve to eat an apple. However, in the Enoch tradition evil does not enter the world through Adam and Eve but through the fallen angels who take human women as wives. The evidence is that the Jesus movement adopted a hybrid version of these two myths in which Eve committed adultery with the snake who was really the chief of the fallen angels, Satan. This is why her firstborn son, Cain, becomes a murderer.[71] Through Cain, everyone alive has the seed of the devil inside him or herself.

How then can mankind be redeemed? The story of Adam and Eve is the second creation in Genesis. The Jesus movement believed that the original creation was spiritual and that in this first creation Adam was made hermaphrodite, male and female. To return to this first creation a person has to find and merge with their spiritual component. For a man, the spirit is female, an image of the first spiritual Eve. So recovering the spiritual Eve undoes the sin of the fleshy Eve. We find just this concept in the Gospel of Philip which was included in Nag Hammadi Codex II immediately after the Gospel of Thomas:

> *When Eve was still in Adam death did not exist. When she was separated from him death came into being. If he enters again and attains his former self, death will be no more. (Gospel of Philip II 68:22-26)*

In 6.13.1 by making the two one, the disciples become "sons of man". The "son of man" is a title of Jesus. So any disciple (male or female) who can recover their spiritual image will become like Jesus and undo the results of the adultery of their fleshy mother, Eve.

All of this shows that Thomas 106 fits well in the place in which we find it, coming after 6.13. Yet it is also very clearly a duplicate, and if we do not delete it, our total will be wrong. What is going on? I believe that the saying has been deliberately added to change the total number of sayings to 109 and so safeguard the secret of the Gospel. We are then given some strong clues that we are supposed to "lose" the saying, to restore the pattern of 108. Let us now look at these clues.

## Moving the mountain

The links between 6.13.1 and 6.13 are all in the first half of the saying. The second half, about moving the mountain, is very similar to 3.11:

> *3.11 Jesus said: "If **two make peace** with one another in this house alone, they shall say to **the mountain, 'Move away' and it shall move.**" (Th. 48)*

> *6.13.1 Jesus said: "When you **make the two one**, you shall be sons of man, and when you say: '**Mountain, move away,' he shall be moved.**" (Th. 106)*

We have seen that for 3.11 "moving the mountain" is the clue that we must move the next two sayings. It is almost inconceivable that the same phrase would not play a similar role in 6.13.1 if it really is an original saying. The wording however differs. In 3.11 we have "*If two make peace with one another in this house*" indicating two sayings in the eighteen are to be moved. In 6.3.1 we have "*make the two one*" which is telling us to make two sayings into one by eliminating a saying as a duplicate or merging it with another saying. For saying 3.11, the two following sayings contain clues that they are to be moved. There are no such clues in the sayings around 6.13.1. So it is 6.13.1 itself that must be removed.

## No place to rest

There is another clue that the saying is to be moved but not to a new position. The phrase "*you shall be sons of man*," recalls the only other place in which "son of man" is found in Thomas:

> 5.13 *Jesus said: "[The foxes have] the[ir dens] and the birds have [their] nests, but **the son of man has no place to lay his head and to rest**." (Th. 86)*

So becoming a "son of man" means that you will have "*no place to lay your head and rest.*" Saying 16.13.1 is to move but not find a home. This contrasts to the two sayings that come after 3.11. These both contain clues that they are to be moved to another position and then stay there or "rest":

- Saying 3.12 has "*for you came from there, and shall go there again*".
- Saying 3.13 says that the sign of the father is "*a movement and a rest.*"

The link between 16.13.1 and 15.13 is reinforced by their positions. They are in equivalent places in the fifth and sixth eighteen (taking the position of 16.13.1 to be the same as 16.13 to which it is linked.)

## The shepherd and the lost sheep

The third clue is the saying that comes after 6.13.1:

> *6.14 Jesus said: "The kingdom is like a shepherd who had a hundred sheep. One of them, the largest, went astray. He left the ninety-nine and sought after the one till he found it. Having labored, he said to the sheep: I love you more than the ninety-nine." (Th. 107)*

This famous saying is also found in Matthew and Luke.[72] Is the lost sheep a cryptic reference to the saying 6.13.1 which must leave the flock of sayings? If so then how is this flock positioned in the Gospel? We have 100 sheep and not 108. But we must not forget the shepherd! Including him in our flock gives 101 sayings. If the "shepherd" is saying 6.14 then the "sheep" he watches over must be the preceding 100 sayings starting at 1.5 and ending with 6.13.1. When 6.13.1 goes astray, the number of sayings will be reduced to 99, or 100 including the shepherd. So eight sayings are excluded from flock and shepherd. The shepherd saying is so positioned that the 100 sayings are centered in the Gospel. The excluded sayings are thus symmetric: four come at the beginning before the flock and four at the end, after the shepherd. This is illustrated by the diagram:

### The Shepherd and the Lost Sheep

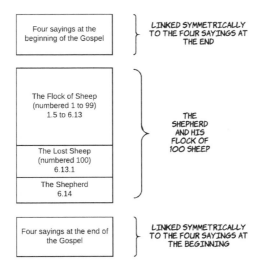

The structure draws attention to the two groups of four sayings at the beginning and end of the Gospel. We shall see that these two groups of four sayings are symmetrically linked to each other. So for example, the fourth saying is linked to the fourth from the end. These connections emphasize the countdown to the final saying which is linked with the first.

Why is the lost sheep larger/greater than the others? This feature is found only in the Thomas version, which suggests that it has something to do with the lost saying. Saying 6.13.1 is certainly not large in the sense of being the longest saying. Nor does it appear to be more important than the other sayings. However, perhaps we need to think in riddle terms. We have 100 sayings, and the Gospel needs to identify one of them as the saying to be moved. Unlike real sheep, our sayings occur in a particular order so that we can number them 1 to 100. So maybe the "largest" sheep is the one with the largest number. This would be 100, which is saying 6.13.1.

In Thomas, many sayings do double or triple duty with multiple levels of meaning. Almost certainly, the shepherd saying is an existing parable that has been modified to fulfill a new role in Thomas in which it alludes to the "lost" saying. But this does not explain why the lost sheep is loved more than the other sheep, so there must be another deeper and more profound meaning. In this deeper meaning, the shepherd undoubtedly stands for Jesus who is the good shepherd in early Christian art. In the Gospels, the lost sheep is a sinner, but I do not think this is correct. Why should one sinner be loved more than ninety-nine of the faithful? Instead, I think the lost sheep represents those Gentiles who are part of the new spiritual Israel, and the ninety-nine sheep are the traditionally minded Jews. Jesus loves the Gentile convert more than those Jews who reject him. The meaning would then be similar to the next but one saying, 6.16, in which a man plowing a field finds a treasure that the original owners did not realize was there.

## *The fourth three and the eighteens*

It is time to return to the symmetrical structure of the second half of the Gospel. The fourth three consists of three sayings, each of which is closely linked to a saying in one of the first three eighteens. First, we have a condemnation of the Pharisees:

> *6.10 And Jesus said: "Woe to them, the Pharisees! For they are like a dog sleeping in the manger of some oxen; for he neither eats, nor does he let the oxen eat." (Th. 102)*

This is very similar in meaning to 3.12R (the original 3.2 which has been reordered) where the Pharisees and scribes have taken the keys of knowledge and do not go in or permit others to go in. The second saying is about guarding against robbers:

> *6.11 Jesus said: Blessed is the man who knows in what part the robbers are coming, that he may rise and gather his [domain] and gird up his loins before they come in. (Th. 103)*

This time the saying is very close to the middle part of saying 2.2: *"Therefore I say this: If the Lord of the house knows that the thief is coming, he will keep watch before he comes, and will not let him dig into his house of his kingdom to carry off his vessels."*[73] The third saying is about fasting and praying:

> *6.12 They said [to him]: "Come, pray today and fast." Jesus said: "What is the sin that I have done, or in what have I been defeated? But when the bridegroom comes out of the bridal chamber, then let them fast and pray." (Th. 104)*

This corresponds to sayings 1.5 and 1.6R, which reject prayer, fasting, and almsgiving. So each of the sayings in the fourth three is closely linked to another saying in each of the first three eighteens. They are so similar that they essentially repeat the meaning of the earlier sayings. Moreover, they are linked in reverse order, which is what we would expect from a chiastic, symmetrical structure in which the end is matched to the beginning:

- 6.10 is linked to 3.12R
- 6.11 is linked to 2.2
- 6.12 is linked to 1.5&1.6R

There is no denying the links. The pattern, however, might be dismissed as coincidence, except that we will find something very similar in the next three.

## The fifth three and the sixes

Each of the sayings of the fifth three is linked to a saying in the first eighteen. It starts with 6.13 about father and mother:

> 6.13 Jesus said: "He who shall know father and mother shall be called the son of a whore." (Th. 105)

We have seen that the mother is Eve, and the saying is about the sowing of the demons within mankind through her adultery with the serpent, the devil.[74] The saying can be twinned with one in the first eighteen:

> 1.14 Jesus said: "When you see he who was not born of woman, throw yourselves down upon your face and worship him. He is your father." (Th. 15)

Saying 6.13 implies that everyone is the son or daughter of a whore because all mankind are the sons and daughters of Eve. Through the adultery of Eve, mankind has been corrupted with the evil seed sown by the devil. All who are born of woman are descended from Eve, so only one not born of woman would be free of corruption. Saying 1.14 tells us that such a one is the father of the Christians—meaning here not God but Jesus. The two sayings are linked, and this link helps us to understand the wording of 1.14. The next saying is the parable of the good shepherd which we have already considered in relation to 1.13.1. But this saying also has remarkable similarities to the fisherman saying (1.7) in which man is like a wise fisherman who casts his net into the sea and draws up many little fish and one great fish. He throws the little fish away but keeps the one big fish. We have seen that this is a parable about the kingdom of heaven, which is represented by the large fish. The little fish are the things of the world that the disciple must put aside for the kingdom. There are a number of points of similarity between the two parables:

- Both parables have a human (shepherd, man) and a number of living creatures (sheep, fish).
- In both parables, one of the creatures is larger than the others.
- In both parables, the human abandons the lesser creatures for the one that is large.
- Both parables use the identical word meaning "trouble" or "labor" to describe why the large creature is chosen. The fish is chosen without trouble whereas the sheep is chosen because the shepherd has labored.

Given this closeness, we would expect the two to mean the same thing, but they don't! The shepherd represents Jesus (taking the deeper original meaning rather than the riddle meaning) and the fisherman a disciple. It is one of the mysteries of the Gospel of Thomas how two sayings that are so similar in form can have completely different meanings. But this would be explained if the two have been crafted to resemble each other closely to establish a link.

The last saying in the three is 6.15:

> *6.15 Jesus said: "Whoever drinks from my mouth shall become like me; I myself will become he, and the hidden thing shall appear to him." (Th. 108)*

Jesus in this saying is spiritual and his essence can pass into the disciple. The saying continues the theme of the hidden secrets that will be revealed. It is linked to the symmetrical saying in the first eighteen:

> *1.4 Jesus said: "Know what is in front of you and that which is hidden from you will be revealed to you. For there is nothing hidden that will not appear." (Th. 5)*

The link between these two sayings is obvious; both concern the hidden thing that will be revealed. The two sayings are fourth from the end and fourth from the beginning. So this is part of the first four sayings being linked symmetrically to the last four.

Each of the sayings in the fifth three is connected to another saying in the first eighteen. Put this together with the previous three, and we can see the pattern:

Fourth three is linked to first half of the Gospel:

- 6.10 links to the third eighteen (3.12R)
- 6.11 links to the second eighteen (2.2)
- 6.12 links to the first eighteen (1.5&1.6R)

Fifth three is linked to first eighteen:

- 6.13 links to the third six (1.14)
- 6.14 links to the second six (1.07)
- 6.15 links to the first six (1.4)

The connections start with the second half of the last eighteen. The first three are linked in reverse order to the first half of the Gospel and the next three to the first eighteen. This reverse order is exactly what we would expect from a symmetrical, chiastic arrangement in which the first becomes last, and the last first. So once again we see a structure that has been carefully crafted and hidden in the Gospel.

## *The first and last eighteens*

The sixth eighteen has been building to a climax, which is also the climax of the whole Gospel. It must contain the revelation spoken of in the keystone saying 6.1, the final revelation which will make the disciples amazed. To complete the pattern, the final three should be linked to the first three as follows:

- 6.16 linked to 1.3.
- 6.17 linked to 1.2.
- 6.18 linked to 1.1.

Taking the first link, saying 6.16 is about a treasure hidden in a field that neither the owner of the field nor his son suspects. Eventually, the field is sold to a man who plows and finds the treasure. We can see the man and his son who originally own the field represent the Jewish establishment; the priests and Pharisees. There is a treasure hidden in the scriptures that they guard, but they do not understand its nature. Instead, it is the outsider, such as a Jew from the excluded sects, or a Gentile, who find the treasure. This is very consistent with sayings such as Thomas 38 and Thomas 102. After the man finds the treasure, he lends *"money at interest to whomsoever he chose."* Here the lending of money at interest is intended to be interpreted spiritually, unlike the symmetrical saying 6.3 where the money is literal. The idea is that by sharing spiritual wealth with others, a person becomes richer themselves. This is also the meaning of 4.8, where the wealthy man hesitates before using his riches to sow, reap, and plant, which would increase his spiritual wealth further.

In the symmetrical reordered saying in the first three, 1.3R, Jesus promises: *"I will give you what eye did not see, what ear did not hear, and hand did not touch, and which did not enter into the heart of man."* The two sayings are linked because in both cases there is something hidden and un-guessed at which is now revealed and uncovered.

The next link concerns the second from last saying:

> 6.17 Jesus said: *"The heavens shall be rolled up and the earth in your presence, and he who lives out of the living one shall not see death."* His disciples said to him: *"On what day will the kingdom come?"* *"It comes not with observation. They will not say: Behold, that side or: Behold there! But the kingdom of the father is spread out upon the earth, and men do not see it."* (Th. 111 & 113)

This is linked to the second saying 1.2. The two are "bookend" sayings that have long been known to link the start and end of the Gospel.[75] Under the conventional numbering, these sayings are Thomas 3 and Thomas 113—although our 6.17 includes both Thomas 111 and 113. In both sayings, the kingdom is present but not to be discerned in a physical sense.

Saying 6.17 is also linked with the saying in the same position in the first eighteen, 1.17. In both cases, the disciples ask about the end, and in both cases, Jesus challenges their expectation that the kingdom exists at a certain time.

We have already seen that 1.17 is linked to the symmetrical saying within the eighteen, 1.2. So we have a triangle of linked sayings; 1.2, 1.17 and 6.17. (These links are covered in more detail in Appendix III.) The triangle is shown in the diagram.

## Triangle of links between first and last eighteens

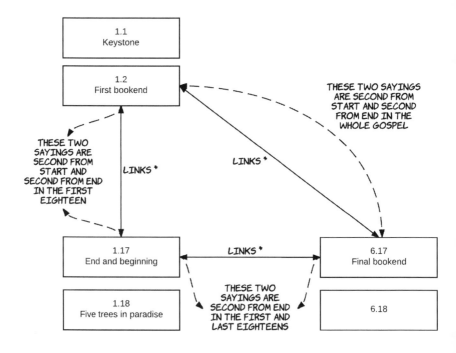

\* See Chapter Appendix for details on links

SAYINGS WHICH ARE LINKED BY CONTENT AND VOCABULARY ARE IN SYMMETRICAL POSITIONS!

## A quadrilateral of sayings

We can go one further by bringing in saying 5.18, the question not answered. There are connections between Thomas 91 (5.18) and Thomas 113 and these links become more extensive when we combine Thomas 111 with Thomas 113 to make 6.17. This supports our conclusion that Thomas 111 and 113 were originally two parts of one saying.

Saying 5.18 is also linked with the first bookend saying, 1.2. (All these links are again covered in Appendix III.) So we can extend our triangle to a quadrilateral, as shown in the diagram.

We see that these four sayings are associated with a spider's web of links. The relationship between 1.2 and 6.17 (the two bookend sayings) depends only on the symmetry between the beginning and end of the Gospel. But the other relationships only make sense under the Thomas Code structure and are evidence for the structure.

Together, the four sayings present a sophisticated cosmology that is a development of the apocalyptic viewpoint. Those in the apocalyptic movement looked for the end of the earth that was expected to occur in the near future, bringing in the kingdom of God. The Gospel of Thomas retains the idea that the earth will come to an end, but it sees both physical reality and physical time as an illusion. Because there is no such thing as time, the disciples can experience both the end, by observing the apocalypse, and the beginning, standing at the moment of creation. If you examine the heaven and earth, you will not see the kingdom of God, and yet the kingdom lies spread out over the face of heaven and earth.

## Links between first and last eighteens including 5.18

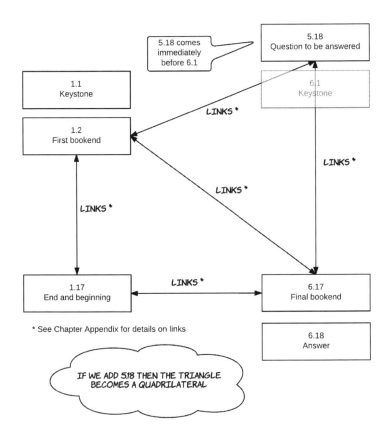

This cosmology is the key to understanding much of Thomas. The ultimate reality is not the physical world but the spiritual kingdom of God that exists in all times and places. It is implicit in this that Jesus himself belongs in the spiritual reality and not in the world.

Is this cosmology the final revelation in Thomas, which will make the disciples "amazed"? We have found links between 5.18 and 6.17 and 1.2, yet all these links concern Jesus' response to the disciples' question in 5.18. However, the keystone saying tells us that Jesus did not answer the question "in those days" meaning in the fifth eighteen. So Jesus' response in 5.18 is not the answer. And we have not found any links between the question ("Who are you...?") and these other sayings. Although saying 6.17 is intimately related to the question saying 5.18, we must reject it as the answer.

## *The final answer*

We should remind ourselves again of the keystone saying:

> 6.1 *Jesus said: "Seek, and you shall find; but those things you asked me in those days, I did not tell you then. Now I wish to tell them, and you seek not after them." (Th. 92)*

There are three reasons why saying 6.18, rather than 6.17, must be the answer indicated by 6.1:

- Saying 6.17, the second from last, is linked with the first bookend 1.2 which is the second saying in the Gospel. But we would expect the final revelation, the climax of the whole Gospel, to come in the last saying, 6.18, which is symmetrical with the first keystone saying.
- As the question is in the last saying of the fifth eighteen, it is appropriate for the answer to be in the last saying of the sixth eighteen.
- Most significantly, we are looking for a saying in which the disciples do not ask Jesus a question. But 6.17 is the only saying in the whole of the last eighteen where the disciples do, in fact, ask Jesus a question. So whoever drafted the keystone saying is telling us to move on from 6.17 to the next saying, 6.18.

Everything points towards 6.18 as the answer:

> 6.18 *Simon Peter said to them: "Let Mary come out from us, for women are not worthy of the life." Jesus said: "Behold, I shall lead her, that I may make her male, so that she will also be a living spirit resembling you males. For*

*every woman who makes herself male shall enter into the
kingdom of heaven."*

This saying is perhaps the most controversial in the Gospel! Indeed, there are many, including Steven Davies, who do not believe that it is original but a later, second-century addition that was added to the end of the Gospel. We will reject this view, not least because symmetry tells us that there must be a saying after the second bookend, 6.17.

We can regard the "Simon Peter" in this saying as a later addition. This combination first occurs in the Gospel of Matthew, and the idea of Peter being opposed to Mary is also found in the second-century Gospel of Mary. The name Simon Peter is also found, along with Matthew, in 1.12. It is likely that these names were added at a time when the users of Thomas were coming into conflict with the proto-orthodox church that looked to Simon Peter for apostolic authority and to the Gospel of Matthew as its principal Gospel. So the names of these proto-orthodox authorities were substituted for the original unnamed disciples in certain places where those disciples said something particularly obtuse.

The phrase "the kingdom of heaven" is also sometimes regarded as indicating a later second-century origin for this saying. The phrase is typical for the Gospel of Matthew, which is dated to c80 AD. However, this is not the only place in Thomas that uses the "kingdom of heaven." Although Thomas normally uses the phrase "the kingdom" or the "kingdom of the Father," in three sayings it is the "kingdom of heaven."[76] The Gospel of Mark does not use the "kingdom of heaven" but that does not mean that it was not in circulation before Matthew! The author of Matthew would not have made up an entirely new phrase for the kingdom and must have taken it from somewhere. Most likely we have a variety of parallel expressions for the kingdom (the kingdom, the kingdom of the Father, of God, and of heaven) in early use so that each gospel writer chose whichever they preferred.

The main problem with Thomas 114 (6.18) in many people's eyes is that it is misogynist. But to interpret the saying in this way is to impose our own cultural norms on the saying. The idea that women should not participate with men in religious studies was mainstream in first-century Judea. Admittedly the attitude of "Simon Peter," that Mary should leave the disciples because women are not worthy of "the life," is extreme even for the first century, but then the purpose of the saying is to rebut this rejection of the female. However, what really causes great embarrassment for modern day Thomas enthusiasts, and which gives great delight to the much larger anti-Thomas camp, is that to enter into the kingdom women must "become male." This appears to give spiritual superiority to the male over the female.

The problem, once again, is that commentators do not take Thomas seriously. We must interpret this saying, not in the light of our modern opinions but the light of the Gospel of Thomas and its worldview. The phraseology here is virtually identical to Thomas 22 where Jesus says the disciples will enter into the kingdom: "... *when you make the male and the female into a single one, that the male be not male nor the female female...*" We have seen the interpretation of this, that it is about the merger of a person and their spirit into a single one, with the spirit being seen as contra-sexual, male for a woman and female for a man. In 6.18, Mary will become "*a living spirit resembling you males.*" It is not Mary who will be male but her spirit! A person must merge with their spiritual husband or wife to get back to the initial state of completeness of the first creation when Adam was made male-female in the image of God. So any woman who wishes to enter the kingdom of heaven must "*make herself male.*" The unstated corollary is that a man must make himself female! But this is not about a person becoming transsexual. It is a case of spiritual union. In the physical sense, a man remains a man, and a woman remains a woman.

**Links between 6.18 and 6.17**

Let us return to that phrase "the kingdom of heaven" that ends 6.18. The saying actually finishes with a phrase that can be literally translated as "of the heavens" which is the same Coptic phrase that starts 6.17. So the two sayings are bracketed, starting and ending with the same expression. This is one of a number of clues that saying 6.18 should be considered alongside 6.17.

Another link is the word for "out." Saying 6.18 starts *"Let Mary come out from us."* The same Coptic word is used at the end of 6.17; *"the kingdom of the Father is spread out upon the earth, and men do not see it."* It is also used in 6.17 for saying that the kingdom *"comes not with observation,"* which is literally "a look outward." The word for "out" is admittedly common in Thomas. It is often used to express either one who is out of the light/kingdom or one who is unable to look properly outward.

The disciple who would expel Mary says she is not worthy of "life." In reply, Jesus promises to make her a "living spirit." This also ties in with something in 6.17: *"he who lives out of the living one shall not see death."* The Incipit tells us that Jesus is the living one, so when Jesus makes Mary a "living spirit" she literally becomes one "who lives out of the living one" and so will not see death.

This suggests that 6.17 and 6.18 are ironically linking those who cannot see Mary for what she is, with those who look upon the earth and cannot see the kingdom.


### Behold, I shall lead her

We have seen how sayings 6.17, 1.2, and 5.18 are all closely linked, so it should not be surprising that 6.18 shares vocabulary with 1.2 as well as 6.17. One such link between 1.2, 16.17, and 6.18 is the Coptic word translated *"Behold,"* which appears in all three. In 1.2, it is spoken by *"those who lead you"* who say the kingdom is in the sky or the sea. In 6.17, it is used by those who think that the kingdom will appear in one place or another. In 6.18, by contrast, the expression is spoken by Jesus himself, who says about Mary, *"Behold, I shall lead her."* The Coptic expression for "lead" is the same here also. So Jesus' audience in 1.2 is led by those with erroneous opinions, unlike Mary in 6.18, who is led by Jesus himself. Those with wrong opinions use *"Behold"* to express their incorrect views of the kingdom, whereas

Jesus uses *"Behold"* to tell his audience about Mary. Unlike those in traditional positions of authority, it is Mary who has true spiritual authority because Jesus leads her.

It is not just vocabulary that is common between 1.2 and 6.18. Saying 6.18 invokes 2.16R (Th. 22) through the female becoming male, but 1.2 also invokes 2.16R through the inside and the outside: *"...the kingdom is inside you and outside you."*

## Thomas 114 must be original

The links with other sayings are the proof that 6.18 (Th. 114) must be original. These similarities would not be there if 6.18 were a saying that was tacked onto the end of the Gospel in the second century. We must see it as part of the original Gospel, carefully crafted to link into 5.18, 6.17, and 1.2. Just as 6.17 and 1.2 resonate with 5.18, so also 6.18 resonates with 6.17 and 1.2. Besides, symmetry requires that a saying should come after the final bookend.

## Mary is the final answer

It is to 6.18 that we must look for the answer to the question posed in 5.18: *"Tell us who you are."* The answer is *"Behold I will lead her"* indicating Mary. This answer will shock anyone brought up on the historical Jesus: he is a spiritual force and not to be physically discerned. The disciples look for him in the heavens or the earth, but he rebukes them: *"he who is in your presence you do not know."* Jesus is in front of them, but they cannot see him. He is present with them through the shaman Mary. This is where all the clues have been leading. Mary has been led to become a living male spirit. No one else in Thomas is described as a "living spirit." The term, coming as it does at the end of the Gospel, links back to the Incipit where the sayings are spoken by *"Jesus who lives."* It is Jesus who is Mary's *"living spirit"* and the authority for her teaching. It is Mary who is one with Jesus.

## *The woman and the loaves*

There is one saying in the last eighteen that we have passed over. This is 6.4 where a woman hides yeast in dough to make loaves.

> *6.4 Jesus said: "The kingdom of the Father is like a woman who took a little yeast and [hid] it in some dough; she made large loaves of it. He that has ears, let him hear." (Th. 96)*

We have seen how in the miracle of the loaves and fishes, the yeast represents a number. Does "yeast" also have a numeric meaning in this saying? Although the saying does not contain any numbers, there is a version in Matthew (and also Luke) that does:[77]

> *He told them another parable. "The kingdom of heaven is like leaven (yeast) that a woman took and hid in three measures of flour, till it was all leavened." (Matthew 13:33 ESV)*

It would seem that the Coptic Thomas version has lost the detail of the three measures. So what is the yeast? It brings in the kingdom of heaven, so it is not the yeast of the Pharisees and Herod, which is the number 5. The clue is that fact that the yeast is "hidden" in three measures. The number 3 is the number of God the Father. To hide the yeast among three measures of flour involves the pattern:

flour - yeast - flour - yeast - flour

We are back to the Thomas Code! The three measures of flour must represent the number 3, and the yeast must be 2. So we get:

$$3 \cdot 2 \cdot 3 \cdot 2 \cdot 3$$

The "large loaves" would be the Gospel of Thomas, and the woman, Mary. She has fed the movement with the Gospel, and she has hidden Jesus within it.

The disciples look for Jesus on the earth, as a man of flesh and blood, or in the heavens, as the anticipated appearance in the skies that will bring in the end times. Yet the whole time Jesus has been right there before them. He has come spiritually through the medium of the prophetess, who many think should not even be allowed to remain with the disciples because she is a woman. It is Mary who is the leader and founder of the Jesus movement, and the movement's supreme human authority. The stone that the builders rejected has become the cornerstone.

# 16

# Postscript

## Who wrote Thomas?

So we come to the final question of the authorship of Thomas. The Coptic version of the Gospel says that the words were written by Didymus Judas Thomas. Neither Didymus nor Thomas is a real name – they both mean "twin." Judas is the supposed brother of Jesus (not Judas Iscariot the betrayer). In my book, *The Rock and the Tower*, I discuss the authorship of the Gospel and propose that it was originally called "the Gospel of the Twin."[78] Judas, the brother of Jesus, would only have become associated with the Gospel in the second century as Christians wondered who was this twin of Jesus. Following the invention of Judas Thomas an extensive literature develops in Syria around him, including the Acts of Thomas in which he travels to India. However, the Gospel is always called the Gospel of Thomas and never the Gospel of Judas. The key piece of evidence for Judas not being associated with the Gospel in the first century comes from the Gospel of John, which was written around 100 AD. The author of John used the Gospel of Thomas extensively as a source but he has both Thomas and Judas in his Gospel as two separate characters. So his version of the Gospel of Thomas could not have been attributed to Judas Thomas.

The first mention of the disciple Thomas is in the Gospel of Mark.[79] The practice of attributing a later writing to a person who was a supposed eyewitness was common among the early Christians. We find it, for example, in three of the four New Testament Gospels. The universal assumption among scholars is that the Gospel of Thomas was

231

named after the obscure disciple who was one of the Twelve. But what has not been considered seriously is the idea that with Thomas the process worked the other way around, so that the author of Mark invented the disciple Thomas because he was well acquainted with the Gospel of that name.

We have seen that Thomas must be earlier than the Gospels of Luke and Matthew because the five in a house saying that expresses the structure of Thomas is embedded within those two Gospels. It must also be older than Mark because the two miracles of the loaves and fishes in that Gospel are a mathematical puzzle which leads to the sequence that has been used to encode Thomas. Whoever put Thomas in its final form came up with the first version of the miracles of the loaves and fishes, the version that was used by the author of Mark as a source. So the author of Mark would have been familiar with the Gospel of Thomas and thought that there must have been a disciple of that name.

In the Coptic version of Thomas, the "twin" occurs twice, first in Aramaic as Thomas and then in Greek as Didymus. The conventional explanation is that a Greek speaker who did not realize that Thomas meant "twin" but who thought it was a name, translated "twin" a second time into Didymus. However, with the Thomas Code we can see why the "twin" should be repeated in the original. The phrase "the twin twin" alludes to the two 2s that represent Jesus in the Code. The Gospel of Thomas actually consists of a collection of sayings by Jesus, so it is appropriate for the "twin" to mean Jesus. The twin is also an allusion to Mary who is bound to Jesus through spiritual twinship.

Most likely the Gospel was attributed to Didymus Thomas in the original. There is a piece of evidence that supports this. In the Gospel of John, there are two references to "Thomas called Didymus."[80] This shows that the two names are being conflated together by the end of the first century. The author of John has probably taken the names from the Gospel of Thomas. He would have had access to a Greek copy of the Gospel, so assuming that Thomas was written in Greek, the name "Didymus Thomas" cannot be a translation error.

So how to explain this strange term "Didymus Thomas"? It must be yet another riddle. The creators of Thomas have expressed "twin" in the two languages that were familiar to them, Greek and Aramaic, to create the fictitious author. His name literally means "twin twin" and is a cryptic reference to the two 2s in the Thomas Code. It is all a play on words and numbers. But the author of Mark took this Thomas literally and made him into a disciple. Then, in the second century, Christians began identifying this supposed twin of Jesus with Judas, brother of Jesus.

In the Gospel of Thomas, we reach back before the Gospels, yet it is unlike anything that conventional scholars would expect from the early Jesus movement. The Gospel of Thomas is clever, very clever. It is cleverer than anything in the New Testament, and this ironically was its downfall. People preferred the simple story and explanations of the New Testament Gospels, rather than the paradoxes of the Gospel of Thomas. The sayings are terse and enigmatic; they function like riddles, intended to hide as much as to reveal. The Gospel is self-aware, using deliberate contradiction and paradox. Underlying it all is a structure based on the Greek mathematics of prime numbers, upon which a spiritual meaning is assigned. The sayings allude to this structure in a way that is almost playful. All of which indicates a sophisticated Roman work.

Yet there is another aspect of Thomas. Through it blows the wind of the Judean desert; the words of a powerful yet primitive, intelligence. The only way to make sense of this apparent contradiction is that it is the work of two different minds. The original sayings would have come from the prophetess Mary. They would have been created over a period of decades and would have circulated independently long before the Gospel of Thomas was assembled. In *The Rock and the Tower*, I trace the history of Mary, how she started in the wilderness in Judea, before moving to Jerusalem and eventually Rome where she met her martyrdom at the hands of the anti-Christ, Nero. It is this diverse history that explains the disparate nature of Thomas. The second hand at work in the Gospel is easy to identify. Mary appointed two brothers to rule her church. They were known as her "sons" and were probably nephews or other relatives. On the right hand was James who ruled the church from Jerusalem. Most likely the appointment of James was simultaneous with Mary's relocation to Rome. On the left hand was James' brother John, who was also called Mark. It was John Mark who, in the second part of her life, was the closest person to Mary. He accompanied her everywhere and acted as her secretary. This means he must have been relatively well educated because only a small minority could write at the time. No less than three of the major works of the New Testament became attributed to him; the Gospel of Mark, the Gospel of John, and the Book of Revelation. Although he wrote none of these, he was regarded as the preeminent authority for written accounts.

Both John Mark and Mary were in Rome at the time the Gospel of Thomas would have taken its final form. John was a clever man living in the most sophisticated city in the world. He was in the prime of life, his late thirties or early forties, whereas Mary was now an elderly woman. It is easy to see how John Mark became influenced by Roman culture. The Jesus movement was beginning to penetrate into aristocratic Roman households that were far from the Judean peasants who were its original audience.

So I think it is to John Mark that we can attribute the mathematical influence on the Gospel of Thomas. Working together with Mary, he would have placed the earlier sayings into a clever new structure. If this is correct, we can date the Gospel to the 50s, or very early 60s AD.

There is one clue that supports a date in the late 50s. It is at just this time that Paul wrote a letter to the church in Rome, and it is in this very letter that Simon Gathercole identifies the best candidate for the Gospel of Thomas being influenced by Paul. He suggests that Thomas 53 (3.16) on circumcision has been influenced by Paul's argument in Romans 2:25-3:2.[81] I think it is quite possible that this is indeed the case; circumcision was Paul's "hot topic" and the conclusion of Paul's argument, that it is circumcision in the spirit that is an advantage, ties in very well with the wording of Thomas 53. Romans is very different from Paul's other letters; longer, more coherent, and unique for being written for no obvious reason to a church with which he had no connection. In *The Rock and the Tower*, I suggest that Paul's real motivation for writing Romans was to set out his theology to influence Mary who is discretely greeted in Romans 16:6.[82] On the subject of circumcision, Paul may have succeeded in his aim, with Mary and John Mark sufficiently impressed to include an anti-circumcision saying in their new Gospel of the Twin. With a conventional dating of Romans to 57-58 AD, this would enable us to date the final form of Thomas to within a year or two of 58 AD.

In just a few years both Mary and Paul would be martyred in the persecution of Nero.[83] Although we have no reliable information about the fate of John Mark, it is likely that he also died in this persecution. His brother James had already been beheaded on the orders of Herod, a tragedy that seems to have left its mark on Mary (it is predicted to Mary in Luke that *"a sword will pierce through your own soul also" (Luke 2:35)*). In fact, virtually the whole original leadership structure was wiped out under persecution just as the movement was expanding rapidly throughout the Roman Empire. The result was complete confusion with no central authority. It was in this environment that a new idea of Jesus began to emerge, that he was a man who had lived and died in the recent past in Judea. This was reflected in a number of gospels that were written by outsiders; Mark, then Matthew, then Luke and then John. Each was aware of its predecessors, and each developed the story further. The Gospel of Thomas was extensively copied, and yet Mary died too early for it to become established as the preeminent authority. It was the new literalistic gospels that filled the vacuum. As they became accepted as the true account of Jesus' life, the use of Thomas began to decline. Thomas seemed increasingly odd when viewed through the worldview of the four Gospels and eventually it was declared as heretical.

The secret of the hidden mathematical structure of Thomas must have been lost almost from the beginning. We have a record from the early second-century Christian, Papias, of a Gospel written down in Rome by Mark. Conventional Christians have long identified this as the Gospel of Mark, even though Papias' description does not match our Gospel of Mark. Papias says that Mark wrote a Gospel of sayings and that it was unordered.[84] This is very much how Thomas has been seen through the ages. Ironically, it was actually exquisitely ordered, but people had forgotten the secret required to read it.[85]

After Constantine the Great, the church acquired great political power, and monks were forbidden from copying heretical gospels such as Thomas. Doctrines, such as the infallibility of Scripture, including the New Testament, became enshrined in the theology of the newly powerful church. Such doctrines were completely opposed to the real teachings of the early Jesus movement, which rejected the authority of all laws and texts, in favor of the living spirit of Jesus within. But such spiritual anarchy did not suit the bishops and priests. Once the principle of biblical inerrancy had been formulated and enforced, it stopped further inquiry. So the Gospel of Thomas disappeared completely from the world for well over a thousand years. Only at the end of the worst conflict in human history did that which had been hidden and buried become revealed again, just as the Gospel had promised.

# Note from the author

Dear reader,

I hope you enjoyed *The Thomas Code*. If you found the book interesting (not to say controversial!) then why not receive my free e-mail newsletter? This will keep you updated with developments including news, research, and upcoming books. You can subscribe at:

JesusOrigins.com/news

We live in exciting times, with new perspectives on the nature of Jesus and the origins of Christianity. Subscribe to be part of this!

Best wishes,
S.P. Laurie

# THE GOSPEL OF THOMAS

## *Structured and numbered according to The Thomas Code*

The Gospel of Thomas in the following pages is an attempt to reconstruct the Gospel in its original form and structure. Sayings have been renumbered according to the eighteen (1 to 6) in which they occur and their position within the eighteen (1 to 18). The traditional numbering is shown in brackets at the end of each saying.

Although it is convenient to number the Gospel by the eighteens this is only one level of ordering. Within each eighteen, the structure of threes and sixes is indicated by lines. A short line divides the groups of three and a longer line the groups of sixes.

The basis for the reconstruction is the complete Coptic copy of the Gospel. As discussed in the book, I believe that the Coptic text is very good, although not perfect, and a better representation of the original than the earlier Greek fragments. There are no changes made to the text until the last eighteen where it is necessary to delete four duplicate sayings. Three of the four have been repositioned as alternative versions next to the original copies of the sayings. (In one case, 5.14, I have preferred the duplicate wording.) As explained in the text, Thomas 106 is a special case by itself. It has been renumbered as 6.13.1 and not counted within the structure. The demarcation of individual sayings mostly follows the traditional numbering with a few differences that are discussed in the book.

For the first three eighteens, there are two versions that differ only in the order of some of the sayings. The first version is the original order. In the second reordered version, two pairs of sayings in each eighteen have had their positions swapped. As discussed throughout this book, this reordered version recreates the Gospel as its original authors intended us to read it. Where a saying has been moved, it has been renumbered according to its new position with the addition of an "R." It is also numbered in its original position without an "R."

The major resource for the translation was Grondin's Interlinear.[86] Numerous translations have also been consulted including those by DeConick,[87] Blatz,[88] Lambdin,[89] Davies,[90] Valantasis,[91] and Cartlidge.[92]

## Incipit

These are the hidden words that the living Jesus spoke, and Didymus Judas Thomas wrote down. And he said this: "Whoever finds the meaning of these words will not taste death." (Incipit & Th. 1)

# *First eighteen*

1.1 Jesus said: "Let him who seeks not stop seeking until he finds, and when he finds he will be troubled, and if he is troubled he will become amazed, and he will become king over the all of it." (Th. 2)

1.2 Jesus said: "If those who lead you say to you: 'Behold, the kingdom is in the sky' then the birds of the sky will become first before you. If they say to you: 'It is in the sea' then the fish will become first before you. Rather the kingdom is inside you and outside you. When you should know yourselves, then you shall be known, and you shall realize that you are the sons of the living Father. But if, however, you do not know yourselves, then you are in poverty, and you are poverty." (Th. 3)

1.3 Jesus said: "The man aged in days will not hesitate to ask a little child of seven days about the place of life, and he will live. For many who are first shall become last and they will become a single one." (Th. 4)

———

1.4 Jesus said: "Know what is in front of you and that which is hidden from you will be revealed to you. For there is nothing hidden that will not appear." (Th. 5)

1.5 His disciples asked him and said to him: "Do you want us to fast? And how shall we pray? Shall we give alms? And what rules for what we should not eat?" Jesus said: "Do not lie; and that which you hate, do not do. For all things are revealed before heaven. For there is nothing hidden which shall not appear forth, and there is nothing covered which shall not be revealed." (Th. 6)

1.6 Jesus said: "Blessed is the lion which the man will eat, and the lion become man. And cursed is the man whom the lion will eat, and the lion become man." (Th. 7)

1.7. And he said: "Man is like a wise fisherman, who cast his net into the sea. He drew it up from the sea full of little fish. Among them the wise fisherman found a good large fish. He cast out all of the little fish, down into the sea; he chose the large fish without trouble. He that has ears to hear, let him hear." (Th. 8)

1.8 Jesus said: "Behold, the sower came out, he filled his hand, he cast. Some indeed fell upon the road; the birds came and gathered them. Others fell onto the rock, and sent no root down to the earth nor did they sprout any sheaths up to the sky. And others fell onto the thorns; they choked the seed, and the worm ate them. And others fell onto the good earth, and gave good fruit up to the sky, sixty per measure and a hundred and twenty per measure." (Th. 9)

1.9 Jesus said: "I have cast fire upon the world, and behold I watch over it until it burns." (Th. 10)

––––––––

1.10 Jesus said: "This heaven shall pass away, and that which is above it shall pass away. And the dead are not alive and the living will not die. In the days you were eating that which is dead you were making it alive. When you come into the light, what will you do? On the day when you were one, you were made two. But when you have become two, what will you do?" (Th. 11)

1.11 The disciples said to Jesus: "We know you will go from us. Who shall be great over us?" Jesus said to them: "In the place to which you come, you shall go to James the Just for whom the heaven and earth came into being." (Th. 12)

1.12 Jesus said to his disciples: "Make a comparison to me, and tell me whom I am like." Simon Peter said to him: "You are like a righteous angel." Matthew said to him: "You are like a wise philosopher." Thomas said to him: "Master, my mouth will not allow me to speak whom you are like." Jesus said: "I am not your master, because you have drunk, you have become drunk from the bubbling spring that I have measured out." And he took him, went aside, and spoke to him three words. Now when Thomas came to his companions, they asked him: "What did Jesus say to you?" Thomas said to them: "If I speak to you one of the words he has spoken to me, you will take up stones and cast them at me, and fire will come out of the stones and burn you." (Th. 13)

———————————

1.13 Jesus said to them: "If you fast, you will beget a sin for yourselves; and if you pray, you will be condemned; and if you give alms, you will do evil to your spirits. And if you go into any land and walk in its regions, if they should receive you, eat what they set before you. Heal the sick among them. For that which goes into your mouth will not defile you. Rather that which comes out of your mouth is that which will defile you." (Th. 14)

1.14 Jesus said: "When you see he who was not born of woman, throw yourselves down upon your face and worship him. He is your father." (Th. 15)

1.15 Jesus said: "Perhaps men think that I am come to cast peace upon the world, and know not that I am come to cast divisions upon the earth; fire, sword, war. For five will be in a house, three will be against two, and two against three, the father against the son and the son against the father; and they shall stand as single-ones." (Th. 16)

———————

1.16 Jesus said: I will give you what eye did not see, what ear did not hear, and hand did not touch, and which did not enter into the heart of man. (Th. 17)

1.17 The disciples said to Jesus: "Tell us how our end shall be." Jesus said: "Have you discovered then the beginning, that you seek after the end? For where the beginning is, the end will be also. Blessed is he who will stand in the beginning, and he will know the end and not taste of death." (Th. 18)

1.18 Jesus said: "Blessed is he who was before he came into being. If you should be my disciples and listen to my words, these stones will minister to you. For you have five trees in Paradise which do not move summer and winter, and their leaves do not fall. He who knows them will not taste of death." (Th. 19)

## First eighteen reordered

1.1 Jesus said: "Let him who seeks not stop seeking until he finds, and when he finds he will be troubled, and if he is troubled he will become amazed, and he will become king over the all of it." (Th. 2)

1.2 Jesus said: "If those who lead you say to you: 'Behold, the kingdom is in the sky' then the birds of the sky will become first before you. If they say to you: 'It is in the sea' then the fish will become first before you. Rather the kingdom is inside you and outside you. When you should know yourselves, then you shall be known, and you shall realize that you are the sons of the living Father. But if, however, you do not know yourselves, then you are in poverty, and you are poverty." (Th. 3)

1.3R Jesus said: I will give you what eye did not see, what ear did not hear, and hand did not touch, and which did not enter into the heart of man. (Th. 17)

---

1.4 Jesus said: "Know what is in front of you and that which is hidden from you will be revealed to you. For there is nothing hidden that will not appear." (Th. 5)

1.5 His disciples asked him and said to him: "Do you want us to fast? And how shall we pray? Shall we give alms? And what rules for what we should not eat?" Jesus said: "Do not lie; and that which you hate, do not do. For all things are revealed before heaven. For there is nothing hidden which shall not appear forth, and there is nothing covered which shall not be revealed." (Th. 6)

1.6R Jesus said to them: "If you fast, you will beget a sin for yourselves; and if you pray, you will be condemned; and if you give alms, you will do evil to your spirits. And if you go into any land and walk in its regions, if they should receive you, eat what they set before you. Heal the sick among them. For that which goes into your mouth will not defile you. Rather that which comes out of your mouth, is that which will defile you." (Th. 14)

---

1.7. And he said: "Man is like a wise fisherman, who cast his net into the sea. He drew it up from the sea full of little fish. Among them the wise fisherman found a good large fish. He cast out all of the little fish, down into the sea; he chose the large fish without trouble. He that has ears to hear, let him hear." (Th. 8)

1.8 Jesus said: "Behold, the sower came out, he filled his hand, he cast. Some indeed fell upon the road; the birds came and gathered them. Others fell onto the rock, and sent no root down to the earth nor did they sprout any sheaths up to the sky. And others fell onto the thorns; they choked the seed, and the worm ate them. And others fell onto the good earth, and gave good fruit up to the sky, sixty per measure and a hundred and twenty per measure." (Th. 9)

1.9 Jesus said: "I have cast fire upon the world, and behold I watch over it until it burns." (Th. 10)

---

1.10 Jesus said: "This heaven shall pass away, and that which is above it shall pass away. And the dead are not alive and the living will not die. In the days you were eating that which is dead you were making it alive. When you come into the light, what will you do? On the day when you were one, you were made two. But when you have become two, what will you do?" (Th. 11)

1.11 The disciples said to Jesus: "We know you will go from us. Who shall be great over us?" Jesus said to them: "In the place to which you come, you shall go to James the Just for whom the heaven and earth came into being." (Th. 12)

1.12 Jesus said to his disciples: "Make a comparison to me, and tell me whom I am like." Simon Peter said to him: "You are like a righteous angel." Matthew said to him: "You are like a wise philosopher." Thomas said to him: "Master, my mouth will not allow me to speak whom you are like." Jesus said: "I am not your master, because you have drunk, you have become drunk from the bubbling spring that I have measured out." And he took him, went aside, and spoke to him three words. Now when Thomas came to his companions, they asked him: "What did Jesus say to you?" Thomas said to them: "If I speak to you one of the words he has spoken to me, you will take up stones and cast them at me, and fire will come out of the stones and burn you." (Th. 13)

---

1.13R Jesus said: "Blessed is the lion which the man will eat, and the lion become man. And cursed is the man whom the lion will eat, and the lion become man." (Th. 7)

1.14 Jesus said: "When you see he who was not born of woman, throw yourselves down upon your face and worship him. He is your father." (Th. 15)

1.15 Jesus said: "Perhaps men think that I am come to cast peace upon the world, and know not that I am come to cast divisions upon the earth; fire, sword, war. For five will be in a house, three will be against two, and two against three, the father against the son and the son against the father; and they shall stand as single-ones." (Th. 16)

---

1.16R Jesus said: "The man aged in days will not hesitate to ask a little child of seven days about the place of life, and he will live. For many who are first shall become last and they will become a single one." (Th. 4)

1.17 The disciples said to Jesus: "Tell us how our end shall be." Jesus said: "Have you discovered then the beginning, that you seek after the end? For where the beginning is, the end will be also. Blessed is he who will stand in the beginning, and he will know the end and not taste of death." (Th. 18)

1.18 Jesus said: "Blessed is he who was before he came into being. If you should be my disciples and listen to my words, these stones will minister to you. For you have five trees in Paradise which do not move summer and winter, and their leaves do not fall. He who knows them will not taste of death." (Th. 19)

## *Second eighteen*

2.1 The disciples said to Jesus: "Tell us what the kingdom of heaven is like." He said to them: "It is like a grain of mustard, smaller than all seeds; when, however, it falls onto tilled earth, it sends out a great branch, and becomes shelter for the birds of the sky." (Th. 20)

2.2 Mary said to Jesus: "Whom are your disciples like?" He said: "They are like children dwelling in a field which is not theirs. When the Lords of the field come, they will say: 'Give our field back to us.' They strip naked in their presence to give it back to them, and they give their field to them. Therefore I say this: If the Lord of the house knows that the thief is coming, he will keep watch before he comes, and will not let him dig into his house of his kingdom to carry off his vessels. You, then, keep watch from the beginning of the world. Gird up your loins with great strength, that the robbers may not find a way to come at you, since the help you will look for, they will find. May there be among you a man of understanding; when the fruit was ripe, he came quickly, his sickle in his hand, and reaped it. He that has ears to hear, let him hear." (Th. 21)

2.3 Jesus saw some little ones at the breast. He said to his disciples: "These little ones at the breast are like those who enter into the kingdom." They said to him: "Then if we be little ones, shall we enter the kingdom?" Jesus said to them: "When you make the two one, and when you make the inside as the outside, and the outside as the inside, and the upper side as the lower side; and when you make the male and the female into a single one, that the male be not male nor the female female; when you make eyes in the place of an eye, and a hand in place of a hand, and a foot in place of a foot, an image in place of an image, then you will enter into [the kingdom]." (Th. 22)

———

2.4 Jesus said: "I shall choose you, one out of a thousand, and two out of ten thousand, and they shall stand as a single one." (Th. 23)

2.5. His disciples said: "Show us the place where you are, for it is necessary for us to seek after it." He said to them: "He that has ears, let him hear. There is light within a man of light, and he becomes light to the whole world. If he does not become light, he is darkness." (Th. 24)

2.6 Jesus said: "Love your brother as your soul; guard him as the pupil of your eye." (Th. 25)

––––––––––––––––

2.7 Jesus said: "The mote which is in your brother's eye, you see; the beam, however, in your eye, you do not see. When you cast out the beam from your own eye, then you will see to cast out the mote from your brother's eye." (Th. 26)

2.8 Jesus said: If you do not fast from the world, you will not find the kingdom; if you do not keep the Sabbath as Sabbath, you will not see the father. (Th. 27)

2.9 Jesus said: "I stood in the midst of the world, and I appeared to them in the flesh. I found them all drunk, I found none among them thirsting; and my soul was afflicted for the sons of men, for they are blind in their mind and do not see, for they came into the world empty; they seek also to depart from the world empty, but now they are drunk. When they have thrown off their wine, then they will repent." (Th. 28)

––––––––

2.10 Jesus said: "If the flesh came into being because of the spirit, it is a marvel; but if the spirit because of the body, it is a marvel of marvels. But as for me, I marvel at this, how this great wealth has settled in this poverty." (Th. 29)

2.11 Jesus said: "Where there are three gods, they are gods; where there are two or one, I myself exist with him." (Th. 30)

2.12 Jesus said: "No prophet is accepted in his own village; a physician does not heal those who know him." (Th. 31)

---

2.13 Jesus said: "A city that is built on a high mountain and fortified cannot fall, nor can it be hidden." (Th. 32)

2.14 Jesus said: "What you shall hear in your ear, proclaim to the other ear on your housetops. For no man lights a lamp and puts it under a bushel, nor does he put it in a hidden place; but he puts it upon the lamp-stand, that all who go in and come out may see its light." (Th. 33)

2.15 Jesus said: "If a blind man leads a blind man, they both fall into a pit." (Th. 34)

---

2.16 Jesus said: "No one can go into the strong man's house and take it/him by force, unless he bind his hands; then he will rob his house." (Th. 35)

2.17 Jesus said: "Do not be anxious from morning to evening and from evening to morning about what you shall put on." (Th. 36)

2.18 His disciples said: "On what day will you appear to us, and on what day will we look upon you?" Jesus said: "When you strip naked and are not ashamed, and take your garments and put them beneath your feet like little children and trample them, then [you will see] the son of the living one and you shall not fear." (Th. 37)

## Second eighteen reordered

2.1 The disciples said to Jesus: "Tell us what the kingdom of heaven is like." He said to them: "It is like a grain of mustard, smaller than all seeds; when, however, it falls onto tilled earth, it sends out a great branch, and becomes shelter for the birds of the sky." (Th. 20)

2.2 Mary said to Jesus: "Whom are your disciples like?" He said: "They are like children dwelling in a field which is not theirs. When the Lords of the field come, they will say: 'Give our field back to us.' They strip naked in their presence to give it back to them, and they give their field to them. Therefore I say this: If the Lord of the house knows that the thief is coming, he will keep watch before he comes, and will not let him dig into his house of his kingdom to carry off his vessels. You, then, keep watch from the beginning of the world. Gird up your loins with great strength, that the robbers may not find a way to come at you, since the help you will look for, they will find. May there be among you a man of understanding; when the fruit was ripe, he came quickly, his sickle in his hand, and reaped it. He that has ears to hear, let him hear." (Th. 21)

2.3R Jesus said: "No one can go into the strong man's house and take it/him by force, unless he bind his hands; then he will rob his house." (Th. 35)

———————

2.4 Jesus said: "I shall choose you, one out of a thousand, and two out of ten thousand, and they shall stand as a single one." (Th. 23)

2.5. His disciples said: "Show us the place where you are, for it is necessary for us to seek after it." He said to them: "He that has ears, let him hear. There is light within a man of light, and he becomes light to the whole world. If he does not become light, he is darkness." (Th. 24)

2.6R Jesus said: "A city that is built on a high mountain and fortified cannot fall, nor can it be hidden." (Th. 32)

———————

2.7 Jesus said: "The mote which is in your brother's eye, you see; the beam, however, in your eye, you do not see. When you cast out the beam from your own eye, then you will see to cast out the mote from your brother's eye." (Th. 26)

2.8 Jesus said: If you do not fast from the world, you will not find the kingdom; if you do not keep the Sabbath as Sabbath, you will not see the father. (Th. 27)

2.9 Jesus said: "I stood in the midst of the world, and I appeared to them in the flesh. I found them all drunk, I found none among them thirsting; and my soul was afflicted for the sons of men, for they are blind in their mind and do not see, for they came into the world empty; they seek also to depart from the world empty, but now they are drunk. When they have thrown off their wine, then they will repent." (Th. 28)

----

2.10 Jesus said: "If the flesh came into being because of the spirit, it is a marvel; but if the spirit because of the body, it is a marvel of marvels. But as for me, I marvel at this, how this great wealth has settled in this poverty." (Th. 29)

2.11 Jesus said: "Where there are three gods, they are gods; where there are two or one, I myself exist with him." (Th. 30)

2.12 Jesus said: "No prophet is accepted in his own village; a physician does not heal those who know him." (Th. 31)

----

2.13R Jesus said: "Love your brother as your soul; guard him as the pupil of your eye." (Th. 25)

2.14 Jesus said: "What you shall hear in your ear, proclaim to the other ear on your housetops. For no man lights a lamp and puts it under a bushel, nor does he put it in a hidden place; but he puts it upon the lamp-stand, that all who go in and come out may see its light." (Th. 33)

2.15 Jesus said: "If a blind man leads a blind man, they both fall into a pit." (Th. 34)

----

2.16R Jesus saw some little ones at the breast. He said to his disciples: "These little ones at the breast are like those who enter into the kingdom." They said to him: "Then if we be little ones, shall we enter the kingdom?" Jesus said to them: "When you make the two one, and when you make the inside as the outside, and the outside as the inside, and the upper side as the lower side; and when you make the male and the female into a single one, that the male be not male nor the female female; when you make eyes in the place of an eye, and a hand in place of a hand, and a foot in place of a foot, an image in place of an image, then you will enter into [the kingdom]." (Th. 22)

2.17 Jesus said: "Do not be anxious from morning to evening and from evening to morning about what you shall put on." (Th. 36)

2.18 His disciples said: "On what day will you appear to us, and on what day will we look upon you?" Jesus said: "When you strip naked and are not ashamed, and take your garments and put them beneath your feet like little children and trample them, then [you will see] the son of the living one and you shall not fear." (Th. 37)

# *Third eighteen*

3.1 Jesus said: "Many times have you desired to hear these words which I speak to you, and you have none other from whom to hear them. Some days will come when you will seek after me, and you will not find me." (Th. 38)

3.2 Jesus said: "The Pharisees and the scribes have taken the keys of knowledge; they have hidden them. They did not go in, and those who wanted to go in they did not allow. You, however, be as cunning as serpents and as innocent as doves." (Th. 38)

3.3 Jesus said: "A vine was planted apart from the Father, and since it is not established it will be pulled up by its roots and destroyed." (Th. 40)

---

3.4 Jesus said: "He who has in his hand, to him shall be given; and he who has not, from him shall be taken even the little that he has." (Th. 41)

3.5 Jesus said: "Become passers-by." (Th. 42)

3.6 His disciples said to him: "Who are you, that you speak these things to us?" "From what I say to you, you do not understand who I am, but you have become as the Jews; for they love the tree and hate its fruit, and they love the fruit and hate the tree." (Th. 43)

---

3.7 Jesus said: "Whoever blasphemes against the Father will be forgiven, and whoever blasphemes against the Son will be forgiven but whoever blasphemes against the holy spirit will not be forgiven, either on earth or in heaven." (Th. 44)

3.8 Jesus said: "They do not harvest grapes from thorns, nor gather figs from thistles; they do not yield fruit. A good man brings forth a good thing from his treasure; a bad man bring forth evil things from his evil treasure which is in his heart, and he says evil things; for out of the abundance of his heart he brings forth evil things." (Th. 45)

3.9 Jesus said: "From Adam to John the Baptist there is none born of woman who is higher than John the Baptist, so as to lower his eyes. I spoke however this: He who shall be among you as a little one shall know the kingdom, and shall be raised up above John." (Th. 46)

————

3.10 Jesus said: "A man cannot ride two horses or draw two bows, and nor can a servant serve two masters; or he will honor the one and despise the other. A man does not drink old wine and immediately desire to drink new wine; and they do not pour new wine into old wineskins, lest they burst, nor do they pour old wine into new wineskins, lest it spoil. They do not sew an old patch on a new garment, because a split will come." (Th. 47)

3.11 Jesus said: "If two make peace with one another in this house alone, they shall say to the mountain, 'Move away' and it shall move." (Th. 48)

3.12 Jesus said: "Blessed are the single-ones and the chosen, for you shall find the kingdom; for you came from there, and shall go there again." (Th. 49)

————————

3.13 Jesus said: "If they say to you, 'From where have you come?' Tell them, 'We have come from the light, the place where the light came into being by his hand himself. He [stood], and he revealed himself in their image.' If they say to you: 'Are you him?' say, 'We are his sons, and we are the chosen of the living father.' If they ask you, 'What is the sign of your Father in you?' tell them, 'It is a movement and a rest.'" (Th. 50)

3.14 His disciples said to him: "On what day will the rest of the dead come? And on what day will the new world come?" He said to them, "That which you look for has come, but you know it not." (Th. 51)

3.15 His disciples said to him: "Twenty-four prophets spoke in Israel, and they all spoke of you." He said to them: "You have left out the living one in your presence and have spoken about the dead." (Th. 52)

———

3.16 His disciples said to him: "Is circumcision beneficial or not?" He said to them: "Were it beneficial, their father would beget them from their mother circumcised. But the true circumcision in spirit is entirely profitable." (Th. 53)

3.17 Jesus said: "Blessed are the poor, for yours is the kingdom of heaven." (Th. 54)

3.18 Jesus said: "Whoever does not hate his father and his mother cannot be my disciple, and whoever does not hate his brothers and his sisters and take up his cross like me, he shall not be worthy of me." (Th. 55)

## *Third eighteen reordered*

3.1 Jesus said: "Many times have you desired to hear these words which I speak to you, and you have none other from whom to hear them. Some days will come when you will seek after me, and you will not find me." (Th. 38)

3.2R Jesus said: "Blessed are the single-ones and the chosen, for you shall find the kingdom; for you came from there, and shall go there again." (Th. 49)

3.3 Jesus said: "A vine was planted apart from the Father, and since it is not established it will be pulled up by its roots and destroyed." (Th. 40)

———

3.4 Jesus said: "He who has in his hand, to him shall be given; and he who has not, from him shall be taken even the little that he has." (Th. 41)

3.5 Jesus said: "Become passers-by." (Th. 42)

3.6 His disciples said to him: "Who are you, that you speak these things to us?" "From what I say to you, you do not understand who I am, but you have become as the Jews; for they love the tree and hate its fruit, and they love the fruit and hate the tree." (Th. 43)

---

3.7 Jesus said: "Whoever blasphemes against the Father will be forgiven, and whoever blasphemes against the Son will be forgiven but whoever blasphemes against the holy spirit will not be forgiven, either on earth or in heaven." (Th. 44)

3.8R Jesus said: "If they say to you, 'From where have you come?' Tell them, 'We have come from the light, the place where the light came into being by his hand himself. He [stood], and he revealed himself in their image.' If they say to you: 'Are you him?' say, 'We are his sons, and we are the chosen of the living father.' If they ask you, 'What is the sign of your Father in you?' tell them, 'It is a movement and a rest.'" (Th. 50)

3.9 Jesus said: "From Adam to John the Baptist there is none born of woman who is higher than John the Baptist, so as to lower his eyes. I spoke however this: He who shall be among you as a little one shall know the kingdom, and shall be raised up above John." (Th. 46)

---

3.10 Jesus said: "A man cannot ride two horses or draw two bows, and nor can a servant serve two masters; or he will honor the one and despise the other. A man does not drink old wine and immediately desire to drink new wine; and they do not pour new wine into old wineskins, lest they burst, nor do they pour old wine into new wineskins, lest it spoil. They do not sew an old patch on a new garment, because a split will come." (Th. 47)

3.11 Jesus said: "If two make peace with one another in this house alone, they shall say to the mountain, 'Move away' and it shall move." (Th. 48)

3.12R Jesus said: "The Pharisees and the scribes have taken the keys of knowledge; they have hidden them. They did not go in, and those who wanted to go in they did not allow. You, however, be as cunning as serpents and as innocent as doves." (Th. 38)

---

3.13R Jesus said: "They do not harvest grapes from thorns, nor gather figs from thistles; they do not yield fruit. A good man brings forth a good thing from his treasure; a bad man bring forth evil things from his evil treasure which is in his heart, and he says evil things; for out of the abundance of his heart he brings forth evil things." (Th. 45)

3.14 His disciples said to him: "On what day will the rest of the dead come? And on what day will the new world come?" He said to them, "That which you look for has come, but you know it not." (Th. 51)

3.15 His disciples said to him: "Twenty-four prophets spoke in Israel, and they all spoke of you." He said to them: "You have left out the living one in your presence and have spoken about the dead." (Th. 52)

---

3.16 His disciples said to him: "Is circumcision beneficial or not?" He said to them: "Were it beneficial, their father would beget them from their mother circumcised. But the true circumcision in spirit is entirely profitable." (Th. 53)

3.17 Jesus said: "Blessed are the poor, for yours is the kingdom of heaven." (Th. 54)

3.18 Jesus said: "Whoever does not hate his father and his mother cannot be my disciple, and whoever does not hate his brothers and his sisters and take up his cross like me, he shall not be worthy of me." (Th. 55)

# *Fourth eighteen*

4.1 Jesus said: "He who has known the world has found a corpse, and he who has found a corpse, the world is not worthy of him." (Th. 56)

4.2 Jesus said: "The kingdom of the Father is like a man who had [good] seed. His enemy came by night, he sowed a weed among the good seed. The man did not allow them to pull up the weed. He said to them: 'So that you do not go to pull up the weed, and pull up the grain with it.' For on the day of harvest the weeds will be visible and will be pulled up and burned." (Th. 57)

4.3 Jesus said: "Blessed is the man who has been troubled. He has found life." (Th. 58)

---

4.4 Jesus said: "Look upon he who lives while you are living, lest you die, and seek to see him, and you are not able to." (Th. 59)

4.5 They saw a Samaritan carrying a lamb going into Judaea. He said to his disciples: "That one is around the lamb." They said to him: "That he may kill it and eat it." He said to them: "While it is living he will not eat it. Only if he kill it and it becomes a corpse." They said: "Otherwise he cannot do it." He said to them: "You also, seek for yourselves a place within rest, so that you do not become corpses and be eaten." (Th. 60)

4.6 Jesus said: "Two shall rest upon a bed; one shall die, the other live." Salome said: "Who are you man? While out of one, you have climbed onto my bed [couch], and ate from my table." Jesus said to her: "I am he who is from that which is equal; to me was given of the things of my Father." "I am your disciple." "Therefore I say, when he should be equal he will be filled with light, but when he should be divided he will be filled with darkness." (Th. 61)

---

4.7 Jesus said: "I tell my mysteries to those [who are worthy] of my mysteries. What your right hand shall do, let not your left hand know what it does." (Th. 62)

4.8 Jesus said: "There was a wealthy man who had many riches. He said: 'I will use my riches that I may sow and reap and plant, and fill my treasure house with fruit, that I may have need of nothing.' These were his thoughts in his heart. And in that night he died. He that has ears, let him hear." (Th. 63)

4.9 Jesus said: "A man was having some guests, and when he had prepared the dinner he sent his servant to call the guests. He came to the first; he said to him: 'My Lord calls you.' He said: 'I have money with some merchants. They are coming to me in the evening. I will go and give them orders. Please excuse me from the dinner.' He went to another; he said to him: 'My Lord calls you.' He said to him: 'I have bought a house, and they require a day of my time. I will not be available.' He came to another; he said to him: 'My master calls you.' He said to him: 'My friend is about to be married, and I am to hold a dinner. I shall not be able to come. Please excuse me from the dinner.' He went to another; he said to him: 'My master calls you.' He said him: 'I have bought a village; I go to collect the rent. I shall not be able to come. Please excuse me.' The servant came, he said to his master: 'Those whom you summoned to the dinner have excused themselves.' The master said to his servant: 'Go out to the roads. Bring those whom you shall find, that they may dine.' The buyers and the merchants [will] not [enter] the places of my Father." (Th. 64)

———

4.10 He said: "A good man had a vineyard. He gave it to some tenants that they might work it, and he receive the fruit from their hand. He sent his servant, that the tenants might give him the fruit of the vineyard. They seized his servant, they beat him, and almost killed him. The servant came and told his master. His master said: 'Perhaps they did not know him.' He sent another servant; the tenants beat the other one. Then the master sent his son. He said: 'Perhaps they will be ashamed before my son.' Those tenants, since they knew that he was the heir to the vineyard, they seized him and killed him. He that has ears, let him hear." (Th. 65)

4.11 Jesus said: "Show me the stone which the builders rejected; it is the cornerstone." (Th. 66)

4.12 Jesus said: "He who knows everything, but lacks himself, lacks everything." (Th. 67)

———————————

4.13 Jesus said: "Blessed are you when they hate you, and persecute you, and they do not find a place in the place where they persecuted you." (Th. 68)

4.14 Jesus said: "Blessed are they who have been persecuted in their mind; they are those who have known the father in truth." (Th. 69a)

4.15 "Blessed are those who are hungry, that they may fill the belly of he who desires." (Th. 69b)

———————

4.16 Jesus said: "When you begat that one in yourselves, he who you have will save you. If you do not have that one in you, he that you do not have will kill you." (Th. 70)

4.17 Jesus said: "I will des[troy this] house, and none shall be able to build it [again]." (Th. 71)

4.18 [A man said] to him: Speak to my brothers, that they may divide my father's possessions with me. He said to him: "O man, who made me a divider?" He turned to his disciples. He said to them: "Truly, do I exist as one who divides?" (Th. 72)

## *Fifth eighteen*

5.1 Jesus said: "The harvest indeed is great, but the laborers are few; but pray to the Lord, so he might send laborers into the harvest." (Th. 73)

5.2 He said: "Lord, there are many around the well, but no one in the well." Jesus said: "There are many standing at the door, but the single ones are they who shall enter the bridal chamber." (Th. 74 & 75)

5.3 Jesus said: "The kingdom of the Father is like a merchant who had some goods; he found a pearl. That merchant was wise. He sold the goods, and bought for himself the pearl alone. You also, seek after his treasure which does not perish but endures, where moth does not enter to eat, nor does worm destroy." (Th. 76)

---

5.4 Jesus said: "I am the light that is over them all. I am the all of it, the all of it came out of me and the all of it bursts up to me. Split a timber, I am there. Raise up the stone, and you shall find me there." (Th. 77)

5.5 Jesus said: "Why did you come out to the field? To see a reed shaken by the wind? And to see a man clothed in soft garments [like your] kings and your powerful ones? These are clothed in soft garments and they cannot know the truth." (Th. 78)

5.6 A woman in the crowd said to him: "Blessed is the womb which bore you, and the breasts which nourished you." He said to her: "Blessed are they who have heard the word of the Father and have truly kept it. For there shall be days when you will say: Blessed is the womb which has not conceived, and the breasts which have not given suck." (Th. 79)

---

5.7 Jesus said: "Whoever has known the world has found the body, and whoever has found the body, the world is not worthy of him." (Th. 80)

5.8 Jesus said: "Whoever has become rich, let him become king, and he who has power let him renounce it." (Th. 81)

*Duplicates 5.7/5.8:*

*Jesus said: "He who has found the world and become rich, let him deny the world." (Th. 110)*

*Jesus says: "He who shall find himself, of him the world is not worthy." (Interpolation in Th. 111)*

5.9 Jesus said: "He who is close to me is close to the fire, and he who is far from me is far from the kingdom." (Th. 82)

———

5.10 Jesus said: "The images are revealed to the man, and the light which is in them is hidden in the image of the light of the father. He will be revealed forth, and his image is hidden by his light." (Th. 83)

5.11 Jesus said: "The days you look upon your likeness, you rejoice; but when you look upon your images which came to be before you, they neither die nor become manifest, how much will you bear?" (Th. 84)

5.12 Jesus said: "Adam came into being out of a great power and a great richness, and he was not worthy of you. For if he had been worthy, he [would] not [have tasted of death]." (Th. 85)

———

5.13 Jesus said: "[The foxes have] the[ir dens] and the birds have [their] nests, but the son of man has no place to lay his head and to rest." (Th. 86)

5.14 Jesus said: "Woe to the flesh which depends upon the soul; woe to the soul which depends upon the flesh." (Th. 112)

*Duplicate:*

*Jesus said: "Wretched is the body which depends on a body, and wretched is the soul which depends on these two." (Th. 87)*

5.15 Jesus said: "The angels come to you, and the prophets, and they give to you what is yours; and you also, give what you have and say to yourselves: On which day do they come and take what is theirs?" (Th. 88)

————

5.16 Jesus said: "Why do you wash the outside of the cup? Do you not understand that whoever made the inside is also he who made the outside?" (Th. 89)

5.17 Jesus said: "Come to me, for easy is my yoke and my lordship is gentle, and you shall find rest for yourselves." (Th. 90)

5.18 They said to him: "Tell us who you are so that we may believe in you." He said to them: "You examine the face of the heavens and the earth, but he who is in your presence you do not know, and you do not know how to examine this moment." (Th. 91)

# Sixth eighteen

6.1 Jesus said: "Seek, and you shall find; but those things you asked me in those days, I did not tell you then. Now I wish to tell them, and you seek not after them." (Th. 92)

*Alternative start to 6.1: Jesus [said]: "He who seeks will find, [and he who knocks] it will be opened to him." (Th. 94)*

6.2 "Do not give that which is holy to the dogs, lest they cast them on the dung heap; do not cast pearls to the swine lest they become [...]." (Th. 93)

6.3 [Jesus said]: "If you have money, do not lend it at interest, but give [it] to him from whom you will not take it back." (Th. 95)

———————

6.4 Jesus said: "The kingdom of the Father is like a woman who took a little yeast and [hid] it in some dough; she made large loaves of it. He that has ears, let him hear." (Th. 96)

6.5 Jesus said: "The kingdom of the [Father] is like a woman carrying a jar full of meal; walking on a road a long way the handle of the jar broke; the meal poured out behind her on the road. She did not know, she did not realize her loss. When she came into her house, she put the jar down; she found it empty." (Th. 97)

6.6 Jesus said: "The kingdom of the Father is like a man wanting to kill a powerful one. He drew the sword in his house and drove it into the wall, that he might know that his hand would be strong. Then he slew the powerful one." (Th. 98)

———————

6.7 The disciples said to him: "Your brothers and you mother are standing outside." He said to them: "Those here who do the will of my Father, these are my brothers and my mother; these are they who shall enter into the kingdom of my Father." (Th. 99)

6.8 They showed Jesus a gold piece and said to him: "They who belong to Caesar demand the taxes from us." He said to them: "Give what is Caesar's to Caesar, give what is God's to God, and that which is mine give to me." (Th. 100)

6.9 Jesus said: "He who shall not hate his father and mother like me cannot be my [disciple], and he who shall [not] love [his father] and his mother like me cannot be my [disciple]; for my mother [...] but my true [mother] gave me life." (Th. 101)

———————

6.10 And Jesus said: "Woe to them, the Pharisees! For they are like a dog sleeping in the manger of some oxen; for he neither eats, nor does he let the oxen eat." (Th. 102)

6.11 Jesus said: Blessed is the man who knows in what part the robbers are coming, that he may rise and gather his [domain] and gird up his loins before they come in. (Th. 103)

6.12 They said [to him]: "Come, pray today and fast." Jesus said: "What is the sin that I have done, or in what have I been defeated? But when the bridegroom comes out of the bridal chamber, then let them fast and pray." (Th. 104)

——————————————

6.13 Jesus said: "He who shall know father and mother shall be called the son of a whore." (Th. 105)

[6.13.1 Jesus said: "When you make the two one, you shall be sons of man, and when you say: 'Mountain, move away,' he shall be moved." (Th. 106)]

6.14 Jesus said: "The kingdom is like a shepherd who had a hundred sheep. One of them, the largest, went astray. He left the ninety-nine and sought after the one till he found it. Having labored, he said to the sheep: I love you more than the ninety-nine." (Th. 107)

6.15 Jesus said: "Whoever drinks from my mouth shall become like me; I myself will become he, and the hidden thing shall appear to him." (Th. 108)

————

6.16 Jesus said: "The kingdom is like a man who had in his field a [hidden] treasure about which he did not know; and [after] he died he left it to his [son. The] son also did not know; he took (possession of) that field and sold it. The man who bought it came to plough, and [found] the treasure. He began to lend money at interest to whomsoever he chose." (Th. 109)

6.17 Jesus said: "The heavens shall be rolled up and the earth in your presence, and he who lives out of the living one shall not see death." His disciples said to him: "On what day will the kingdom come?" "It comes not with observation. They will not say: Behold, that side or: Behold there! But the kingdom of the father is spread out upon the earth, and men do not see it." (Th. 111 & 113)

6.18 Simon Peter said to them: "Let Mary come out from us, for women are not worthy of the life." Jesus said: "Behold, I shall lead her, that I may make her male, so that she will also be a living spirit resembling you males. For every woman who makes herself male shall enter into the kingdom of heaven." (Th. 114)

*(Th. 110 duplicate moved to 5.7-8)*

*(Th. 111 interpolation moved to 5.7-8)*

*(Th. 112 duplicate moved to 5.14)*

# Acknowledgements

I would like to thank my wife, Angela, for her comments on the manuscript and her proofreading skills. As ever, her support and encouragement have been vital.

Thanks also to Christina Cutting for copyediting and converting my British English to US English. And to Jay McNair who has done an admirable job of typesetting both the print and e-book versions.

# APPENDICES

# Appendix I

# The "five in a house" saying in Luke and Matthew

This appendix considers the relationship between the Luke, Matthew, Micah and Thomas versions of the "five in a house" saying. It supplements the material in Chapter 4.

## Why Luke must have used Thomas

This is the Luke version of 1.15:

> "I came to cast fire on the earth, and would that it were already kindled! I have a baptism to be baptized with, and how great is my distress until it is accomplished! Do you think that I have come to give peace on earth? No, I tell you, but rather division. For from now on in one house there will be five divided, three against two and two against three. They will be divided, father against son and son against father, mother against daughter and daughter against mother, mother-in-law against her daughter-in-law and daughter-in-law against mother-in-law." (Luke 12:49-53 ESV)

As in the Thomas version, Jesus has come to cast fire and does not bring peace but rather divisions. However, it has all been considerably toned down. The fire is explicitly connected with the spirit and is brought by Jesus' "baptism," being his crucifixion and resurrection. This idea of the spirit being represented as fire is also found in Acts, in which the author of Luke describes the spirit as coming down

275

in tongues of flame at Pentecost. Luke does not have the "sword" and "war" of Thomas but goes straight from "divisions" to the arguments within a household. We have seen how the sword and armed conflict do appear in Luke but have been relocated to the arrest of Jesus. The link with violence is more explicit in the Matthew version:

> "Do not think that I have come to bring peace to the earth. I have not come to bring peace, but a sword. For I have come to set a man against his father, and a daughter against her mother, and a daughter-in-law against her mother-in-law. And a person's enemies will be those of his own household." (Matthew 10:34-36 ESV)

Under the conventional explanation, Luke is either using Matthew or both are using the supposed (but probably fictitious!) lost sayings Gospel called "Q." The two Gospels contain a lot of shared material not found in the first synoptic Gospel, Mark, and if Q did not exist, then Luke must have copied Matthew directly. However, when we look at the above passage in Luke, we can find features that are inexplicable if Luke only had Matthew as a source. Instead, the author of Luke must have had access to both Matthew and the version of the saying found in Thomas.

### Why should Luke expand Matthew?

There is no reason why Luke should introduce the concept of the "three" and "two" unless this was in the author's source. The "two" and "three" are not found directly in Matthew. They are implicit in Matthew once we realize that the younger generation consists of three individuals (son, daughter, and daughter-in-law) and the older generation has two individuals (father, mother/mother-in-law). But this is not obvious from a casual reading!

## Why does Luke expand the opposed pairs to include the older generation against the younger?

The point of the Matthew passage and its source in Micah is that those of the younger generation are rebelling against their elders. However, Luke changes this so that as well as the younger generation being against the older generation, the older is also against the younger. So we get, for example, "mother against daughter and daughter against mother." There must be something in the author of Luke's source to justify this change.

## The order of the relationships in Luke is wrong

The Gospel of Luke develops the relationships to explain "three against two and two against three" in a most pedantic fashion. But the order is wrong! We should have:

Son against father, father against son
Daughter against mother, mother against daughter
Daughter-in-law against mother-in-law, mother-in-law against
    daughter

It should be in this order because:

1. It would give "three against two and two against three."
2. It is consistent with Matthew, which starts with "a man against his father" etc.

But Luke does not have this! Instead, it reverses the order of each pair:

"Father against son, son against father,"
"Mother against daughter, daughter against mother,"
"Mother-in-law against daughter, daughter-in-law against
    mother-in-law,"

This is not "three against two and two against three" but "two against three and three against two"!

## Luke must have used Thomas as well as Matthew

Each one of these otherwise inexplicable features of the Luke version relates to something in Thomas:

> Thomas has the "three against two and two against three."
> Thomas has opposed pairs so that the younger is against the older and the older against the younger.
> Thomas has "the father against the son and the son against the father," which is the same way and order that Luke starts the list of three opposed pairs.

What the author of Luke has done is to start with 1.15 and has expanded the relationships to be consistent with Matthew by including "mother against daughter" and "mother-in-law against daughter-in-law". So the author of Luke must have had both the Thomas and Matthew variants of the saying.

# *Matthew, Micah and Thomas*

So we come to the Matthew version:

> *"Do not think that I have come to bring peace to the earth. I have not come to bring peace, but a sword. For I have come to set a man against his father, and a daughter against her mother, and a daughter-in-law against her mother-in-law. And a person's enemies will be those of his own household." (Matthew 10:34-36 ESV)*

Like Thomas, it has "peace" and "sword." However, the saying the makes clear that the conflict is within a family. This is why "fire" and "war" should be omitted. The Matthew version is much closer to the ultimate source in Micah:

> *Believe not in a friend, trust not in a leader, From her who is lying in thy bosom keep the openings of thy mouth. For a son is dishonoring a father, A daughter hath stood against her mother, A daughter-in-law against her moth-*

*er-in-law, The enemies of each [are] the men of his house.*
*(Micah 5:5-6)*

The point of the Micah passage is justifying the exile as a just pun-
ishment by YHWH. It was the supposed degenerate behavior of the
Jews that led to the defeat by the Babylonians. The law of YHWH was
to respect your elders; one of the Ten Commandments is to honor
your father and mother. Also, a wife should obey her husband. But
before the exile, the inhabitants of Judea and Jerusalem had turned
these commands on their head. A man can no longer trust his wife.
The younger generation dishonor and oppose the older generation.
As a result of these moral failings, Judah will be punished by defeat
at the hands of the Babylonians and the exile.

There are two key points concerning the use of Micah by Matthew:

- The use of the Micah passage does not make any sense in the
  context of Matthew.
- Matthew contains additions to the Micah passage that we
  would not expect unless the author of Matthew had another
  source they were following.

### Why does Matthew quote the Micah passage?

In Matthew, the Micah passage is connected to the difficulties
that the Jesus movement will bring upon families: *"Whoever loves
father or mother more than me is not worthy of me, and whoever loves son
or daughter more than me is not worthy of me."* (Matthew 10:37) This
is a toned-down version of the instruction to put aside father and
mother. But going against your father and mother is what Micah is
condemning! So quoting Micah only serves to emphasize how the
Jesus movement is going against the law of YHWH. Elsewhere, the
author of Matthew is keen to emphasize that the law has not been
abolished but still applies.

## Why does Matthew bring in a sword to the Micah quote?

There is no sword in the Micah quote. A sword does appear a little before the Micah passage, but this is the Babylonian sword that will fall upon Jerusalem. In Matthew, the sword is used quite differently as a metaphor for the family disagreements. Why should Matthew introduce the sword in this way?

We must again emphasize how politically sensitive this point is. The Matthew passage specifically says that Jesus has not come to bring peace to the earth but a sword. This, on its face, is an incitement to war and violence. It would be reckless to introduce this aspect into a saying about family disagreements. Instead, it must have come from the author of Matthew's source.

The solution to these points is that the author of Matthew must be reacting to a source that is embarrassing and which they are attempting to tame. This is explained if the author of Matthew has (i) 1.15 from Thomas and (ii) has recognized the connection to Micah:

- He attempts to downplay the incitement to violence by eliminating "war" and "fire" and relating the sword to family disagreements.

- He reverts to the Micah version to avoid reference to the older generation being against the younger, which is contrary to Jewish law. The line "the father against the son and the son against the father" would have been particularly offensive because it also suggests a conflict between the Father, God, and the Son, Jesus.

Neither Luke nor Matthew explicitly has the last line of 1.15, that they will stand as single ones. However, Luke may be equating the "single one" with the one who strikes off the ear of the high priest's servant. And Matthew would have assumed it is covered by the last line of Micah: *"The enemies of each [are] the men of his house."*

# Appendix II

# Reconstruction of the "three gods" saying

This appendix considers the original form of the "three gods" saying, Thomas 30. It supplements the material in Chapter 5.

## The reconstruction of 2.11 (Th. 30)

We have essentially three separate versions of this saying. One in Coptic Thomas, one from the Greek papyrus fragments, and a passage in the Gospel of Matthew. The three versions are:

Coptic:

> *Jesus said: "Where there are three gods, they are gods; where there are two or one, I myself exist with him."*

Greek:

> *Jesus said: "Where there are three, they are gods. And where there is one, [I say] I am with him. Lift the stone and you will find me there. Split the timber and I am there."*

Matthew:

> *Truly, I say to you, whatever you bind on earth shall be bound in heaven, and whatever you loose on earth shall be loosed in heaven. Again I say to you, if two of you agree on earth about anything they ask, it will be done for them by my Father in heaven. For where two or three are gathered in my name, there am I among them." Matthew 18:18-20*

The challenge is to recreate the original saying that could give rise to these three variants.

### Which version is closest to the original?

The second half of the two Thomas versions differ, so which is closest to the original? The Coptic has "two" and "one" whereas the Greek just has "one." To compound the confusion, the related Matthew saying has "three" and "two." However, we should prefer the Coptic version for three reasons:

1. The sequence "three," "two," and then "one" which is found in the Coptic makes sense!

2. If Matthew is based on the Thomas saying, then the author of Matthew must have had a version with "two" in the second half. (Matthew does not have "one," but this is to be expected because "one" would not at all suit the meaning that the author of Matthew gives to the saying.)

3. There is evidence that the Greek version of 2.3 has been subject to modification. It has an additional sub-saying appended to the end: *"Lift the stone and you will find me there. Split the timber and I am there."* In the Coptic Gospel, this is part of Thomas 77, and there is evidence that supports this as being the original placing. Most significantly, there is a passage in the Gospel of John which shows links to Thomas 77, including the sub-saying.[93] It would seem that the author of John knew a version of Thomas 77 which was very like our Coptic copy. If so then the sub-saying originally belonged with Thomas 77 and has been moved in the Greek copy to Thomas 30.

### The reconstruction

We will reconstruct the original as being very close, but not identical, to the Coptic:

> *Where there are three (gods) they are gods; where there are*
> *two I am there; where there is one I am with him. (Recon-*
> *struction of 2.11)*

This makes more sense than the existing Coptic. It ties in with 1.15 in that we have the countdown from three, two, and one, with three being God and two being Jesus. We will now show how we can get from this reconstruction to each of the three extant early versions.


## The Coptic

The Coptic has abbreviated the saying by missing out the element in bold below and replacing it by "or":

> *Where there are three gods they are gods; where there are*
> *two [I am there; where there is] one I am with him.*

Such a change would make sense to a copyist or translator as the original wording appears to be redundant.


## The Greek

The Greek has done something more interesting. It has omitted the second element in bold:

> *Where there are three they are gods; [where there are*
> *two I am there;] where there is one I am with him.*

This element has been replaced by the reordered end of Thomas 77. We can see that the omitted phrase suggests the replacement:

> *"where there are two I am there"*

Replaced by:

> *"Lift the stone and you will find me there. Split the timber*
> *and I am there."*

Note that this sub-saying gives two places where Jesus is, the stone and the timber!

## Matthew

The author of Matthew has applied a Jewish understanding to the saying by relating it to the only place in scripture where people are called gods, Psalm 82.

> I said, "You are gods, sons of the Most High, all of you; nevertheless, like men you shall die, and fall like any prince." Arise, O God, judge the earth; for you shall inherit all the nations! (Psalm 82:6-8)

This was interpreted by the Jews as applying to the Sanhedrin, the human council of God on earth. The author of Matthew concludes that the meaning of 2.3 is that a gathering of three Christians are called "gods" because they have the power to "judge the earth" as a new Sanhedrin council. He extends the three to two because of the next line in 2.3, which says that Jesus is with the two. So he gives any two or three the power to "loose and bind," a power which his Gospel has already granted to Peter earlier. So he concludes that the saying is about three or two Christians being given authority when gathered together. The "one" does not fit this interpretation and so is omitted. However, Jesus does say that the two or three have to be gathered "in my name" which may be the author of Matthew's interpretation of "where there is one I am with him."

## Direct evidence for the reconstruction

We can find direct early evidence that supports the reconstruction showing that it did exist in this form. The evidence is from the fourth-century Commentary on the Diatessaron by Ephrem 14.24.[94] The Diatessaron was a harmony of the four gospels produced by Tatian and probably written in Syriac. Tatian mostly follows Matthew's order and is commenting on the Matthew text above when he quotes extracts from what is obviously a version of Thomas 30. These extracts appear in reverse order:[95]

> *"Where one is, I [am there]"*
>
> *"Where two are, I [am there]"*
>
> *"When there are three..."*

The last is the start of the phrase "Where there are three (gods) they are gods." The commentary does not give the remainder of this phrase but says that when there are three they are assembled in the church, the *"perfect body, the seal of the Messiah."* Ephrem is trying to make sense of the saying in relation to the Diatessaron, which follows Matthew at this point. The original version of the saying probably had "gods," but Ephrem interpreted this in relation to the Matthew account, so that the assembly of gods becomes the church, which draws its divine status from Jesus. The other two extracts of the saying are almost identical to the reconstruction.

We conclude that Ephrem writing in the fourth-century must have had access to a saying that is very like our reconstruction.

# Appendix III

# Links between the beginning and the end of the Gospel

This Appendix sets out the links between sayings in the first and last eighteens together with the question saying, 5.18. It supplements the material in Chapter 15.

## Links between 1.2, 6.17 and 5.18

**Question saying (5.18)**

Question:

> *They said to him: "Tell us who you are so that we may believe in you."*

Response:

> *He said to them: "You examine the face of the heavens and the earth, but he who is in your presence you do not know, and you do not know how to examine this moment." (Th. 91)*

**Second from last in the Gospel (last bookend)**

> *6.17 Jesus said: "The heavens shall be rolled up and the earth in your presence, and he who lives out of the living one shall not see death." His disciples said to him: "On what day will the kingdom come?" "It comes not with*

*observation. They will not say: Behold, that side or: Behold there! But the kingdom of the father is spread out upon the earth, and men do not see it." (Th. 111 & 113)*

## Second from first in the Gospel (first bookend)

*1.2 Jesus said: "If those who lead you say to you: 'Behold, the kingdom is in the sky' then the birds of the sky will become first before you. If they say to you: 'It is in the sea' then the fish will become first before you. Rather the kingdom is inside you and outside you. When you should know yourselves, then you shall be known, and you shall realize that you are the sons of the living Father. But if, however, you do not know yourselves, then you are in poverty, and you are poverty." (Th. 3)*

We will cover the links between these three saying under the headings below.

## Heavens, earth and sea

All three sayings reject two physical places. In 5.18 and 6.17, it is the heavens (or sky) and the earth. In 1.2, it is the idea that the kingdom is in the sky or sea that is rejected.

Similar phraseology is used in both the response in 5.18 and saying 6.17. Both mention the heavens and earth, and they both have an identical Coptic phrase translated as "in your presence." In 5.18 the disciples do not know the one in their presence, whereas in 6.17, the heaven and earth are rolled up in their presence. The disciples think that reality is what is before them, but Jesus challenges this notion by saying that reality will be dissolved in plain view.

## The kingdom is not to be visibly discerned

Both 6.17 and 1.2 use similar terminology to express this concept. In 6.17 they will not say about the kingdom: *"Behold, that side or: Behold there!."* In 1.2 those *"who lead you"* say *"Behold, the kingdom is in the sky"* or *"It is in the sea"* but are wrong. In 6.17, the kingdom is *"spread out upon the earth, and men do not see it,"* whereas, in 1.2 it is *"inside you and outside you."*

## Knowing the Living One

All three have similar terminology about knowing the living one:

- 5.18: *"...he who is in your presence you do not know..."*
- 6.17: *"The heavens shall be rolled up and the earth in your presence, and he who lives out of the living one shall not see death."*
- 1.2 *"When you should know yourselves, then you shall be known, and you shall realize that you are the sons of the living Father."*

## Saying 6.17 as a reverse of 5.18

We can see that 6.17 is a reversal of the response to 5.18. Everything in the response corresponds to something in 6.17, but in the opposite sense:

- In 5.18 the disciples examine heaven and earth, but in 6.17 these are dissolved in front of them.
- In 5.18 the disciples do not know the one in their presence (Jesus), but in 6.17 if they live in the living one (Jesus) then they will not know death.
- In 5.18 the disciples do not examine this moment, but in 6.17 they ask Jesus when the kingdom will come. In response, he tells them it is already spread out upon the earth.

It is significant that these links cross the divide between Thomas 111 and 113, as do the links between 1.2 and 6.17. This supports the idea that Thomas 111 and 113 are two parts of one saying.

## *Links to the "end and beginning" saying 1.17*

Saying 1.2 is linked to 1.17, which is the symmetrical saying in the first eighteen, so we should not be surprised to find links between 1.17 and 6.17. Moreover, these two sayings also occupy identical positions in the first and final eighteens. The links are:

- In both sayings, the disciples ask Jesus very similar questions. In 1.17, "Tell us how our end shall be"; and in 6.17, "On what day will the kingdom come?"
- In both cases, Jesus denies the concept of the kingdom coming at the "end." In 1.17, he tells them to look to the beginning, and in 6.17 that the kingdom is spread upon the earth.
- In 1.17 Jesus promises that one who stands in the beginning "will know the end and not taste of death." In saying 6.17, the disciples will know the end by observing the dissolution of heaven and earth and "he who lives in the living one shall not see death.

# Appendix IV

# Reconstructing the last eighteen

It is in the last eighteen that we encounter the greatest problems for reconstructing the original Gospel. According to the conventional numbering, we have five too many sayings. There are three separate areas of uncertainty:

Thomas 92-94
Thomas 106
Thomas 110-113

In the first two areas, I have deleted one saying in each as duplicates. In the last area, I have deleted two sayings, edited one saying, and combined Thomas 111 and 113 as one saying. However, although the changes in the final group are the most extensive, this is also the area about which we can be most confident. Coming immediately before the ending, it is the most natural point to insert additional material. It is clear from Thomas 111 that additional material has indeed been added. And there is evidence that supports Thomas 111 and 113 being two parts of one saying. We will take each of the areas in turn.

## *Recreating the first three: Thomas 92-94*

Our starting point is that the three sayings Thomas 96, 97 and 98 must constitute the second three of the eighteen because they all start with the formula "The kingdom of the Father...." This means that the four sayings which under the conventional numbering come before Thomas 96, must form the first three of the eighteen. These sayings are:

*Jesus said: "Seek, and you shall find; but those things you asked me in those days, I did not tell you then. Now I wish to tell them, and you seek not after them." (Th. 92)*

*"Do not give that which is holy to the dogs, lest they cast them on the dung heap; do not cast pearls to the swine lest they become [...]." (Th. 93)*

*Jesus [said]: "He who seeks will find, [and he who knocks] it will be opened to him." (Th. 94)*

*[Jesus said]: "If you have money, do not lend it at interest, but give [it] to him from whom you will not take it back." (Th. 95)*

There is no reason to suppose that Thomas 95 is not an original stand-alone saying. Also if it is third in the eighteen, then it is symmetrical with the third from last, 6.16, which also mentions lending money at interest. So assigning Thomas 95 as 6.3, we then have to reduce Thomas 92-94 to two sayings. There are two points to note:

- Thomas 94 seems redundant as it largely repeats the start of Thomas 92. It only adds "and he who knocks it will be opened to him" which has a similar meaning to the first part, "he who seeks will find..."
- Thomas 93 does not have a "Jesus said" or "He said" statement at the beginning and so could be the continuation of Thomas 92.

These point to two different ways in which to reconstruct the first three. There is, however, another important piece of evidence. There is a passage in Matthew that is related to these Thomas sayings:

*"Do not give dogs what is holy, and do not throw your pearls before pigs, lest they trample them underfoot and turn to attack you.*

*"Ask, and it will be given to you; seek, and you will find; knock, and it will be opened to you. For everyone who asks receives, and the one who seeks finds, and to the one who knocks it will be opened. Or which one of you, if his son asks him for bread, will give him a stone? Or if he asks for a fish, will give him a serpent? If you then, who are evil, know how to give good gifts to your children, how much more will your Father who is in heaven give good things to those who ask him!" (Matthew 7:6-11 ESV)*

The saying about dogs and swine in Matthew is devoid of context whereas in Thomas it follows on logically from Jesus talking about a secret that will be revealed.[96] It would seem that the author of Matthew's source for the second section was something like:

Ask, and it will be given to you; seek, and you will find; knock, and it will be opened to you.

Everything that comes afterward is an elaboration of this. Indeed, the entire line *"For everyone who asks receives, and the one who seeks finds, and to the one who knocks it will be opened"* is redundant as it just repeats the first line. As always, it is simple to know when two passages are linked, and the Matthew passage is closely linked to Thomas 92-94. It is much harder to know which came first. The Matthew passage does not resolve the problem for us as the link can be explained in two different ways in our two different options. We will now consider these options.

## Eliminate Thomas 94

This approach is taken in the main reconstruction. It assumes that a copyist was faced with two different variations of Thomas 92. One started "Jesus said: Seek, and you shall find" and the other with, "Jesus said: He who seeks will find, and he who knocks it will be opened to him." He keeps the full first version of the saying. But he is unwilling to discard the variation completely, so he adds the alternative beginning as a separate saying.

How do we explain the fact that Matthew also has *"seek, and you will find; knock, and it will be opened to you"* following on from the dogs and swine saying? If Thomas 94 were not in the original Gospel, then it would have been added by a copyist who would have been very familiar with the most popular Gospel, that of Matthew. So he positions his alternative in the same place it occupies in Matthew.

If we accept this solution, then the author of Matthew's source must have been the version of Thomas 92 that included knocking and opening. This version would have all the elements that Matthew has; seeking and finding, knocking and opening, asking and answering. He follows the lead of Thomas 93 by making what is asked for as something that is eaten; bread/stones, fish/snake. But if we look at the line that must have been his original source it is very similar to Thomas and would have originally meant some revelation, a meaning that is lost in Matthew.

## Combine Thomas 92 and Thomas 93

If we took this approach then we would have an alternative reconstruction of the first three as below:

> *6.1(A) Jesus said: "Seek, and you shall find; but those things you asked me in those days, I did not tell you then. Now I wish to tell them, and you seek not after them. Do not give that which is holy to the dogs, lest they cast them on the dung heap; do not cast pearls to the swine lest they become [...]."" (Th. 92&93)*

> *6.2(A) Jesus [said]: "He who seeks will find, [and he who knocks] it will be opened to him." (Th. 94)*

> *6.3 [Jesus said]: "If you have money, do not lend it at interest, but give [it] to him from whom you will not take it back." (Th. 95)*

This approach has some advantages. It is not necessary to delete any saying or to hypothesize that Thomas 93 has lost a "Jesus said." Instead, it would be the conventional numbering that is wrong.

It would also explain why in Matthew seeking/finding and knocking/opening follows on from the dogs and swine. The author of Matthew has followed the lead of Thomas 94 to which he incorporates elements from Thomas 92.

This solution, however, is not favored because it has a number of disadvantages:

- It complicates the keystone saying 6.1.
- The two parts of 6.1(A), Thomas 92 and Thomas 93, are quite different in subject matter.
- Thomas 94 is redundant within the three.

None of these disadvantages is fatal, and we cannot completely rule out this alternative. However, eliminating Thomas 94 gives a neater solution.

## Thomas 106

Originally I deleted this saying as a duplicate of Thomas 48. The two are very similar:

> *Jesus said: "If two make peace with one another in this house alone, they shall say to the mountain, 'Move away' and it shall move." (Th. 48)*

> *Jesus said: "When you make the two one, you shall be sons of man, and when you say: 'Mountain, move away,' he shall be moved." (Th. 106)*

As discussed in Chapter 15, I now think that Thomas 106 was deliberately added as an "extra" which we are supposed to remove. So I have numbered it as 6.13.1 but eliminated it from the structure.

# *Thomas 110-113*

This is where we have to make some radical changes! The first three sayings are shown below:

> *Jesus said: "He who has found the world and become rich, let him deny the world." (Th. 110)*

> *Jesus said: "The heavens shall be rolled up and the earth in your presence, and he who lives out of the living one shall not see death" because Jesus says: "He who shall find himself, of him the world is not worthy." (Th. 111)*

> *Jesus said: "Woe to the flesh which depends upon the soul; woe to the soul which depends upon the flesh." (Th. 112)*

Something has clearly gone wrong in Thomas 111, where someone has added the statement *"because Jesus says:..."* This is the clearest evidence of an interpolation in the whole Gospel. But this saying is surrounded by two others that are duplicates. We can see why Thomas 110 should have been added immediately after Thomas 109 since that saying ends with the man lending money at interest, which seems inconsistent with the rest of the Gospel. The addition of Thomas 110 corrects the literal interpretation of this notion by saying that the rich should deny the world. This is then echoed again in the last part of Thomas 111. The saying that comes after this interpolation, Thomas 112, is another duplicate. If we remove both duplicates and the interpolation in Thomas 111, we get just this:

> *Jesus said: "The heavens shall be rolled up and the earth in your presence, and he who lives out of the living one shall not see death."*

Which is followed by Thomas 113:

> *His disciples said to him: "On what day will the kingdom come?" "It comes not with observation. They will not say: Behold, that side or: Behold there! But the kingdom of the*

*father is spread out upon the earth, and men do not see it."*
*(Th. 113)*

Thomas 113 does not contain a "Jesus said" statement that would indicate a separate saying. In fact, the two make better sense as a single dialogue, starting with Jesus making a statement about the end of the world, with the disciples then asking about the time, before Jesus replies that the kingdom does not come with observation. This gives a startling contradiction between the two parts of the saying; Jesus first states that the heavens and the earth will be rolled up "in your presence" but then says in the second part of the saying that the kingdom does not come with observation but is already spread out upon the earth. The Gospel loves contradiction, although many of its early readers did not! So a copyist may have split up the saying to avoid such a blatant inconsistency, which would explain why interpolations were made between the two parts.

How can we be sure of this conclusion? When we put the two halves together to make 6.17, we find links between this and other important sayings. The links cross over the boundary of the two sayings and are evidence that they originally belonged together.

# Notes

1 Bernard P. Grenfell, and Arthur S. Hunt, *Sayings of our Lord from an Early Greek Papyrus* (London: Egypt Exploration Fund, Frowde, 1897).

2 The Papyrus is now referred to as P.Oxy 1. The "1" means that it was the first papyrus to be found and catalogued from the site.

3 Bernard P. Grenfell, and Arthur S. Hunt, *New Sayings of Jesus* and *Fragment of a Lost Gospel* (New York: Egypt Exploration Fund, Oxford University Press, 1904). The two fragments are now known as P.Oxy. 654, and P.Oxy. 655.

4 The source for the discovery story is James M. Robinson, "Introduction; 3. The Discovery", *The Nag Hammadi Library in English*, Revised Edition, (Leiden: Brill, 1988), pp. 22-26. There is a good retelling of the story in Elaine Pagels, *The Gnostic Gospels* (London: Penguin Books, 1982) pp. 13-17.

5 Mark Goodacre, *How Reliable is the Story of the Nag Hammadi Discovery?*, Journal for the Study of the New Testament 35(4) (2013), 303–322.

6 The idea that the find was the result of a deliberate search for antiquities is supported by the location which is very close to some sixth-dynasty tombs which had been reused by early Christian hermits. Goodacre repeats an earlier account of the discovery from Jean Doresse which is simpler and less sensational than the Robinson account. In this account Doresse speculates that the find may actually have come from one of these tombs (ibid. p. 315). In some alternative versions of the story a skeleton was found alongside the jar (ibid. n. 13, p. 307) which may indicate that the jar was buried in a grave.

7 There may also have been a monetary consideration as Robinson was in the habit of paying his informants, including Muhammed 'Ali, for their stories (ibid. pp. 314-5).

8 Elaine Pagels, *The Gnostic Gospels* (London: Penguin Books, 1982) p. 130.

9 Of the fifty-two tractates, six were duplicated within the collection and six more were copies of already known works. So the Nag Hammadi collection contained forty new texts. See: James M. Robinson, "Introduction; 2. The Manuscripts", *The Nag Hammadi Library in English*.

10 Bernard P. Grenfell, and Arthur S. Hunt, *Sayings of our Lord from an Early Greek Papyrus* p. 16.

11 Helmut Koester, Introduction to "The Gospel of Thomas" in *The Nag Hammadi Library in English*, Revised Edition, Ed. James M. Robinson (Leiden: Brill, 1988). See also the essays by Koester in James M Robinson and Helmut Koester, *Trajectories through Early Christianity*, (Philadelphia: Fortress Press, 1971) and in particular "One Jesus and Four Primitive Gospels". In relation to "proverbial sayings" in *Thomas*, Koester says: "...there is no reason to

assume that they were drawn from the synoptic Gospels. Rather, *Thomas*'s source must have been a very primitive collection of proverbs, a collection which was incorporated into Matthew's and Luke's common source Q and thus became the basis of the materials used by Matt. 5-7 and Luke 6 for their "Sermons," and which was also known to Mark." Helmut Koester "One Jesus and Four Primitive Gospels", p.182.

12  Stevan Davies, 'Mark's use of the Gospel of Thomas' in *Neotestamentica* 30 (2)(1996), pp. 307-334. Stevan Davies and Kevin Johnson 'Mark's use of the Gospel of Thomas, Part 2' in *Neotestamentica* 31 (2) (1997), pp. 233-261.

13  Stevan Davies, *The Gospel of Thomas and Christian Wisdom* 2nd edn (California: Bardic Press) p. 3.

14  Stephen Patterson, *The Gospel of Thomas and Jesus*, (Sonoma CA: Polebridge Press, 1993), p. 120.

15  Nicholas Perrin, *Thomas and Tatian: The Relationship between the Gospel of Thomas and the Diatessaron*, (Atlanta: Society of Biblical Literature, 2002). See also "The Syriac Gospel of Thomas" in *Thomas, the Other Gospel*, (London: SPCK, 2007) pp. 73-106.

16  This seems a fatal objection to Perrin's theory. It would require Thomas to have been written almost immediately after the Diatessaron in 173 and then equally rapidly translated from Syriac to Greek. A very large number of copies of the new Gospel would then have to be made (copying by hand!) and transported as far as Oxyrhynchus in Egypt where the earliest fragment has been dated to c200 AD. In "The Syriac Gospel of Thomas", p.97-99, Perrin suggests that Syriac texts were routinely translated into a Greek so that Thomas could have been translated "in as little as a few weeks"! He sees no reason why Thomas should not have been extensively reproduced so that a copy found its way to Oxyrhynchus by 200. Although this is physically possible, it requires a very unlikely chain of events. Statistically, the probability of survival for any physical copy of a text is extremely low. The three fragments of Thomas found at Oxyrhynchus were small fragments of three separate copies of Thomas and they have all been dated to the first half of the third century. It would require an enormous number of copies of Thomas to be in circulation among Christians at this time to leave this physical evidence. Why should a newly written Gospel become this popular so quickly?

17  April DeConick, *Recovering the Original Gospel of Thomas* (London: T&T Clark International, 2005) and *The Original Gospel of Thomas in Translation* (London: T&T Clark International, 2006).

18  Mark Goodacre, *Thomas and the Gospels: The making of an apocryphal text* (London: SPCK, 2012). Simon Gathercole, *The Composition of the Gospel of Thomas: Original Language and Influences*, (New York: Cambridge University Press, 2014).

19  Mark Goodacre, *Thomas and the Gospels: The making of an apocryphal text* Chapter 9, pp. 169-71. Although Goodacre argues throughout his book that

Thomas is later than the Synoptics, his dating of the Gospel to c140 is based on an interpretation of a single saying, Thomas 68. He follows a suggestion of Hans-Martin Schenke that this saying is a reference to the expulsion of the Jews from Jerusalem after the Bar Kochba rebellion in 135. In a blog post I argue that this is not the case and that the "place" that those who persecute the disciples are being excluded from is actually the kingdom of heaven. <http://splaurie.com/gospel-of-thomas/thomas-68/#more-168> [accessed 8 Sept. 2017]

20  April DeConick, *Recovering the Original Gospel of Thomas*, chapter 4.

21  Stevan Davies interviewed by Christopher Skinner, 8/11/2009, Crux Sola blog <https://cruxsolablog.com/2009/11/08/interview-with-stevan-davies-part-i/> [accessed 17/3/2017].

22  Stevan Davies, "1994 SBL paper: Does the Gospel of Thomas has a meaning?" in *The Gospel of Thomas and Christian Wisdom* 2nd edn. (California: Bardic Press), p.167.

23  ibid. pp. 167-8.

24  Ibid. pp. 156-67.

25  Ibid. pp. 167-8.

26  S. P. Laurie, *The Rock and the Tower* (London: Hypostasis, 2016), Chapter 37-38, pp. 621-48.

27  Proof: All prime numbers except 2 are odd. So the sum of any two primes is an even number unless one of the two primes is 2. But any even number, other than 2, is not a prime. So the only possible pair of successive primes that could add to another prime are 2 and the next prime 3. These add to 5 which is a prime number.

28  Proof: All primes except 2 are odd. So the difference between any two primes will be an even number unless one of the two primes is 2. As 3 is an odd number, we can only get 3 as the difference between two primes if one of the primes is 2. So the other prime must be 5, as 3= 5-2. So the pair {2,5} is the only pair of primes which have a difference of 3.

29  Proof: If we add any two factors from {2,3} the answer must be either 4 or 5 or 6. We can only get 4 by adding 2+2, and 6 by adding 3+3. So if we want to get the same answer from adding any two consecutive factors, then 2 and 3 must alternate to give the sum of 5. As we have more 3s than 2s, we must start and end with 3, giving the sequence 3·2·3·2·3.

30  Stevan Davies, "1994 SBL paper: Does the Gospel of Thomas has a meaning?" *in The Gospel of Thomas and Christian Wisdom* 2nd edn. p.167.

31  Genesis 1:26-27.

32  Genesis 2:7-8; 18-25.

33  Matthew 10:34-6; Luke 12:49-53

34  Mark 4:13-20.

35  For example of an apocalyptic interpretation, see the Interpretative comment for logion 16.1-2 in April DeConick, *The Original Gospel of Thomas in Translation* (London: T&T Clark International, 2006), p.93.

36  Simon Gathercole, *The Composition of the Gospel of Thomas: Original Language and Influences*, First paperback ed., (New York: Cambridge University Press, 2014), Chapter 3: Saying 16.4, pp.56-7.

37  Klijn, A. F. J., "The single one in the Gospel of Thomas" in *Journal of Biblical Literature*, Vol. 81, No. 3 (Sep., 1962), pp. 271-278.

38  Grondin's interlinear translation at <http://www.gospel-thomas.net> [accessed 14/9/2017].

39  Stevan Davies, "Mark's use of the Gospel of Thomas" in *Neotestamentica* 30 (2)(1996), pp. 307-334.

40  1 Cor. 1:13.

41  The text actually has "destroyed" instead of equal, but this reading does not make sense. Most translations assume that "destroyed" is a scribal error for "equal" as the two words are similar in Coptic.

42  S. P. Laurie, *The Rock and the Tower*, Chapter 16, pp. 239-248.

43  Mark 4:3-8.

44  The translation is based on the ESV with a few minor changes.

45  Matthew 16:12.

46  In fact, the original source behind the Mark account may only have had the "yeast of Herod." It is possible that the author of Mark added in the Pharisees for the same reason that the author of Matthew was to later add the Sadducees.

47  Mark 1:17.

48  April DeConick, *Recovering the Original Gospel of Thomas*, Chapter 4, pp. 113-30. See also *The Original Gospel of Thomas in Translation*, Chapter 2, pp. 25-31. DeConick divides many of the sayings into sub-sayings, but I have only shown the saying number in the table.

49  April DeConick, *Recovering the Original Gospel of Thomas*, pp. 113-4.

50  S. P. Laurie, *The Rock and the Tower*, Chapter 32, pp. 524-529.

51  Translation by John Bostock and HT Riley, <http://data.perseus.org/citations/urn:cts:latinLit:phi0978.phi001.perseus-eng1:19.54>.

52  Song of Song 2:15.

53  Luke 13:32.

54  Mark 3:15.

55  2 Cor. 12:7-9.

56  1 Cor. 11:30.

57  For Paul's views on marriage, see 1 Corinthians 7 and in particular 7:28.

58  Mark Goodacre, *Thomas and the Gospels: The making of an apocryphal text* Chapter 7, pp. 119-121.

59  The probability has been calculated by stochastic simulation. Each simulation involves assigning the sayings to random positions within the eighteen

and then counting how many of each of two groups of six sayings appear in the same position in the threes. A total of 2.5 million simulations were carried out and 1,439 had at least five of each group of six in the same position. This gives a probability of 1,439/2,500,000 = 0.00058 or 1/1737.

60 The calculation is as above but with one of the two groups consisting of five sayings. The number of simulations with at least 5 out of 6 and 4 out of 5 in the same position is 4,966. This gives a probability of 4,966/2,500,000 = 0.00199 or 1/503.

61 The probability is calculated from the stochastic simulation as above. The calculation determines which simulations have both (i) five out of six sayings in the same position of a three for each of the two groups and (ii) the vacant positions falling on sayings 12 and 13. A total of 21 simulations met both of these conditions. This gives a probability of 21/2,500,000 = 0.0000084 or 1/119,047.

62 1 Cor. 3:1-3.

63 Matthew 22:1-10.

64 Luke 14:16-24.

65 Mark 14:58.

66 In "Does the Gospel of Thomas has a meaning?" *in The Gospel of Thomas and Christian Wisdom* 2nd edn. p.167., Stevan Davies takes Thomas 73, 74 and 75 as one saying. Although I agree that Thomas 74 is not spoken by Jesus but addressed to Jesus and should be merged with 75, I do not see why 73 should be brought into this combined saying. Thomas 74 and 75 are closely linked in form and subject matter but this is not the case with Thomas 73. Also both 73 and 75 have a "Jesus said" statement which would mean that the combined saying would be unique in having two "Jesus said" statements. Both Thomas 73 and Thomas 74 have the word 'Lord" and this would function as a catchword linking 73 and 74/5.

67 Galatians 4:1-10. See S. P. Laurie, *The Rock and the Tower,* Chapter 15, pp. 219-223 for a discussion of this passage.

68 DeConick offers the alternative explanation that "angels and prophets" mean the disciples. The saying would then by aimed at the ordinary community member who is being told to support wandering disciples in return for their teaching and preaching. (See DeConick, The Original Gospel of Thomas in Translation, Thomas 88.) There are two problems with this interpretation. First, it neglects the very specific symmetrical structure of the saying which must have some significance. Second, it is considerable stretch to interpret "angels and prophets" as meaning the disciples. The word "prophets" would normally mean the prophets of Israel who supposedly wrote the Jewish scriptures. The Jesus movement also believed that the law had been brought through angels. So "angels and prophets" refers to the two groups who had brought the law, as represented by the Torah and other Jewish scripture.

69  For consideration of the meaning of these sayings about two families see S. P. Laurie, *The Rock and the Tower,* Chapter 28, pp. 460-476.

70  Ibid. Chapter 25, pp. 399-403.

71  Genesis 4:1.

72  Matthew 18:12-13; Luke 15:4-7.

73  The sayings are so close that it could be asked whether Thomas 103 should be eliminated as a duplicate. The justification for not doing this is that Thomas 103 only repeats one part of Thomas 21. We have surmised that the duplicates have arisen where a copyist or translator has come across two variations on a saying so that they are not sure if they are one saying or two. This cannot be the case here because the beginning and end of Thomas 21 are not repeated in Thomas 103. It is unlikely that a copyist would take a section from the middle of a saying and make it a separate "Jesus said" saying in another part of the Gospel.

74  S. P. Laurie, *The Rock and the Tower,* Chapter 25, pp. 399-403.

75  See for example Stevan Davies, *The Gospel of Thomas: Annotated and Explained* (Woodstock, VT: Skylight Paths Publishing, 2002), Introduction xxix.

76  Thomas 20, 54, 114 all use the "kingdom of heaven."

77  The version in Luke 13:21 is essentially the same as Matthew.

78  S. P. Laurie, *The Rock and the Tower,* Chapter 16, pp. 239-248.

79  Mark 3:18.

80  John 11:16; 20:24.

81  Simon Gathercole, *The Composition of the Gospel of Thomas: Original Language and Influences,* First paperback ed., (New York: Cambridge University Press, 2014), pp. 227-233. He also argues for dependence of Thomas 3 on Romans 10.7, but I think this is uncertain. It is more likely that Thomas 3 is a long established saying among the Jesus movement at this time.

82  S. P. Laurie, *The Rock and the Tower,* Chapter 39, pp. 655-58.

83  Ibid. Chapter 40, pp. 669-88.

84  See Bauckham's translation of Papias: *"The Elder used to say: Mark, in his capacity as Peter's interpreter, wrote down accurately as many things as he recalled from memory – though not in an ordered form – of the things either said or done by the Lord."* Later they were placed on order by Matthew: *"Therefore Matthew put the logia in an ordered arrangement in the Hebrew language ..."* Translations from Richard Bauckham, *Jesus and the Eyewitnesses: The Gospels as Eyewitness Testimony* (Grand Rapids: Wm. B Eerdmans, 2006), Chapter 9, p. 203.

85  Papias says that Mark was the secretary/interpreter of Peter. In *The Rock and the Tower* I explain why I think he was actually the "son" and constant companion of Mary. See in particular Chapter 39 and my discussion of the Papias passage in pp. 658-63.

86  Michael W. Grondin, "An Interlinear Translation of the Coptic Gospel of Thomas" at The Gospel of Thomas Resource Centre <http://www.gospel-thomas.net>

87  April D. DeConick, *The Original Gospel of Thomas in Translation* (London: T&T Clark International, 2006).

88  Beate Blatz, "The Coptic Gospel of Thomas" in Wilhelm Schneemelcher Ed., R McL. Wilson trans., *New Testament Apocrypha*, Volume One, (Cambridge: James Clarke & Co, 2003) pp. 110-133.

89  Thomas O. Lambdin, Translation of "The Gospel of Thomas" in James M. Robinson, Ed., *The Nag Hammadi Library in English*, Revised Edition, (Leiden: Brill, 1988).

90  Stevan Davies, *The Gospel of Thomas: Annotated and Explained* (Woodstock, VT: Skylight Paths Publishing, 2002).

91  Richard Valantasis, *The Gospel of Thomas* (London: Routledge, 1997).

92  David R. Cartlidge, "A Translation of the Gospel of Thomas" in Stevan Davies, *The Gospel of Thomas and Christian Wisdom* 2nd edn. (California: Bardic Press), pp. 179-183

93  The use of Thomas 77 by the Gospel of John is in a section with a number of such links. The Thomas saying is:

> *Jesus said: "I am the light that is over them all. I am the all of it, the all of it came out of me and the all of it bursts up to me. Split a timber, I am there. Raise up the stone, and you shall find me there."*
> *(Th. 77)*

In this saying, Jesus makes three "I am" statements. The first is that he is "the light that is over them all" which in John becomes "I am the light of the world":

> *Again Jesus spoke to them, saying, "I am the light of the world. Whoever follows me will not walk in darkness, but will have the light of life." (John 8:12 ESV)*

The Pharisees do not accept this, saying that he testifies of himself. Jesus replies that they do not know where he has come from or where he is going, *"I am with the Father who sent me" (John 8:16)*. This echoes a line at the beginning of John: *"He was in the beginning with God. All things were made through him, and without him was not any thing made that was made." (John 1:1-2 ESV)* which in turn echoes Thomas 77, *"the all of it came out of me."* It seems that Thomas 77 was one of the influences behind the beginning, and that the author of John recalls the beginning here.

There is then a section of John based on other Thomas sayings before we get to the second part of Thomas 77. Jesus is having an argument with the Jews:

> *Your father Abraham rejoiced that he would see my day. He saw it and was glad." So the Jews said to him, "You are not yet fifty years*

*old, and have you seen Abraham?" Jesus said to them, "Truly, truly,*
*I say to you, before Abraham was, I am." (John 8:56-58 ESV)*

First Jesus says that Abraham saw him, and he gives an "I am" statement, that he existed before Abraham. This type of odd statement suggests that the author is using a source which he has misunderstood. The "I am" expression leads us back to Thomas 77, where we have *"Split a timber, I am there"*, the Greek papyrus version of which is *"split the wood, I am there"*. The most famous story concerning Abraham is when God asks him to sacrifice his son Isaac. Genesis says that as soon as he heard God's command, he got up in the morning and *"split the wood for the burnt-offering" (Genesis 22:3)*. The Septuagint Greek version uses the same word for "split" as the Greek papyrus Thomas. As Abraham is about to sacrifice Isaac, an angel of the Lord comes and tells him to stop and sacrifice a ram caught in a thicket instead. There is ambiguity because this angel of YHWH also seems to be called YHWH himself (Genesis 22:15-16). The author of John has interpreted *"split the wood, I am there"* as meaning that Jesus was present at the sacrifice, and was the divine being who gave Abraham his instruction to sacrifice Isaac and who then told him to hold his hand. The fact that the angel is distinct from YHWH, but also seems to be called YHWH, fits in very well with the author of John's belief that the Father and Son are one, and that the Father is seen through the Son. The angel blesses Abraham, and says that his descendants will be numbered like the stars in the sky or the sand on the seashore, and that the nations will be blessed through him.

As for the second half of the second part of the Thomas 77 saying, *"Raise up the stone, and you shall find me there"*, this comes on the very next line:

*So they picked up stones to throw at him, but Jesus hid himself and*
*went out of the temple. (John 8:59 ESV)*

94  See April DeConick, "Literature Parallels, Logion 30.1-2", in *The Original Gospel of Thomas in Translation* (London: T&T Clark International, 2006).

95  The full quote of 14.24 is: "Just as the Messiah took care of his flock in every necessity, so too he offered consolation with regard to the sadness of loneliness, when he said, **Where there is one, I [am there]**, lest all those who are solitary be sad. For he is our joy, and he is with us. **Where there are two, I [am there]**. His grace gives us protection. And **when there are three**, it is like when we are assembled in the Church, which is the perfect body, the seal of the Messiah. The angels in heaven see the face of my Father, that is [through] their prayers." Carmel McCarthy, *Saint Ephrem's commentary on Tatian's Diatessaron*, reprint, (Oxford: Oxford University Press, 2000), p. 225.

96  DeConick makes the point that the positioning in Thomas, unlike Matthew, agrees with the interpretation in the Pseudo-Clementine Recognitions 2.3 and 3.1. See *The Original Gospel of Thomas in Translation* (London: T&T Clark International, 2006), Logion 93.1-2 Interpretative comment, p. 264.

# Bibliography

Bauckham, Richard, *Jesus and the Eyewitnesses: The Gospels as Eyewitness Testimony* (Grand Rapids: Wm. B Eerdmans, 2006)

Blatz, Beate, "The Coptic Gospel of Thomas" in Wilhelm Schneemelcher Ed., R McL. Wilson trans., *New Testament Apocrypha*, Volume One, (Cambridge: James Clarke & Co, 2003) pp. 110-133

Cartlidge, David R., "A Translation of the Gospel of Thomas" in Stevan Davies, *The Gospel of Thomas and Christian Wisdom* 2nd edn. (California: Bardic Press), pp. 179-183

Davies, Stevan, *The Gospel of Thomas and Christian Wisdom* 2nd edn (California: Bardic Press)
—— "1994 SBL paper: Does the Gospel of Thomas has a meaning?" in *The Gospel of Thomas and Christian Wisdom* 2nd edn. (California: Bardic Press)
—— "Mark's use of the Gospel of Thomas" in *Neotestamentica* 30 (2) (1996), pp. 307-334.
—— and Kevin Johnson, "Mark's use of the Gospel of Thomas, Part 2" in *Neotestamentica* 31 (2) (1997), pp. 233-261.
—— *The Gospel of Thomas: Annotated and Explained* (Woodstock, VT: Skylight Paths Publishing, 2002)

DeConick, April D., *Recovering the Original Gospel of Thomas* (London: T&T Clark International, 2005)
—— *The Original Gospel of Thomas in Translation* (London: T&T Clark International, 2006)

Gathercole, Simon, *The Composition of the Gospel of Thomas: Original Language and Influences*, First paperback ed., (New York: Cambridge University Press, 2014)

Goodacre, Mark, *Thomas and the Gospels: The making of an apocryphal text* (London: SPCK, 2012)

—— *How Reliable is the Story of the Nag Hammadi Discovery?*, Journal for the Study of the New Testament 35(4) (2013), 303–322

Grenfell, Bernard P. and Hunt, Arthur S., *Sayings of our Lord from an Early Greek Papyrus* (London: Egypt Exploration Fund, Frowde, 1897)

—— and Hunt, Arthur S., *New Sayings of Jesus* and *Fragment of a Lost Gospel* (New York: Egypt Exploration Fund, Oxford University Press, 1904)

Grondin, Michael W., "An Interlinear Translation of the Coptic Gospel of Thomas" at The Gospel of Thomas Resource Centre <http://www.gospel-thomas.net>

Klijn, A. F. J., "The single one in the Gospel of Thomas" in *Journal of Biblical Literature*, Vol. 81, No. 3 (Sep., 1962), pp. 271-278.

Koester, Helmut, "The Origin and Nature of Diversification in the History of Early Christianity" in James M. Robinson and Helmut Koester, *Trajectories through Early Christianity*, (Philadelphia: Fortress Press, 1971) p 114-157

—— "One Jesus and Four Primitive Gospels" in James M. Robinson and Helmut Koester, *Trajectories through Early Christianity*, (Philadelphia: Fortress Press, 1971) p 158-204

—— "The Structure and Criteria of Early Christian Beliefs" in James M. Robinson and Helmut Koester, *Trajectories through Early Christianity*, (Philadelphia: Fortress Press, 1971) p 205-231

—— Introduction to "The Gospel of Thomas" in James M. Robinson, Ed., *The Nag Hammadi Library in English*, Revised Edition, (Leiden: Brill, 1988)

—— *Ancient Christian Gospels: Their History and Development* (London: SCM Press, 1990)

Lambdin, Thomas O., Translation of "The Gospel of Thomas" in James M. Robinson, Ed., *The Nag Hammadi Library in English*, Revised Edition, (Leiden: Brill, 1988)

Laurie, S. P., *The Rock and the Tower: How Mary created Christianity* (London: Hypostasis, 2016)

McCarthy, Carmel, *Saint Ephrem's Commentary on Tatian's Diatessaron*, reprint, (Oxford: Oxford University Press, 2000)

Meyer, Marvin, "The Beginning of The Gospel of Thomas" in *Secret Gospels: Essays on Thomas and the Secret Gospel of Mark*, (Harrisburg: Trinity Press International, 2003), pp. 39-53
—— "Making Mary Male: The Categories "Male" and "Female"" in *Secret Gospels: Essays on Thomas and the Secret Gospel of Mark* (Harrisburg: Trinity Press International, 2003), pp. 76-95
—— "Gospel of Thomas Saying 114 Revisited" in *Secret Gospels: Essays on Thomas and the Secret Gospel of Mark* (Harrisburg: Trinity Press International, 2003), pp. 96-106

Pagels, Elaine, *The Gnostic Gospels* (London: Penguin Books, 1982)
—— *Beyond Belief* (New York: Random House, 2005)

Patterson, Stephen J., *The Gospel of Thomas and Jesus*, (Sonoma CA: Polebridge Press, 1993)

Perrin, Nicholas, *Thomas and Tatian: The Relationship between the Gospel of Thomas and the Diatessaron* (Atlanta: Society of Biblical Literature, 2002)
—— *Thomas, the Other Gospel*, (London: SPCK, 2007)

Robinson, James M. and Helmut Koester, Trajectories through Early Christianity, (Philadelphia: Fortress Press, 1971)
—— ed., *The Nag Hammadi Library in English*, Revised Edition, (Leiden: Brill, 1988)

Skinner, Christopher W., *What are they saying about the Gospel of Thomas?*, (New Jersey: Paulist Press, 2012)

Valantasis, Richard, *The Gospel of Thomas* (London: Routledge, 1997)

# About the author

S. P. Laurie lives in a cottage in rural Shropshire, England (think of the Shire but without the hobbits!). He read mathematics at Balliol College, Oxford. When not researching Christian origins or writing books he attempts to grow things, often without success. He is also a keen astrophotographer.

For more information on his research and books go to:

JesusOrigins.com

Made in the USA
Middletown, DE
03 January 2019